GW01606112

Meteorology for Glider Pilots

Meteorology for Glider Pilots

C. E. WALLINGTON

JOHN MURRAY

FIFTY ALBEMARLE STREET LONDON

First published 1961
Second edition 1966
Reprinted 1968

Printed in Great Britain by Photolitho by
Unwin Brothers Ltd., Woking and London
and published by John Murray (Publishers) Ltd.

7195 1473 8

Contents

Plates

Preface

No other sport is so interwoven with the ways of the weather as gliding. Very early in his career the glider pilot finds meteorology infused into his initial instruction. Often his early lessons materialise from irritating delays in his training programme; the wind is either too light or too strong, or it rains on the wrong day, or convection is too weak and sporadic. But natural curiosity whetted by minor frustrations prompts him to learn more about the element in which he flies, so from conversations with his instructors and club colleagues and from his sharpened interest in the weather forecasts disseminated by the press, radio and television he gleans something of the practical significance of depressions, fronts and anticyclones.

As his flying ability progresses, however, the pilot's meteorological interest tends to be directed from the broad scale weather features towards the local phenomena which can present both hazards and opportunities for soaring. He experiences the effects of rugged terrain on hill lift and local eddies; he cavorts around in convection currents and, if lucky, he finds himself soaring in lee waves. At this stage his task is not so much to understand or forecast the phenomena in which he soars as to visualise the pattern of lift and to fly correctly within it. At first it is difficult to decide how much of any failure to stay in lift is due to his handling of the aircraft and how much is due to the natural capriciousness of the atmosphere. Flying ability normally improves with experience, but the rate of progress made in understanding the atmosphere varies considerably among the individuals who comprise the gliding fraternity. For some pilots meteorology is a science akin to their own professions, while for others the weather is no more than a topic for casual conversation before their introduction to gliding. Whatever their initial scientific standards, however, most pilots acquire their meteorological knowledge through clubhouse conversation and books on general or aviation meteorology—and as their flying experience increases they begin to find such sources of information inadequate. Casual advice and hints from clubhouse conversation can easily be misinterpreted by the trainee, and semi-experienced pilots are sometimes loath to seek guidance on aspects of meteorology they feel they ought to know already. Elementary books on meteorology usually treat fronts, low level winds, sea breezes, convection and lee waves at too elementary a level for the glider pilot; advanced level books cater mainly for the meteorological specialists and books on aviation meteorology are designed primarily for the power pilot who is likely to attend a formal training course.

The glider pilot's thirst for meteorological knowledge is usually made obvious to any meteorologist, like myself, involved in gliding affairs by the numerous questions he asks at opportune moments. The substance and level of this book is based mainly on such questions put to me by glider pilots in recent years. In the first nine chapters the aim is to cover the necessary meteorological groundwork without specific reference to gliding. Then, having set the broad meteorological scene, the remainder of the book elaborates on those aspects of the subject particularly relevant to soaring flight. Here there has been ample opportunity to incorporate the findings of modern research into the varied facets of convection, sea breezes, lee waves and wind flow in mountainous regions. To help the reader new to meteorology to acquire more familiarity with meteorological charts and real weather situations, actual case histories rather than hypothetical examples are used wherever practicable.

A few facts, figures and rough and ready formulae are interspersed in the text, not so much to enable the reader to forecast for himself as to provide numerical teaching aids for the reader to juggle with in his spare time. Some sections on fronts and the tephigram may also call for thoughtful study rather than perfunctory reading, but in general the level at which the book is pitched has been considered with three main requirements in mind. First and foremost, most gliding club members need a textbook suitable for self-tuition. Secondly, the glider pilot needs to acquire a mature appreciation of the actual weather he encounters; he cannot turn a blind eye to observations which do not fit oversimplified concepts, and if he cannot explain these observations then he should at least understand why they are difficult for his (and perhaps the expert meteorologist's) comprehension. Thirdly, there is a growing need for a textbook suitable for the lectures and short courses on meteorology for gliding which have been inaugurated in recent years and which are envisaged for the future.

Although gliding is an international sport, the accent here is on the gliding meteorology of the British Isles. Material from other lands has been included but to cover too wide a geographical field would have meant sacrificing detail for generality, and it is the details of certain local phenomena which make soaring possible. Nevertheless, although the characteristics of weather and climate vary from country to country, the basic physical processes involved are the same the world over and, once these processes are understood, it is not too difficult for the pilot to adapt his meteorological repertoire to foreign climes.

The international aspect of gliding also poses the problem of selection of units; knots, kilometres per hour, metres and feet should all be familiar to the truly international pilot. To help foster this familiarity I have given a liberal selection of approximately equivalent Continental values alongside the units used in English meteorological practice. This practice entails the use of two temperature scales: degrees Fahrenheit for most ground level observations and degrees Celsius (centigrade) for upper air temperatures, but a familiarity with the approximate conversion from one scale to the other is soon acquired with a little usage.

A sound appreciation of meteorology and of the forecasting services does not, of course, automatically raise a pilot to top class in the soaring world, but it can add considerable interest to his sport, it can forestall many potential hazards, it can help him to perceive and use extra soaring opportunities and it can make him feel more at home in the air. It is not for me to advise on the handling of aircraft on the ground or in the air, but my hope is that by elaborating on the strictly meteorological aspects of gliding I may help literally to broaden the glider pilot's horizons and at the same time reduce whatever worries he may have about his personal knowledge of meteorology.

Much of a practising meteorologist's work entails collecting data or literature from various sources and passing it on to his customers in a suitable form. Therefore, I am indebted to many of my friends in the gliding world for recounting to me their various flying experiences. I have also made use of many scientific papers and gliding articles, and by way of acknowledgement (as well as to provide references for further study) the authors and a selection of their articles are listed at the end of the book.

I must thank Dr R. S. Scorer for introducing me to gliding meteorology and for his guidance particularly in those early days when modern views on lee waves and thermals were just beginning to emerge from post-war research. John Findlater, with his practical enthusiasm, has inspected the script and made suggestions for which I am also grateful, and last, but by no means least, I want to thank my wife for being secretary extraordinary.

C. E. W.

January 1960

NOTE ON THE SECOND EDITION

In response to the increasing demands of the enthusiasts, the second edition has a chapter on the construction of up-to-date weather maps based on the B.B.C. Shipping Bulletins, which are easily obtainable throughout the British Isles. The text of the Meteorological Office Shipping Bulletins is Crown Copyright and is reproduced here by permission.

Since the first edition of the book was published, degrees Celsius (centigrade) has taken precedence over the Fahrenheit scale in meteorological practice in Britain. But, as this change was anticipated, and as both scales are likely to be in use for some time, only a few modifications have been necessary to keep this second edition in step with the transition from one scale to another.

A few modifications have been made to take account of slight changes in the Weather Service, but these are entirely matters concerning organisation and have no bearing on the scientific aspects of the text.

C. E. W.

November 1965

CHAPTER 1

Pressure and Wind

We live at the bottom of an ocean—a great ocean of air encasing the earth and effectively about 200 miles deep. We call this ocean the atmosphere. We feel its undercurrents as winds, sometimes as gales sweeping across the countryside, sometimes as light breezes gently filtering through the trees, but always driven by an illimitable supply of energy—energy from the sun. The linkage between this energy and wind can be described briefly, though rather loosely, as follows. Heat rays from the sun give rise to an uneven distribution of temperature changes over the globe; the tropics receive more radiant heat than the poles, and temperature is quick to rise over desert sands whereas much of the heat received by a marshland is used for evaporation; snow surfaces and the tops of thick cloud layers reflect rather than absorb much of their incident heat rays. This uneven distribution of temperature changes leads to variations in atmospheric pressure and it is these variations which are directly linked with winds over the earth. But the winds themselves affect the temperature distribution by transporting warmth, or cold, or layers of cloud from place to place, and the whole mechanism is geared to the spinning motion of the earth and lubricated by the evaporation and condensation of water in the atmosphere. So the weather we experience can be considered as the by-product of interwoven cycles of events into which the sun injects a daily supply of energy. A convenient starting point for dissecting and understanding the weather machine is an appreciation of atmospheric pressure.

Atmospheric Pressure

The air in the atmosphere is fairly light, but its weight is by no means negligible. At low levels the air is compressed by the weight of the air above it, and the total weight of a column of air extending from the ground to the top of the atmosphere amounts to almost one ton for every square foot of ground it covers—or, in metric units, about one kilogram per square centimetre. This weight of air per unit area is called the *atmospheric pressure*, or sometimes *barometric pressure*, "baros" being the Greek word for "weight."

A vital duty of most meteorological services is to measure the atmospheric pressure at frequent intervals at a large number of observing posts scattered throughout the territories they serve. The most commonly used measuring instrument is the mercury barometer. It is a simple device consisting in principle of mercury

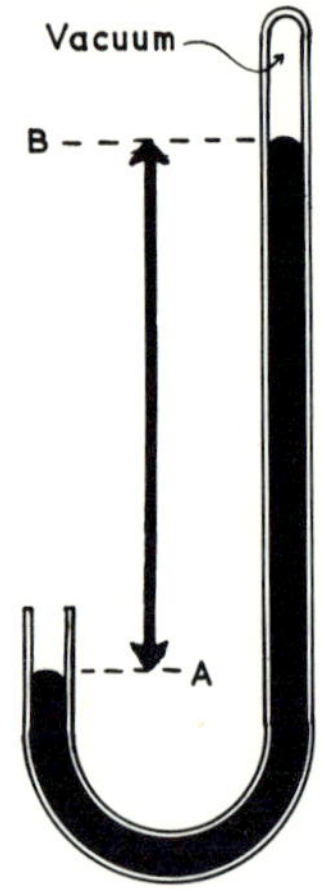

Fig. 1.1. The mercury barometer is a form of balance; the weight of air resting on the mercury surface at *A* exactly balances the weight of mercury in the column between levels *A* and *B*.

in a U-shaped glass tube which is open at one end and closed at the other. As shown in Figure 1.1, the tube is held vertically to form a sort of balance; the weight of air resting on the mercury surface at level *A* exactly balances the weight of mercury in the column between levels *A* and *B*. If the pressure on the exposed surface of the mercury increases, then level *A* is pushed down and *B* rises. Thus the atmospheric pressure can effectively be measured in terms of the length of the mercury column *AB*. In all but freak weather conditions this length lies somewhere between 28 and 31 in. (between about 70 and 80 cm.) at places at or near mean sea-level (M.S.L.). Since horizontal pressure gradients are of primary interest to meteorologists, barometer readings are "reduced" to a standard altitude. In all but generally high level territories M.S.L. is taken as the standard reference level and mercury barometer readings are modified by simple calculation to yield the probable atmospheric pressures at M.S.L. Meteorologists and aviators find it more convenient to talk of pressure in terms of millibars rather than lengths of mercury. By definition a millibar is a pressure of 1,000 dynes per square centimetre, but we need only remember that the range 950 to 1050 mbs. corresponds roughly to the more familiar 28 to 31 in. of mercury.

Taken throughout the year, the mean atmospheric pressure over the British Isles is about 1014 mbs., while the highest and lowest recorded in these isles during the past 100 years are 1054·7 mbs. and 925·5 mbs.

The Pressure Map

As soon as pressure measurements from a number of observing stations are available a pressure map can be plotted. Figure 1.2 shows a typical map for Europe and part of the Atlantic. The observing stations, some of which are ships at sea, are indicated by small circles.

To the right of each "station circle" are the last three figures of the pressure in millibars and tenths of millibars. In other words the 15·0 at Dublin denotes a pressure of 1015·0 mbs. and the 96·4 at the ship near Greenland means 996·4 mbs. This is an international system of plotting pressure on weather maps. In practice there is seldom any doubt in deciding whether "9" or "10" should precede the three plotted figures.

The first step in diagnosing the pressure pattern is to draw *isobars* on the map, isobars being lines joining places having equal pressure. Drawing these lines for the values 996 mbs., 1000 mbs., 1004 mbs. and so on yields the pressure map for 06 GMT 19 May 1957. The pattern reveals two areas of low pressure which we label "*LOW*." They may be referred to as *depressions*, or simply *lows*, while the suitably labelled high-pressure area has the alternative name of *anticyclone*. The pressure map also shows a *trough* (of low pressure), a *ridge* (of high pressure) and a *col*—that is a region of fairly uniform pressure between two highs and two lows. It is difficult to measure the precise dimensions of these features labelled on the pressure map but, roughly speaking, the depression over the North Sea is about 600 miles in diameter and the anticyclone west of Spain covers an area of approximately 1,000 × 500 miles. Meteorologists would consider these dimensions as quite normal. Depressions or anticyclones of less than about 300 miles in diameter would probably

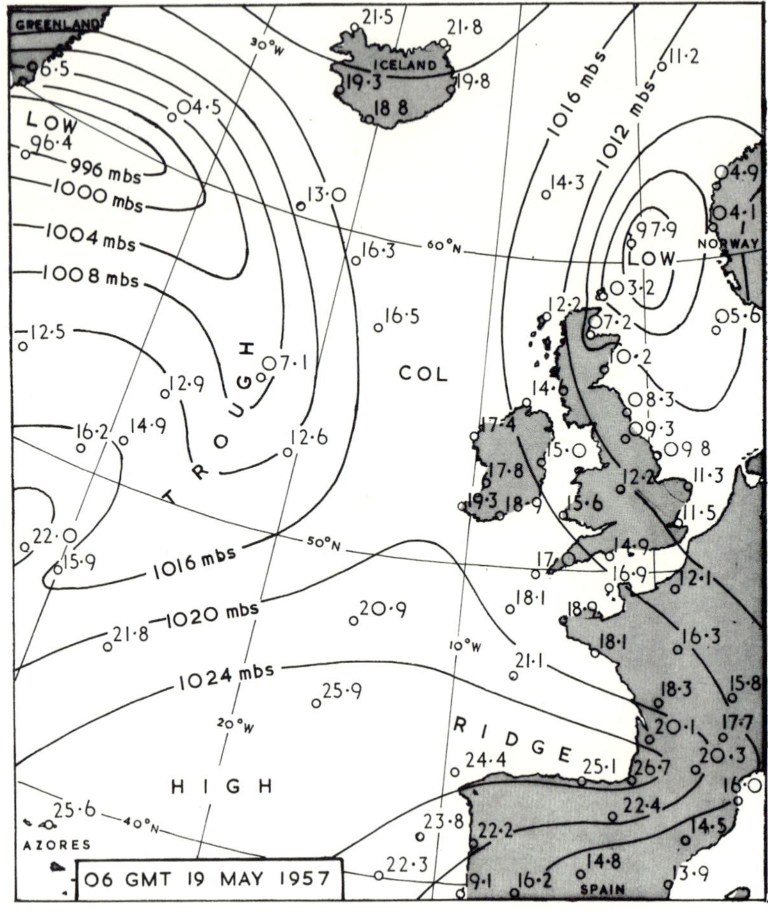

Fig. 1.2. The atmospheric pressure map for 06 GMT 19 May 1957. To the right of each "station circle" are the last three figures of the pressure in millibars and tenths, e.g. 25·6 at the Azores denotes a pressure of 1025·6 mbs. while 96·5 in Greenland means 996·5 mbs.

be described as small but the figures quoted in this chapter should not be taken to define rigid limits; they merely serve to acquaint the reader new to meteorology with the magnitude and character of pressure systems in general.

At most meteorological offices pressure maps are prepared at regular intervals throughout the day and night, the conventional chart times being midnight, 6 a.m., 12 noon and 6 p.m. GMT (or,

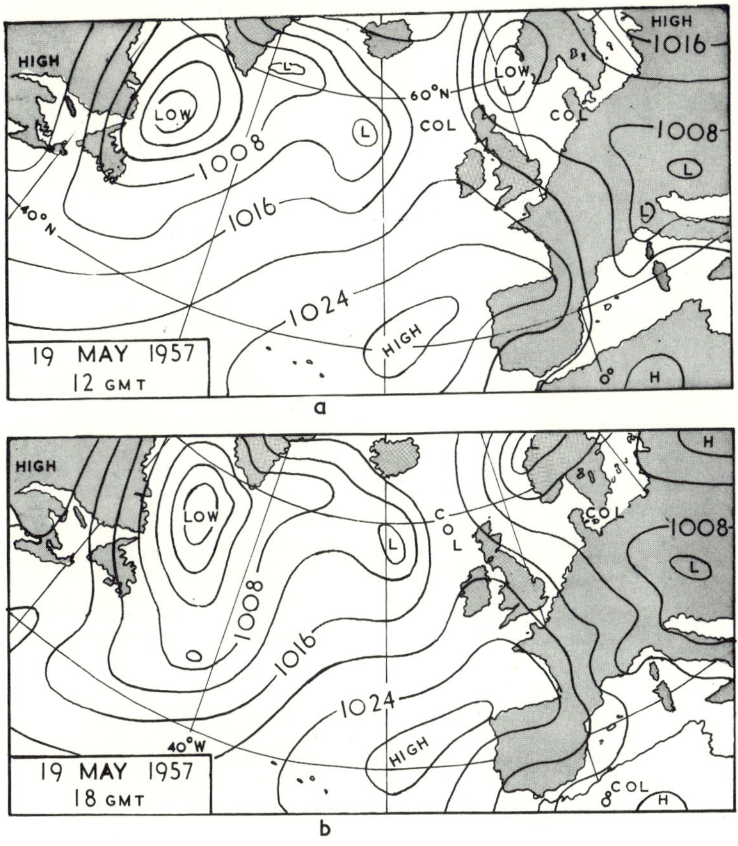

Fig. 1.3. The sequence of six-hourly pressure maps shows the development of a secondary depression over the Atlantic. The last three charts show the tracks of the principal lows and highs with dots to indicate the positions every six hours. *See also* pages 6, 7.

more professionally, 00, 06, 12 and 18 GMT). A number of stations supplement these main charts with intermediate 3-hourly or even hourly maps, and once a sequence of charts is available the movement of current depressions and anticyclones can be measured. For example, in the sequence of charts shown in Figure 1.3 we can trace the movement of the lows and highs by noting their positions every 6 hours. The western half of the first chart, 12 GMT 19 May 1957, is dominated by a large depression from which a trough extends towards the south. By 18 GMT a small new depression had appeared

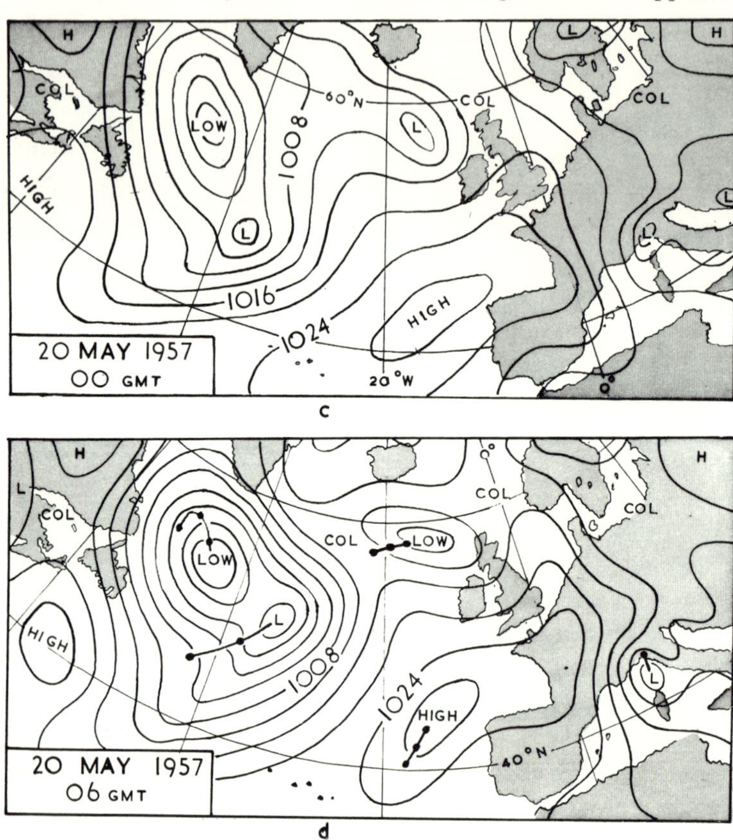

Fig. 1.3—*continued*

in this trough, and during the next 24 hours this *secondary depression* deepened and moved on a curved track towards Iceland. At first it moved along this track at over 40 knots but a gradual deceleration brought the speed down to 20 knots by the end of the sequence. Meanwhile the "primary" depression turned from its northerly track towards the south-east so that the two depressions over the Atlantic showed a tendency to rotate about each other.

A high moved at 10 to 15 knots towards the Bay of Biscay while another smaller anticyclone passed south of Newfoundland at over 40 knots.

Depression speeds of 20 to 30 knots are quite common; small developing depressions, such as the secondary low already described, sometimes move at very high speeds of 60 to 80 knots while very

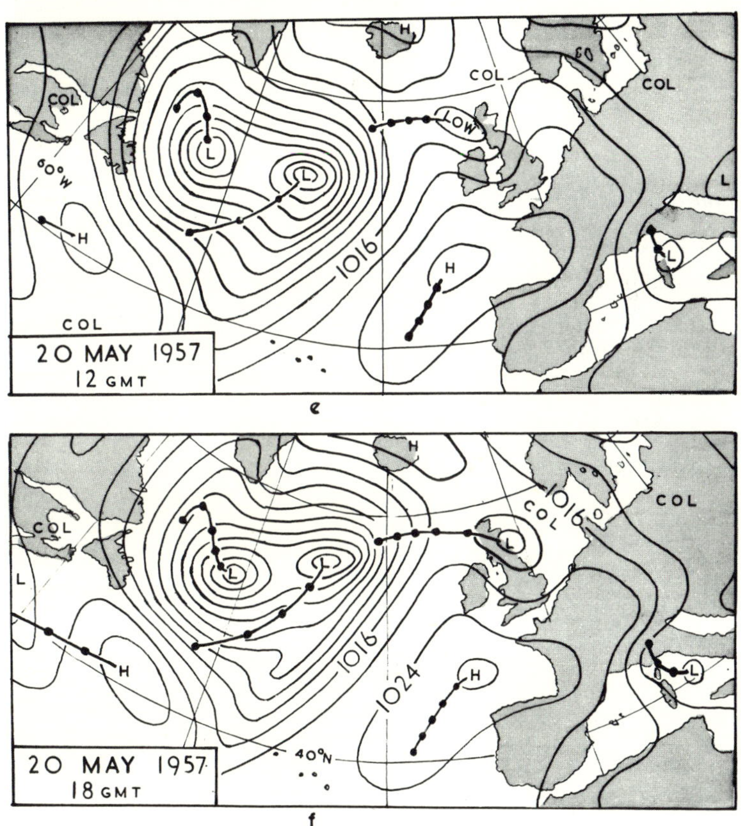

Fig. 1.3—*continued*

low speeds are usually associated with old depressions in process of filling up. The direction of movement of lows varies but over most of the world it is, in a broad sense, from west to east.

Unlike the low pressure systems, anticyclones are seldom resolute travellers. Now and again a high may appear to move very fast but most anticyclones are sluggish and occasionally erratic in their movements. In some regions of the world the tendency for high pressure systems to stagnate is so prevalent that any anticyclone in such a locality is given the appropriate geographical name. The "Azores High," for instance, is a name given to any anticyclone which happens to be stagnating in the neighbourhood of the Azores; the fact that it has a special name indicates the observed predominance, particularly during the summer, of high pressure systems in this region. The "Siberian Anticyclone" is also a commonly used name signifying the persistence of anticyclones over Siberia during the winter.

The movement of air

We have spoken of the movement of depressions and anticyclones but such movement may not be real in the sense that a definite

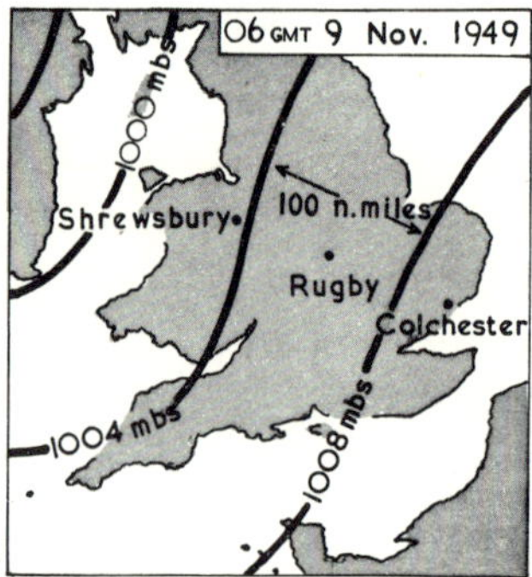

Fig. 1.4. The pressure gradient at 06 GMT 9 November 1949 in the neighbourhood of Rugby was about 4 mbs. per 100 nautical miles.

object moves from place to place. The movement of pressure systems is akin to that of ripples on water; a particular set of ripples may have an observed movement but a cork floating on the surface does not move horizontally with them; it merely bobs up and down as the ripples pass by. So we cannot argue that because a depression moves east the air within it also flows to the east. To determine the actual air movement we must look to the *pressure gradient*, that is the rate at which the atmospheric pressure changes with distance across the isobars. In Figure 1.4 the pressure gradient in the neighbourhood of Rugby is 4 mbs. per 100 miles. In practice it is rarely necessary to express a pressure gradient in actual figures; it is often adequately described as weak or slack when the spacing between the isobars is wide, and strong or tight when the isobars are close together.

The pressure gradient just measured is an indication that any vertical column just south-east of Rugby contains more air by weight than a column covering an equal area to the north-west. Therefore, to make up this deficiency the air would have to flow from south-east to north-west—from the heavy column to the lighter, just as water flows through a sluice gate from the high water side to the low. Figure 1.5 may illustrate the nature of the situation by likening the atmosphere to an ocean of water whose upper surface has been tilted from its normally horizontal position. But the

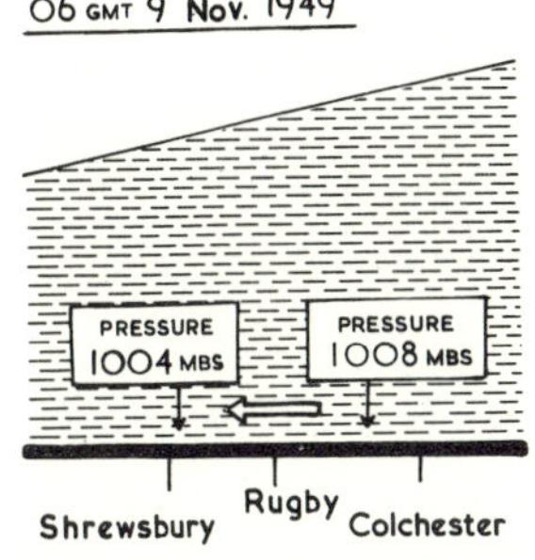

Fig. 1.5. The situation illustrated in Figure 1.4 may be likened to an ocean of water whose upper surface has been tilted from its normally horizontal position. (But in the atmosphere the consequence is not a simple flow from high to low pressure.)

subsequent events are not as simple as the picture suggests. The earth is rotating, and because of this rotation any air moving over the earth's surface is subjected to a force tending to pull it off its course. I offer no easy explanation of this terrestrial trick. Mathematically it can be proved beyond all doubt, but at this stage let us content ourselves with a simple, though by no means complete, analogy. Consider the hypothetical action of an uninformed golfer, who tries to hit a golf ball from Southampton to Newcastle, which lies in a due northerly direction from the south-coast port. The golfer takes his stance and, being uninformed, hits his ball on a bearing of 360 degrees true. But he forgets that the earth's spinning motion gives him and everything with him at 51° N., the latitude of Southampton, a speed of 567 knots in an easterly direction. Even the golf ball has this velocity component when it takes off on its northward flight. Newcastle, however, being at latitude 55° N. has an easterly speed of only 516 knots and therefore lags behind the general rush through space. So the ball drops into the North Sea and the golfer mutters something about a mysterious force deflecting the ball from its intended path. The effect of the earth's spinning motion is indeed so similar to that of an actual force that it is called the *geostrophic force* and, mysterious or not, it has three definite characteristics:

1 In the northern hemisphere the geostrophic force on air moving over the earth's surface acts perpendicularly to the right of the direction of movement of the air (as illustrated in Figure 1.6*a*); south of the Equator the force acts towards the left.

2 The magnitude of the geostrophic force is proportional to the

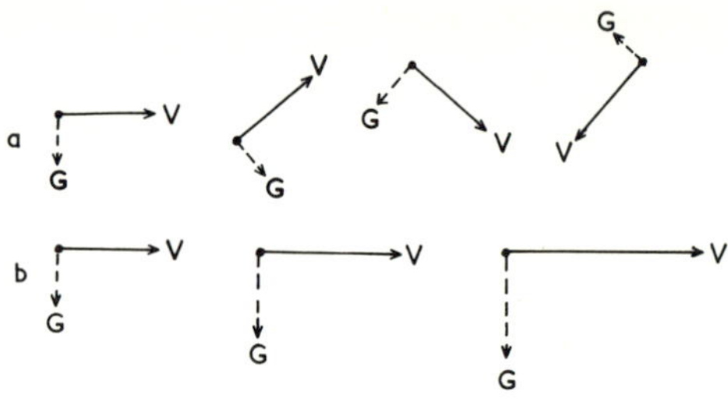

Fig. 1.6. The geostrophic force, *G*, acts at right angles to the velocity, *V*, of the air with a magnitude proportional to the wind speed. In this figure the directions of the geostrophic forces are those applicable to the northern hemisphere. (South of the Equator the directions are reversed.)

speed of the air itself; the faster the air is moving the bigger the geostrophic force (Figure 1.6*b*).

3 The magnitude of the geostrophic force also varies with latitude; it increases from zero at the Equator to a maximum at the poles.

These three characteristics are not easily deduced from either the golfing story or any other simple analogy. But a free imagination is helpful in visualising the geostrophic effect, and, if the golfer's excuse is not convincing, we could also consider such hypothetical problems as playing billiards on a rotating billiard table, or football on a rotating pitch.

The Geostrophic Wind

The geostrophic force (also known as the *Coriolis* force) together with the forces due to atmospheric pressure gradients controls the bulk of air movement in temperate and polar latitudes. To see how this joint control is applied let us suppose that a small parcel of air initially at rest in the northern hemisphere is represented on part of a pressure map by a point between two isobars, say the point at *A* in Figure 1.7. The force due to the pressure gradient will tend to push the parcel across the isobars, from high to low pressure, but as the air starts to move it invites the attention of a geostrophic force which tries to deflect it towards the right of its actual path. Thus the

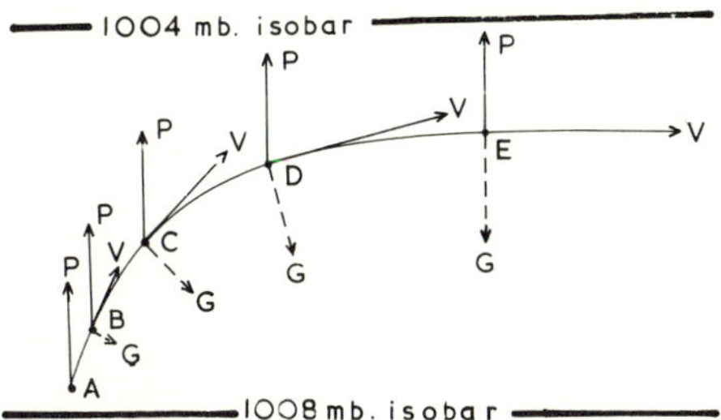

Fig. 1.7. Starting from rest at *A* a parcel of air would soon attain a velocity *V* at *E* such that the geostrophic force, *G*, exactly balances the pressure gradient force, *P*. (The magnitudes of the speeds and forces are proportional to the lengths of the arrows.)

resultant movement will be in a direction somewhere between the directions of the two forces, say from *A* to *B* in the diagram. At this stage of its progress the air is accelerating; therefore the geostrophic force also increases and since it is always directed at right angles to the motion of the air the next section of the air's trajectory is deflected even farther away from its initial direction. So the process goes on until the air is actually moving parallel to the isobars. At this stage, *E*, the geostrophic force is exactly equal in magnitude and opposite in direction to the pressure gradient force (which has remained unchanged throughout the proceedings). This fine balance between the two controlling forces will be preserved as long as the air flows parallel to the isobars with just sufficient speed for the pressure gradient and geostrophic forces to balance each other. Any deviation in direction or speed from this wind velocity can only be temporary; the geostrophic force would be automatically adjusted in favour of restoring the balancing airflow or, to use the correct term, the *geostrophic wind.*

The geostrophic wind speed necessary to maintain the balance is determined by the steepness of the pressure gradient; in Figure 1.8*b* the pressure gradient is double that of 1.8*a*, so for a balanced situation the geostrophic force must be doubled and this is attained when the wind speed also is twice that of 1.8*a*.

Thus we conclude that the pressure gradient and geostrophic forces produce winds which blow parallel to the isobars with speeds proportional to the pressure gradients. The sense of direction can best be remembered by the rule: "If you stand with your back to the wind then the atmospheric pressure decreases towards your left." (This is the rule for the northern hemisphere. South of the Equator the low pressure would be on the right.)

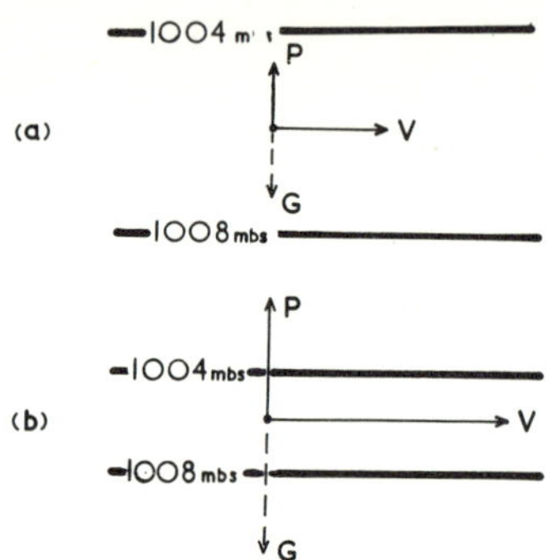

Fig. 1.8. The geostrophic wind speed necessary to maintain the balance between the pressure gradient force, *P*, and the geostrophic force, *G*, is determined by the steepness of the pressure gradient. The steeper the gradient the stronger the geostrophic wind speed.

The airflow is also affected by other forces which have not yet been mentioned, but usually these forces are relatively small and, in general, Nature confirms the deductions we have made. So the pressure map acquires a new significance. To view the current wind systems the pressure gradients at a variety of points can be measured and the corresponding wind arrows can be inserted for easy reference. Such a map would look like that shown in Figure 1.9*a*, but in practice it is rarely necessary to draw wind arrows all over the map. A mere glance at, say, the pressure map of Figure 1.9*b* reveals that there is a north-easterly airstream across Iceland and a broad flow of north-westerly winds across much of Great Britain. For the moment there is no need to worry about precise wind speeds, but until a greater familiarity with pressure charts is attained it may be wise to indicate the direction of the geostrophic winds by marking arrows on some of the isobars.

Trajectories

The pressure chart reveals the current wind systems only for the particular time of the chart. To determine the trajectory, or true

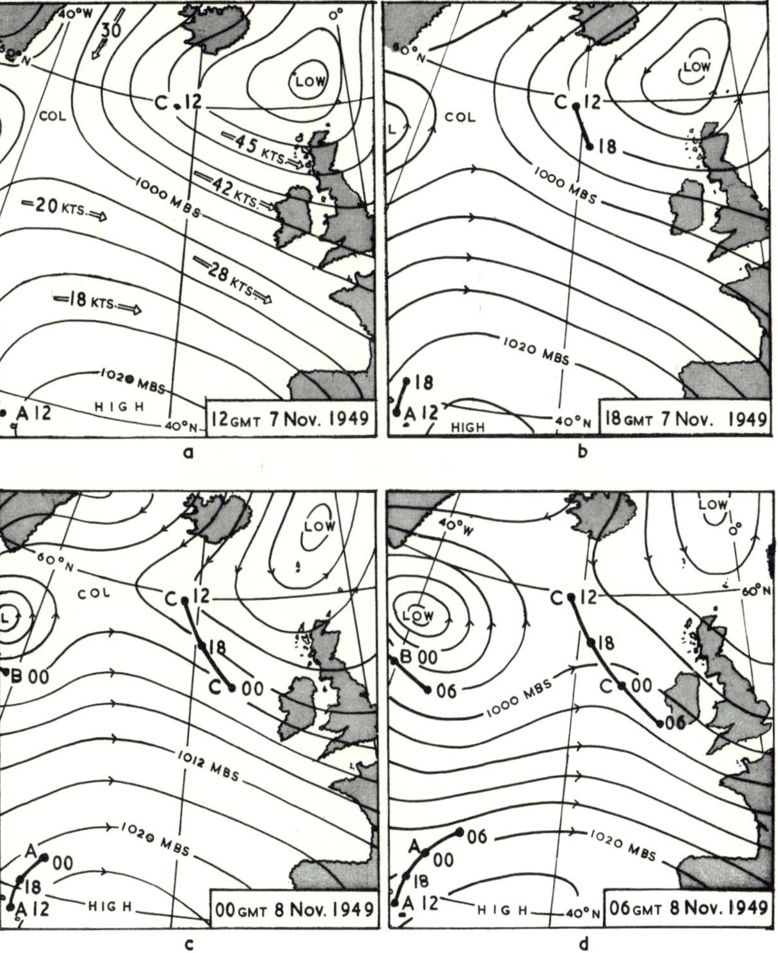

Fig. 1.9. A sequence of charts is used to trace trajectories of the air. Points on the three trajectories are numbered according to the times, e.g. A.12 marks a 12 GMT position of the air whose trajectory is traced from A.12 at 12 GMT 7 November 1949 to the 06 GMT position on 9 November 1949. (Page 14.)
A selection of geostrophic wind speeds has been computed and inserted in Figure 1.9*a*. On the remaining charts arrows on the isobars indicate the sense of direction only of the geostrophic flow.

path, of a parcel of air we need a sequence of pressure maps. In the sequence of Figure 1.9 a parcel of air at position A.12 at 12 GMT 7 November 1949 was moving with the geostrophic wind, 10 knots from the south, at that position at that time, but while the parcel

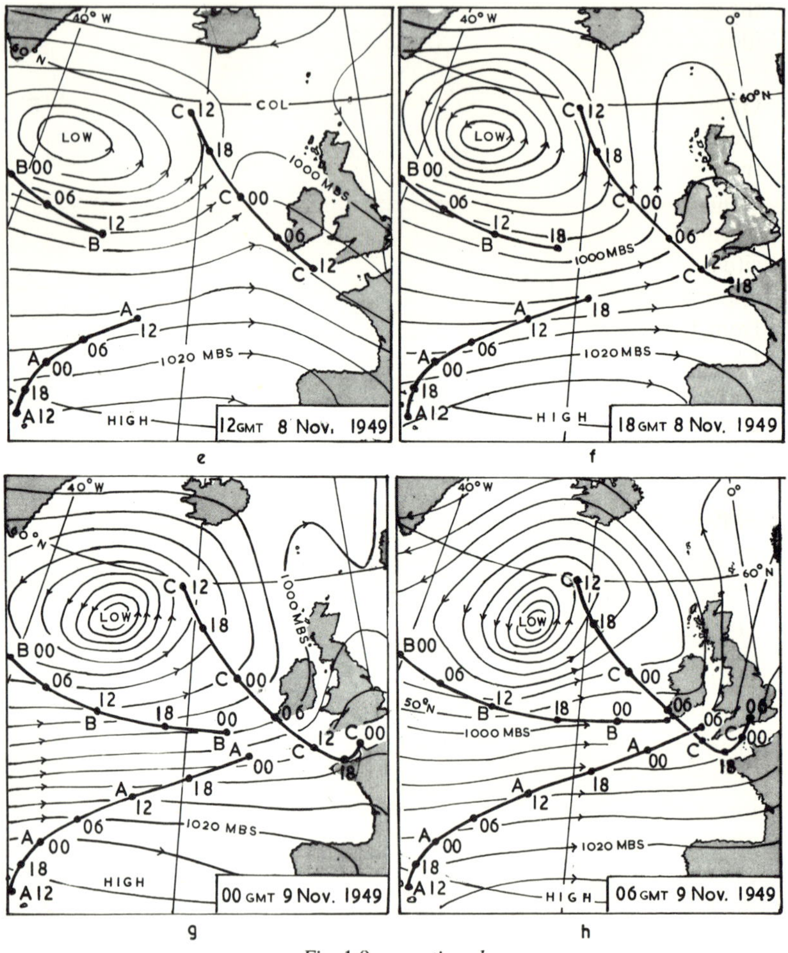

Fig. 1.9.—*continued*

moved the pressure pattern changed so that 6 hours later the parcel then at position A.18 was being propelled by a geostrophic wind of 220/12, i.e. 12 knots *from* a direction of 220 degrees. The complete trajectory of the parcel of air throughout this sequence of charts is along the path A.12, A.18, A.00, ... A.06.

Soon after 06 GMT 9 November this air crossed Wales where it was noticeable for its warmth for the time of the year and its dampness—just as may be expected of air which has travelled a long way over the sea from a comparatively warm region. After tracking the movement of air across other parts of the map we can form some idea of the distribution of warmth and moisture in the air around us.

Trajectory *B* shows the route of rather cold air from south of Greenland towards south-west England, but before studying track *C* look again at Figure 1.4, p. 8. Here the isobars indicate winds from the south-south-west in the neighbourhood of Rugby, but we should be wrong to deduce, from this chart alone, that this air was warm. Trajectory *C*, in Figure 1.9 on the charts leading up to the situation at 06 GMT 9 November 1949, reveals that this air which approached Rugby from the south-south-west had in fact travelled from the cold north-west. After being swept down to the English Channel in the rear of a depression moving away towards the Norwegian Sea, this cold air was caught up in the developing circulation of a succeeding low pressure system. This is how it happened to flow up over England to complete the sandwich of warm air between two masses of cold air at 06 GMT 9 November 1949 over the British Isles. We shall make a more detailed inspection of this sandwich in a later chapter.

Wind observations

In modern meteorological practice wind direction, that is the direction *from* which the wind blows, is reported in degrees true or in points of the compass. In Figure 1.10 showing the relationship between the two angular measures, the apostrophes stand for "by"; for example, NE'N is pronounced "north-east by north." To complete our vocabulary relating to wind direction we must note that the wind *backs* when its direction changes in an anticlockwise sense on Figure 1.10 and *veers* when the direction turns clockwise.

Most meteorological stations have some sort of *anemometer* for measuring wind speed. One type of instrument, of which there are various patterns, is the *cup anemometer* whose basic feature comprises three or four hemispherical cups fixed to a vertical spindle about which the cups can be rotated by the wind. The wind speed is very nearly proportional to the speed of rotation of the spindle and this angular speed can be measured in one of several ways; by using a mechanical counter to record the number of revolutions in a short time interval, or by applying the magnetic drag principle similar to that used in motor car speedometers, or by measuring the current generated by a dynamo driven by the rotating spindle. Inertia prevents cup anemometers from registering the fine details of gusts and lulls usually present in a natural airstream. To obtain such details a recording *pressure tube anemometer* is used. Based on the pitot tube principle with a wind vane to keep the tube pointing into

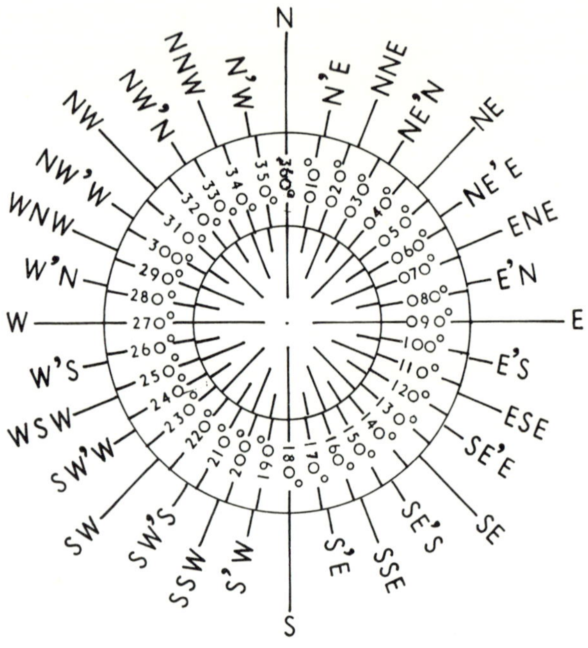

Fig. 1.10. Relationship between degrees true and points of the compass.

wind, this rather expensive and complicated instrument faithfully records fluctuations of wind speed and direction graphically on a cylindrical chart which is rotated by clockwork.

By comparing wind speed estimations with anemometer readings it is not difficult for an observer to learn to estimate wind speed with reasonable accuracy by the feel of the wind on his face or the sound in his ears, but without adequate training and occasional checking he is likely to overestimate the speed of moderate to strong breezes.

Wind speeds are usually reported in knots in English speaking countries, but as a result of pioneer work by Admiral Beaufort, who classified wind forces according to their effect on a "well conditioned man-of-war," the Beaufort wind scale is more familiar to some users of meteorological information. The descriptions and Beaufort equivalents of wind speeds up to 71 knots are tabled below.

WIND SPEEDS AND DESCRIPTIONS

Description	*Speed knots*	*Mean speed knots*	*Beaufort force*	*Terms used in forecasts for the general public*
Calm	Less than 1	0	0	Calm
Light air	1–3	2	1	Light
Light breeze	4–6	5	2	
Gentle breeze	7–10	9	3	
Moderate breeze	11–16	13	4	Moderate
Fresh breeze	17–21	19	5	Fresh
Strong breeze	22–27	24	6	Strong
Moderate gale	28–33	30	7	
Fresh gale	34–40	37	8	Gale
Strong gale	41–47	44	9	Severe gale or storm
Whole gale	48–55	52	10	
Storm	56–63	60	11	
Hurricane	64–71	68	12	

CHAPTER 2

The Nature of the Air

Temperature

To measure temperatures aloft, meteorologists use an apparatus called a radio-sonde; this is a lightweight radio transmitter coupled with devices for measuring pressure, temperature and humidity. The apparatus is carried up into the air by a gas-filled balloon, and while ascending it emits radio signals which can be monitored and translated into pressure, temperature and humidity readings by operators on the ground. The balloon normally ascends to between 60,000 ft. and 80,000 ft. (20,000 m. and 25,000 m.) before bursting and leaving the radio-sonde with a small parachute to check its rate of fall. When plotted against height the temperature readings usually yield graphs of the patterns shown in Figure 2.1. Here the temperature soundings for midday on 12 February 1958 are plotted for seven radio-sonde stations ranging from the tropics to the arctic. The characteristics common to all of these graphs are a decrease of temperature in the lower part of the atmosphere and fairly constant temperature with height at higher levels. In every case the level at which the temperature stops decreasing with height is distinctive enough to merit a special name; it is called the *tropopause*. The lower part of the atmosphere in which the temperature usually decreases with height is called the *troposphere*, and the huge region above forms the *stratosphere*.

The tropopause acts as a sort of lid on cloud formation throughout the world. Clouds are rarely found in the stratosphere, so when discussing cloud structure we can keep our ideas of height and depth in proper perspective by remembering that almost all cloud is confined to the troposphere. At the same time we must not regard the tropopause as a level in the sense of being rigid, flat or horizontal. Apart from transient humps and hollows and a seasonal

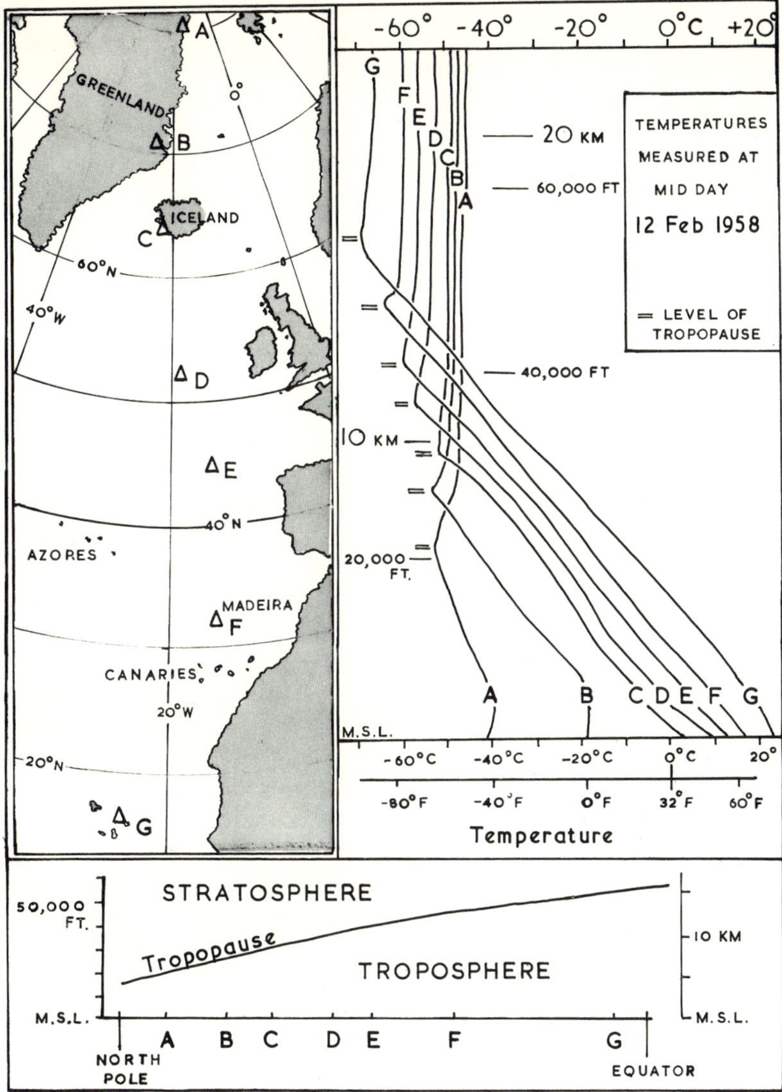

Fig. 2.1. Temperature measurements at the seven radio-sonde stations marked on the map reveal the tropopause to be low towards the North Pole and high towards the Equator.

tendency to rise in the summer and lower in the winter, the tropopause is generally at a high level over the tropics and relatively low over the poles (as illustrated in the lower part of Figure 2.1).

The lapse rate

In many meteorological processes the rate of change of temperature with height plays just as important a rôle as that of the temperature itself and, for brevity, this rate of change is referred to as the *lapse rate*. Figure 2.2 illustrates that the air over Camborne at 03 GMT 5 June 1950 had a lapse rate of about 1·5° C. per 1,000 ft. between 3,700 and 6,000 ft. At lower levels the current weather

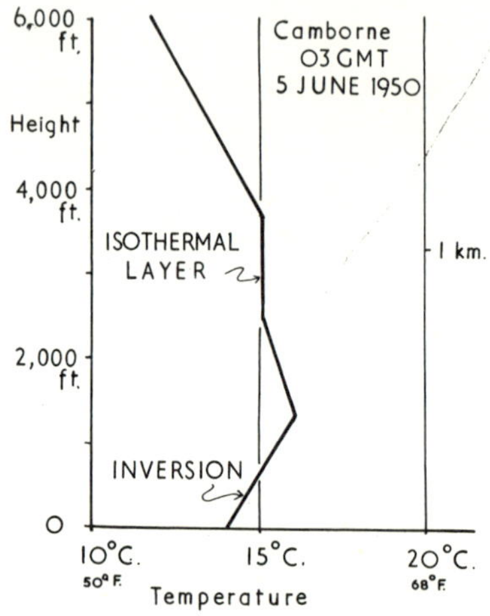

Fig. 2.2. Upper air temperatures for Camborne 03.00 GMT 5 June 1950.

conditions had produced an *isothermal* layer between 2,500 ft. and 3,700 ft., while from ground level up to 1,300 ft. there was an *inversion*—that is a temperature increase with height.

Moisture in the air

If a piece of salt is dropped into a glass of water the salt dissolves and becomes invisible, and if more salt is added this, too, dissolves until a certain limit is reached. At this limit the water is said to be saturated with salt and any more salt added will not dissolve; it will remain solid and visible in the water. In the same way as water has a limited capacity for dissolving salt, so air has a limited capacity for containing invisible, evaporated water—or, to give it its correct name, *water vapour*.

A dry airstream crossing the sea acts almost as though it were a vertical piece of dry blotting paper; it soaks up water which creeps higher and higher from the sea surface—but unlike the blotting paper the air does not readily show its absorbed moisture.

Returning to the salt and water analogy we could try a simple experiment. If the water were warmed we should find it possible to dissolve more salt into it. Then if the water were allowed to cool down to its original temperature again this additional salt would reappear white and solid, thereby demonstrating that the water's capacity for containing invisible salt depends upon its temperature;

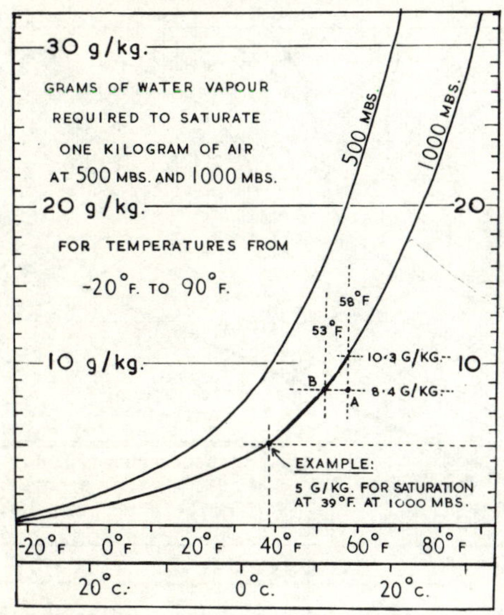

Fig. 2.3. Saturation water vapour content for air at 1000 mbs. and 500 mbs. Points *A* and *B* refer to positions in Fig. 2.4.

the higher the temperature the greater the quantity of salt which can be dissolved into its invisible state. Similarly the capacity of air for holding water vapour also increases with temperature. Pressure, too, has an effect on the air's capacity for water vapour, but only a subsidiary effect. Figure 2.3 shows the experimentally determined relationship between pressure, temperature and saturation water vapour content. The plotted curves indicate how much water vapour is required to saturate air at pressures of 1000 mbs. and 500 mbs. over a range of temperatures. One kilogram of air at, say, a pressure of 1000 mbs. and temperature of 39° F. (4° C.) needs only 5 gms. of water vapour for saturation. If weather conditions contrive to mix, say, 6 gms. of water with 1 kg. of air at 39° F. at 1000 mbs. it is likely that 5 gms. of this water will be in the form of invisible water vapour and the remaining 1 gm. will be liquid water—mostly in the form of minute droplets visible as cloud with perhaps some larger drops of drizzle or rain.

To enhance the realism of Figure 2.3 let us trace the history of a parcel of air which, at 12 GMT 3 May 1956, was approaching the Channel Isles. Dots on the trajectory sketched in Figure 2.4 mark the calculated positions of the parcel for 12-hourly intervals during the

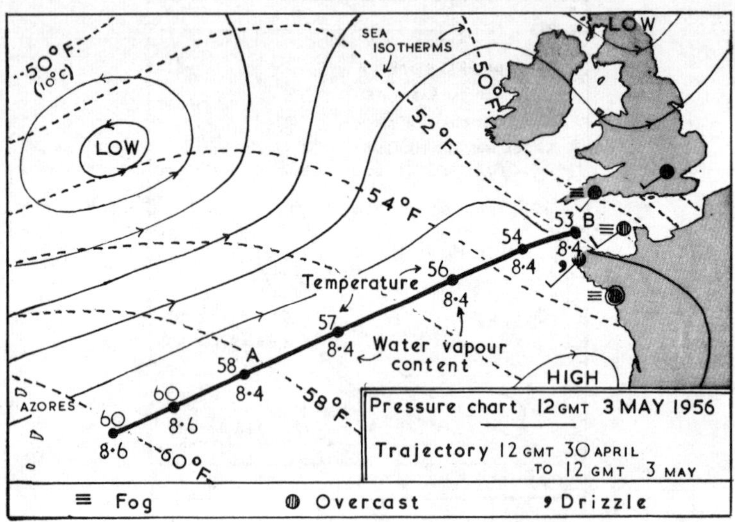

Fig. 2.4 Dots on the thick line mark the positions of warm moist air at 12-hour intervals on its path from the Azores. (50° F. = 10° C., 59° F. = 15° C.)

previous 72 hours. Adjacent to each dot are the temperatures in degrees Fahrenheit and water vapour content in grams per kilogram of dry air. (Both temperature and water vapour content were deduced from meteorological observations made on ships at sea.) We see that after setting off from the Azores with a temperature of 60° F. and a water vapour content of 8·6 g./kg. this particular parcel of air was cooled during its passage over progressively colder sea. During the first 24 hours the water vapour content of the air near sea level was slightly reduced probably due to water vapour seeping up into relatively dry air aloft slightly quicker than it could be replaced at low levels by evaporation from the sea. However, during the subsequent 48 hours the water vapour content of the low level air remained at 8·4 g./kg. so that when the air temperature reached 53° F. at position *B*, the air became saturated. But the air continued to cool down on its progress along the English Channel, so some of the water vapour was obliged to condense into tiny water drops. Millions of these drops fell slowly into the sea, but millions were kept in the air by the turbulent motion of the air itself, and every minute millions more were produced by the condensation now going on. In fact it was hard to see for water drops and what do we find in the observer's log for Jersey at midday 3 May 1956 but "Fog. Visibility 330 yds. (300 metres.)"

Relative humidity and dew point

There are several ways of expressing the dampness of the air. One method, which we have already used, is to state the *water vapour content* in grams per kilogram of dry air. In some circumstances it is more convenient to use other modes of expression. The familiar name, *relative humidity*, denotes the actual water vapour content of the air expressed as a percentage of the amount required for saturation. The linkage between relative humidity, temperature and water vapour content is best illustrated by specific examples. At position *A* in Figure 2.4 air at 58° F. contained 8·4 gms. of water vapour per kilogram of dry air. Reference to Figure 2.3 shows the saturation water vapour content of air at this temperature to be 10·3 g./kg. Therefore, the relative humidity was equal to:

$$\frac{\text{the actual water vapour content}}{\text{the saturation water vapour content}} \times 100 = \frac{8{\cdot}4}{10{\cdot}3} \times 100 = 82\%$$

Similar reasoning leads to 100% for the relative humidity of the air at position *B*.

Another method of expressing the moisture content of the air is to specify its *dew point*; this is the temperature to which the air must be cooled to bring it to the point of saturation. Referring once more to Figures 2.3 and 2.4 we see that the dew point of the air at position *A* must have been 53° F. because if the air had been cooled to this temperature (without adding or subtracting any water vapour) it would have been just saturated. At position *B*, where relative humidity was 100%, both temperature and dew point were 53° F.

These and other forms of expressing the dampness of the air all have their particular uses. Relative humidity indicates the dampness or dryness of the air without specifying the precise amount of water present. In everyday meteorological practice the term dew point is commonly used in conjunction with temperature. But to acquire an understanding of the physical processes of weather it is often more instructive to talk and think in terms of water vapour content; this method of expression does convey the idea that air can contain and carry with it a certain amount of invisible water vapour.

Latent heat

If you were to take the temperature of water being heated in an electric kettle you would observe this temperature to rise steadily to the boiling point of water (100° C. or 212° F. at average M.S.L. pressure) then stay at this temperature until all the water had boiled away. The interpretation of these observations is that during the first stage of this simple, but domestically inconvenient, kitchen experiment heat is being used to raise the temperature of the water, but during the boiling stage heat is used to convert the water into vapour. This heat is carried away with the vapour and is called the *latent heat* of evaporation of water.

Water does not need to be heated to 100° C. before it evaporates; it will evaporate from any moist surface or damp region into relatively dry airstreams, and in doing so the vapour acquires latent heat usually at the expense of the air into which the evaporation takes place.

One of the least impressive but most valuable of the meteorologist's instruments is the "wet and dry bulb" hygrometer. One of two shaded thermometers placed side by side has its bulb covered with muslin kept permanently damp by moisture creeping up through a wick dipped in water. Unless the surrounding air is saturated, water evaporates from the damp muslin and extracts latent heat from the immediate surroundings. Thus the "wet bulb" thermometer is cooled. The drier the airstream flowing past the thermometers the greater the evaporation and the bigger will be the difference between the dry and the wet bulb temperatures. In practice a special slide rule or appropriate tables are used to calculate the relative humidity and dew point from the two thermometer readings.

When water vapour condenses back into liquid form it gives up its latent heat to its surroundings. This release of latent heat by condensation is Nature's principal device for changing the tempo of atmospheric events. We shall see later how such changes are produced; for the moment let us realise the magnitude of the effect by noting that the latent heat released by condensation of only 1 gm. of water vapour is sufficient to raise the temperature of 1 kg. of air about 1° F. (At M.S.L. 1 kg. of air occupies a volume of about 1 cubic metre.) Or it may be more impressive to remark that:

1 calorie of heat is required to raise the temperature of 1 gm. of water 1° C.

About 590 calories are required to evaporate 1 gm. of water.

Pressure variation with height

Because the air at any level in the atmosphere has to support the weight of the air above it, the lower layers are compressed much more than those above. Thus atmospheric pressure decreases as the height increases. The precise relationship between altitude and pressure depends upon the prevailing pressure system and on the temperature, warm air taking up more space than cold and dense air. The rough, round figure relationship between pressure and altitude is :

M.S.L.	1000 mbs.
3,000 ft. (1,000 m.)	900 mbs.
10,000 ft. (3,000 m.)	700 mbs.
20,000 ft. (6,000 m.)	500 mbs.
30,000 ft. (10,000 m.)	300 mbs.

Air which moves upward through the atmosphere is allowed to expand, and descending air is compressed. Vigorous use of a bicycle pump easily illustrates that air can be warmed by compression, but the opposite effect of cooling by expansion is not so obvious in everyday life. It is nevertheless a fact, and the consequence is that, in the atmosphere, ascending air is cooled. Descending air is, of course, compressed and warmed.

Before deducing the ultimate consequences of ascent or descent we must not forget the all-important ingredient, water vapour. Unless some moistening or drying process is going on, a parcel of air and the water vapour it contains move together as a single entity, and if this parcel is cooled by ascent to below its dew point then some of the water vapour will be condensed into liquid water drops. Descent of air, on the other hand, leads to an increase of temperature and a consequent increase of the air's capacity to contain water vapour, so that as air descends in the atmosphere the relative humidity decreases.

The adiabatic lapse rates

The rate at which cooling by ascent or warming during descent occurs is closely regulated by natural laws governing the physical properties of air and water. The temperature of unsaturated air changes at about 3° C. for every 1,000 ft. change of height (1° C. per 100 m.). If, for example, unsaturated air with a temperature of 10° C. rises from M.S.L. to 2,000 ft. (600 m.) its temperature at the new level will be 4° C. This rate of change of 3° C. per 1,000 ft. is known as the *Dry Adiabatic Lapse Rate* (D.A.L.R.). In this context the word "adiabatic" means that this lapse rate applies to air which ascends or descends without exchanging any heat with its surroundings.

We have already noted that ascent of saturated air must be accompanied by condensation. The condensation itself releases latent heat which tends to warm the air—or rather to reduce the rate of cooling taking place. The net result is 1·5° C. per 1,000 ft. (1° C. per 200 m.) for the *Saturated Adiabatic Lapse Rate* (S.A.L.R.) at low levels. At high levels (i.e. low pressures) and low temperatures the saturated water vapour contents are smaller, so the release of latent heat is less effective and the saturated adiabatic lapse rate is not very different from the D.A.L.R.

Radiation of heat

Heat and light are propagated through air and through space in the form of pulses or vibrations known as electro-magnetic waves. Every object, whatever its temperature, emits heat by radiation and also receives heat radiating from its surroundings. If the outgoing radiation from the object exceeds the incoming radiant heat the temperature of the object decreases, but when the net effect is a gain of heat the temperature rises. The intensity of the outgoing radiation depends upon the temperature of the object; the hotter the object the more intense the radiation; but the temperature affects not only the intensity but also the wavelengths on which the radiation takes place. A red-hot object emits electromagnetic waves which are particularly intense for wavelengths of about 0·000035 in. and our eyes interpret such electromagnetic waves as red light.

Bearing in mind the effect of waves on an anchored boat or the reflection and dispersion of waves by a rocky shore, it is not difficult to appreciate that the interaction between electromagnetic waves and the objects they encounter is a complex process whose outcome is critically dependent on the wavelength in relation to the structure, size and weight of the objects encountered. Radiant heat from the sun (*insolation*) arrives at the troposphere mostly on wavelengths between 0·00001 in. and 0·0001 in. This wave band includes short waves (of about 0·000017 in. wavelength) which are particularly prone to scattering by molecules of dry air and water vapour, and since our eyes recognise such electromagnetic waves as blue light we see the sky as a blue canopy above. When larger dust and smoke particles accrue in the atmosphere the blue light from the sun may be almost entirely cut off while longer waves penetrate the haze and make the sun visible as a dull red ball. Although these interactions between solar radiation and the air produce visible effects, their nature is such as to produce only a small direct effect on the temperature of the air. On a cloudless day the bulk of the incoming solar radiation passes through the air almost without heating it. It is the earth's surface that absorbs this heat and this surface warms the air with which it is in contact. The practically incessant stirring motion of the air then spreads this heat upwards into the troposphere. By comparison with the sun's rays radiation of heat from the earth's surface (*terrestrial radiation*) takes place on long wavelengths, about 0·0002 to 0·002 in. Some of this long wave radiation happens to have a direct heating effect on water vapour; damp air can absorb heat radiated from the ground whereas dry air is almost transparent to such radiation. The consequences of this difference between the radiative absorption properties of dry air and water vapour are intricate and varied, but they are often swamped by the stirring motion already mentioned, and, broadly speaking, their net effect is to underline the statement that the air in the troposphere is heated by the earth from below rather than by the sun from above.

The fate of insolation received at the earth's surface depends upon the nature of the surface itself; some surfaces reflect rather than absorb this radiant heat. Snow or ice covered ground, for example, reflects between 40% and 90% of the incident radiation, whereas a dark mould surface will reflect only 10% of the incoming radiant heat. This reflective power (called the *albedo*) varies with the state of the ground; dry sand reflects about 18% (this is equivalent to saying that its albedo is 0·18), while for wet sand the reflection drops to 9% (albedo 0·09). The albedo of a water surface varies according to the sun's zenith angle; for sunshine from directly overhead it is 0·02, when the sun is only 10 degrees above the horizon the water surface albedo is 0·35. Cloud layers also reflect radiation; thin layers not more than 500 ft. (150 m.) thick can reflect between 5% and 65% of the incident radiation, while for thicknesses of about 3,000 ft. (1,000 m.) the reflective power of an extensive layer of cloud is between about 45% and 85%. A cloud layer can reflect radiant heat from both its top and its base.

CHAPTER 3

Introducing the Clouds

Ascending air expands, cools and, if the air is sufficiently moist, some of its accompanying water vapour may condense into a cloud of minute water drops. There is no harm in stressing that statement, for almost all clouds are born in ascending air. So the pertinent question is: what causes the air to rise? High ground? Yes, that is an obvious answer which many a mountaineer can confirm. If air blowing up a mountainside reaches its *condensation level*—the level at which cooling by ascent produces saturation—then cloud will form. Such cloud does not always hug the hill tops; sometimes it appears high in the sky, the air at low levels being relatively dry. On the other hand, it is not uncommon for the low level air to be so moist and condensation to be so prolific that many of the tiny cloud particles coalesce into larger drops which then fall out of the cloud as rain, or if the temperature is low enough as snow. Whatever

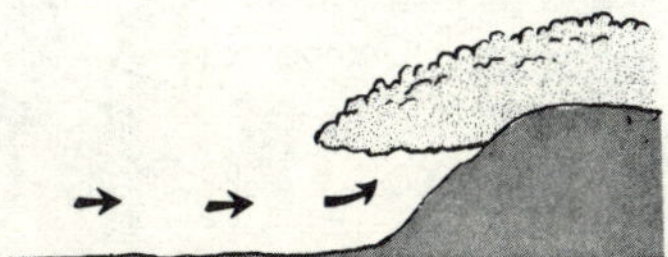

Fig. 3.1. Air flowing up a mountainside cools and if this cooling leads to condensation then orographic cloud will form.

the precise effect may be, this cloud which is produced by air flowing over high ground, as illustrated in Figure 3.1, is called *orographic cloud* and any resultant rainfall is called *orographic rain.*

Convection cloud

Over now from mountains to a weather ship keeping to its ocean station 400 miles west of Ireland. At 15 GMT 9 January 1956 the observer here reported cloud, but there are no mountains over the Atlantic to push the air up high; here the upward motion of the air was brought about by other means. The airstream flowing from the north travelled over progressively warmer sea (see Figure

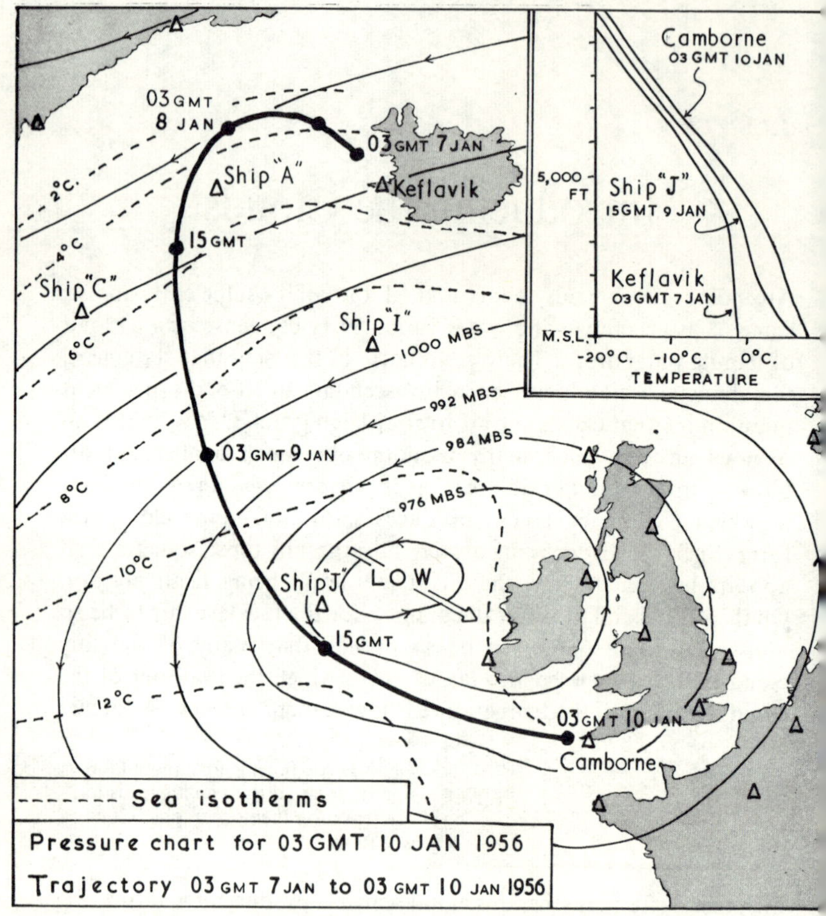

Fig. 3.2. Radio-sonde stations are indicated by the triangles. The trajectory of cold air from the region of Iceland is marked by the thick line with dots at 12-hour intervals. The temperature/height graphs reveal how much the air was warmed during its passage over the progressively warmer sea.

3.2) and the air just skimming over the waves was warmed by the sea itself. When air is warmed it becomes lighter and soon this air near the sea surface became so light and buoyant that bubbles of it began to float up into the air aloft. Because the bulk of the air aloft was

Plate 1 CUMULUS HUMILIS

Small fair-weather cumulus floating in the sky as an Olympia 419 takes off during the 1960 World Gliding Championships at Butzweilerhof, Germany.

fairly cold and therefore somewhat dense the bubbles penetrated to heights of several thousand feet in the atmosphere, and here again the ascent produced cooling, condensation and clouds. These clouds differed in character from the orographic type; they were formed not in a steady upward stream but in bubbles of rising air and the very shape of the clouds confirmed their method of growth. With fairly flat bases at the condensation level, the clouds looked like puffs of cotton wool floating in the sky. Figure 3.3 illustrates

Fig. 3.3 Cloud formed by cooling and condensation in rising convection currents is of the cumulus variety.

their general shape and method of formation, and Plate 1 shows the same type of cloud photographed on another occasion.

Plate 2 CUMULONIMBUS INCUS *R. K. Pilsbury*

The tops of very deep convection cloud usually spread out to give the cloud an anvil shape. Wind shear often stretches the anvil out, and, because this part of the cloud is composed of ice crystals which are slow to evaporate, such anvils occasionally form extensive tongues of cirrus cloud.

Cumulus, as this type of cloud is called, is commonly found in cold and sufficiently moist airstreams which are being heated from below. This low level heating need not be confined to air passing over a progressively warmer surface; it can be generated in another way. As explained in Chapter 2, the nature of clear air is such that heat rays from the sun pass right through the air almost without warming it, just as they pass through the glass of a greenhouse almost without warming the glass itself. It is the ground which is warmed by the sun's rays, and the ground in turn warms the air with which it is in contact. Thus if the air aloft is fairly cold, convection currents will be set up and, if the air is moist enough, cumulus clouds will form. In gliding parlance the upward convection currents are usually called *thermals*.

Convection cloud varies in depth and extent from one weather situation to another. Sometimes the clouds are scattered and shallow, say only 1,000 ft. from base to top; sometimes they tower upwards to 20,000, 30,000 or even 40,000 ft. before spreading out into an anvil-shaped top like that of the *cumulonimbus* cloud in Plate 2. Dark and ominous when viewed from below, these thick convection clouds usually produce heavy showers of rain, hail, sleet or snow and turbulent processes within the cloud sometimes generate thunder and lightning.

Turbulence cloud

A third cause of air being lifted up to its condensation level is turbulence. The friction encountered by an airstream flowing over the ground creates a layer of turbulent air from the ground up to about 1,000 ft. in light breezes, and to about 4,000 or 5,000 ft. in strong winds. A sea surface produces a similar but slightly shallower effect. Unless the wind is very strong this turbulence is seldom violent, but even in a light breeze, when the turbulence is little more than a gentle stirring motion, some of the air at low levels is lifted up through the turbulent layer and if this lifting extends above the condensation level cloud will form in the patterns indicated in Figure 3.4.

Fig. 3.4. A general stirring up of the air at low levels produces stratocumulus type of cloud above the condensation level.

This type of cloud is called *stratocumulus*, although if it forms at a very low level it is usually called *stratus*.

Classification of clouds

We shall learn more about the formation of clouds in subsequent chapters of this book, but before reading these chapters it is as well to acquire some familiarity with the more formal descriptions of cloud types and structure. By international convention, based on world-wide observations, clouds are classified into the ten types listed on the following pages.

Name	*Abbreviations*	*Description*	*Examples of cloud symbols used on Weather Charts*
Cirrus	Ci	Detached white or mostly white clouds in the form of delicate filaments, or patches, or narrow bands.	
Cirrocumulus	Cc Ci-Cu	Thin white patch, sheet or layer of cloud composed of very small elements in the form of grains or ripples more or less regularly arranged; most of the elements have an apparent width of less than one degree.	
Cirrostratus	Cs Ci-St	Translucent, whitish veil of cloud generally producing halo phenomena. (Produced by refraction and reflection of light through the prismatic ice crystals of which the cirrus is formed, the most common of the halo phenomena is a white or slightly coloured ring around the sun or moon ; the angle between the arc of this halo and the sun or moon is 22 degrees.)	
Altocumulus	Ac Alto-Cu	White or grey patch, sheet or layer of cloud composed of rounded masses or rolls; most of the more or less regularly arranged small elements usually have an apparent width of between one and five degrees.	
Altostratus	As Alto-St	Greyish cloud sheet without halo phenomena and through which the sun is barely visible.	
Nimbostratus	Ns Nb-St Nimb-St	Grey cloud layer thick enough to blot out the sun.	
Stratocumulus	Sc St-Cu	Grey or whitish patch, sheet or layer of cloud composed of rounded masses or rolls; most of the more or less regularly arranged small elements have an apparent width of more than five degrees.	

Name	*Abbreviations*	*Description*	*Examples of cloud symbols used on Weather Charts*
Stratus	St	Generally grey cloud layer with fairly uniform base.	—
Cumulus	Cu	Detached clouds developing vertically in the form of rising mounds with cauliflower shaped tops.	⌓
Cumulonimbus	Cb Cu-Nb CuNim Cu-Nimb	Dense cloud with considerable vertical extent, in the form of a mountain or huge towers. At least part of its upper portion is usually smooth or striated, and nearly always flattened; this part spreads out in the shape of an anvil or vast plume.	⧖

Observations have shown that clouds are encountered over a range of altitudes varying from sea level to the tropopause and, by convention, this range is divided into three broad levels: high, medium and low. Each broad level is defined according to the types of cloud it most frequently contains. We have:

Cirrus, cirrocumulus and cirrostratus at *high* levels
Altocumulus at *medium* levels
Stratocumulus and stratus at *low* levels

The two uppermost ranges overlap and their depths vary with latitude, the approximate limits being:

	Polar regions	*Temperate regions*	*Tropical regions*
High	10,000–25,000 ft. (3–8 km.)	16,500–45,000 ft. (5–13 km.)	20,000–60,000 ft. (6–18 km.)
Medium	6,500–13,000 ft. (2–4 km.)	6,500–23,000 ft. (2–7 km.)	6,500–25,000 ft. (2–8 km.)
Low	0–6,500 ft. (0–2 km.)	0–6,500 ft. (0–2 km.)	0–6,500 ft. (0–2 km.)

Cloud types which are not always confined to one of these three broad levels are:

Altostratus which is usually found at medium levels but often extends higher.
Nimbostratus which is almost invariably found at medium levels, but usually extends to both low and high levels.
Cumulus and *cumulonimbus* which usually have their bases at low levels but whose tops may reach medium or high levels.

Observed peculiarities in the shape of clouds and differences in their internal structure have led to the subdivision of most of the cloud types into various species. Three of these species are:

Altocumulus castellanus (Ac cas or Alto-Cu Cast.)
Altocumulus with marked turrets, groups of which seem to be arranged in lines and connected by a common base. The term castellanus may also be applied to Ci, Cc and Sc.
Altocumulus lenticularis (Ac len or Alto-Cu Lent.)
Altocumulus having the shape of lenses or almonds, often very elongated and usually with well-defined outlines.
Stratus fractus (St fra)
Better known as Fracto-stratus (Fr-St). Ragged stratus in irregular shreds. The prefix Fracto- may also be applied to ragged Cu.

In casual conversation description of clouds can easily be amplified by ordinary adjectives such as "woolly," "tufted," "tattered," etc., but, to enhance consistency in cloud observations, better defined though perhaps less graphic international specifications are available for whoever wishes to use them. The specifications applicable to cumulus or cumulonimbus are:

Humilis (hum) Cumulus clouds of only a slight vertical extent; they generally appear flattened.
Mediocris (med) Cumulus clouds of moderate vertical extent, the tops of which show fairly small protuberances.
Congestus (con) Cumulus clouds which are markedly sprouting and are often of great vertical extent; their bulging upper part frequently resembles a cauliflower.
Calvus (cal) Cumulonimbus in which at least some protuberances of the upper part are beginning to lose

their cumiliform outlines but in which no cirriform parts can be distinguished.

Capillatus (cap) Cumulonimbus characterised by the presence, mostly in its upper portion, of a distinct cirriform cloud, frequently having the form of an anvil or vast plume. Cumulonimbus capillatus is usually accompanied by a shower or by a thunderstorm.

Clouds sometimes have supplementary features attached to them or may be accompanied by other usually smaller clouds known as accessory clouds. Five of these supplementary features are:

Mamma (mam) Otherwise known as mammatus. Hanging bulges on the under surface of a cloud.

Virga (vir) Vertical or inclined trails of precipitation ("fallstreaks") attached to the under surface of a cloud which do not reach the earth's surface.

Tuba (tub) Cloud column or inverted cloud cone protruding from a cloud base. Otherwise known as "*funnel cloud*," this type of cloud indicates the intense vortex motion of incipient or fully fledged tornadoes.

Incus (inc) The upper portion of a Cb spread out in the shape of an anvil with a smooth fibrous or striated appearance.

Pileus (pil) An accessory cloud in the form of a cap or hood above or attached to the upper part of a cumiliform cloud.

Cloud observations

At most meteorological observing stations cloud observations comprise three items: the type of cloud, the amount of cloud of this type and the height of the cloud base above the level of observation.

The classification of cloud types has already been described and we should note here that each type refers to the shape and not the method of formation of the cloud. This limitation may, at first, appear to be rather unscientific, but the observer seldom has sufficient information to speculate on why the cloud is there or how it attained its shape; it is wiser for him to report what he actually sees and let others interpret his observations according to their special interests. Frequently more than one type is within view and the observer, with procedural rules and codes to guide him, makes a compromise between brevity and thoroughness in describing the state of the sky.

Cloud amount is usually reported in eighths of the sky covered; 4/8 means half covered; 8/8, completely covered. Sometimes the internationally convened word "*oktas*" is substituted for "eighths."

The measurement or estimation of the height of cloud base ("ceiling" to the Americans) is a task whose difficulty varies considerably with general weather conditions and local facilities. The majority of observers are obliged to make estimations and, however conscientious and experienced an observer may be, he seldom claims to estimate cloud height with a smaller margin of error than 20% of the actual height. Sometimes the accuracy is worse. To appreciate the difficulty of the task we must realise that our eyes are very poor range finders; we judge distances by noting the apparent sizes of familiar objects. The method of estimating the distance away of a two-storey house or the altitude of a glider is virtually to compare the apparent sizes of these objects with the standard sizes we know them to be. But clouds are not confined to a small range of standard sizes; they range from small cloudlets to layers covering the whole sky, and so their apparent size is a fickle guide to their height or their distance away. Their apparent speed of movement is often helpful; the lower the clouds the faster they appear to move, but some idea of the wind speed at the level of cloud base is required in order to decide whether such apparent movement is due to the nearness of the cloud or whether the cloud really is moving quickly in a strong wind.

When 8/8 stratiform cloud is present estimation of its height may occasionally be little more than a plausible guess based on experience. Fortunately, the height of such cloud as this can often be found by instrumental techniques. One method involves measuring the time taken for a hydrogen-filled balloon of predetermined buoyancy to rise from the ground to cloud base. At night time simple trigonometry is used to derive cloud height from the measured angular elevation of the patch of cloud illuminated in the vertical beam of a distant *cloud searchlight*, while for less restricted use a few large airports are equipped with special radar devices or a daytime version of the cloud searchlight, but such devices are expensive and need judicious operators, especially on the occasions when the merging of low stratus with low level haze or smoke defies all attempts to discern a distinctive cloud base.

Naturally the observer best equipped to measure cloud height is the pilot who can fly up or down through cloud base, and on most airfields meteorological observers on the ground build up valuable experience by comparing their estimations with the cloud heights actually measured by pilots in the air.

CHAPTER 4

Frost, Fog and Smoke

Authors of fiction occasionally use the phrase, "blanket of cloud," little knowing how meteorologically apt it is; any low and reasonably thick layer of cloud does indeed act as a blanket for whatever part of the earth it covers. At night the fate of ground without a cloud cover is like that of a teapot without a cosy—it gets cold, or more precisely, it loses heat by radiation. As a natural consequence the air close to the ground is also cooled and its temperature decreases. The effect of this cooling at ground level is usually transmitted upwards into the atmosphere by turbulence rather than by conduction, air being a poor conductor of heat. In light winds the vertical extent of this turbulence is often 1,000 ft. or less, and a marked fall of temperature occurs in the low level layer to which the cooling is confined. Thus on cloudless nights with light winds *nocturnal radiation* of heat from the ground can produce a low level inversion—cold air at low levels with warmer air just above it. Because appreciable energy is needed to lift cold and dense air up into the warmer layer aloft, the presence of a temperature inversion damps down whatever stirring motion exists, and so the cooling is confined to a progressively shallower layer of air. At the end of a calm, clear night it is not unusual for the temperature at 4 ft. above ground level to be about 8° F. more than that at ground level itself and about 10–15° F. less than the temperature at a height of about 1,000 ft.

At ground level the loss of heat by radiation is partly compensated by the conduction of heat upwards through the ground from depths down to about 3 ft. where the earth temperature is extremely slow to change and is usually higher than that at the soil surface on a cold clear night. This upward conduction of heat is not nearly sufficient to compensate for the cooling by radiation at the surface, but, because local variations. In clear calm conditions night temperatures at the surface of light sandy soils (poor conductors of heat) are 5 to 10° F. lower than those at the surface of clay soils.

These local variations of temperature are not nearly so noticeable at heights of a few feet above the ground. At the 4-ft. level the temperature shown by a well-exposed thermometer is usually indicative of the regional effect of night cooling rather than the local differences between one field and the next. In this context a well-exposed thermometer is deemed by convention to be a thermometer shielded from direct radiation (yet well ventilated) situated over short grass well away from buildings, trees or other large objects. To achieve such exposure the meteorologist usually houses the thermometer in a carefully sited double louvred white box called a *Stevenson screen.* Unless otherwise stated, air temperature is usually taken to be this shade temperature at 4 ft. above the ground.

One of the daily tasks of many a weather forecaster is to predict the minimum temperature likely to occur during the night, usually at about dawn, and to help make such a prediction he applies the most appropriate of several methods. One such method, statistically appropriate for geostrophic wind speeds up to 25 knots over central and southern England, is expressed by the formula:

Minimum air temperature (° F.)
= + 0·32 × midday temperature (° F.)
+ 0·75 × predicted average cloud amount in eighths
+ 0·20 × predicted geostrophic wind speed (knots)
+ 0·55 × midday dew point (° F.)
− 4

Minimum air temperature (° C.)
= + 0·32 × midday temperature (° C.)
+ 0·42 × predicted average cloud amount in eighths
+ 0·11 × predicted geostrophic wind speed (knots)
+ 0·55 × midday dew point (° C.)
− 4·5

Although this formula is a rough but practical approximation to the theoretical truth about night cooling, it does at least illustrate the relative importance of the principal factors in the problem.

The formula shows that the lower the midday temperature and the lower the predicted cloud amount the lower will be the temperature during the night, while inclusion of the predicted geostrophic wind speed reminds us that the effect of cooling by radiation is distributed through the lowest few hundred or few thousand feet of the air by turbulence due to the wind; the lighter the wind, the lower will be the upper limit of turbulence, and the shallower the cooled layer, the greater will be the fall in temperature; therefore light winds mean low night temperatures. In assessing the geostrophic wind effect we should recall that surface wind speeds are usually less than the geostrophic speeds; inversions accentuate the difference so that on cold clear nights the wind near ground level may become considerably lighter than the geostrophic wind prevailing just above the top of the inversion.

The significance of the dew point in the formula is twofold. Firstly, it reflects the climatological fact that dry air over the British Isles is often associated with clear, fairly calm weather conditions favourable for plenty of night cooling. Secondly, the dew point is a measure of the amount of water vapour in the air, and water vapour, with its ability to intercept much of the long wave radiation of heat from the ground, can also act as a tenuous blanket covering the earth at night. So it is not surprising that low dew points are associated with cold nights.

To become better acquainted with the relative importance of temperature, cloud amount, geostrophic wind speed and dew point in night cooling we can put some real figures in the minimum temperature formula. For example, for a cloudless night with zero geostrophic wind speed the minimum temperature following a midday temperature and dew point of 60° F. and 40° F. respectively, the predicted minimum air temperature for the night would be just over 37° F. while for a completely overcast night with a 25-knot geostrophic wind and damper conditions characterised by a midday temperature and dew point of 60° F. and 54° F. the meteorologist would forecast scarcely any night cooling at all.

Frost

Air frost occurs when the air temperature decreases to the freezing point of water (32° F. or 0° C.) or below. Such a decrease may be the

Description	*Wind speed less than 10 knots*		*Wind speed 10 knots or more*	
Slight frost	27 to 32° F.	0 to −3·5° C.	31 to 32° F.	−0 to −0·4° C.
Moderate frost	21 to 26° F.	−3·6 to −6·4° C.	28 to 30° F.	−0·5 to −2·4° C.
Severe frost	11 to 20° F.	−6·5 to −11·5° C.	23 to 27° F.	−2·5 to −5·5° C.
Very severe frost	Below 11° F.	Below −11·6° C.	Below 23°F.	Below −5·6° C.

result of the arrival of a freezingly cold airstream, but in the British Isles the commonest cause of frost is nocturnal radiation on clear calm nights. In view of the far more damaging effect of low temperatures in strong winds than in calm conditions forecasters describe the intensity of frost in terms related to both temperature and surface wind speed according to the table on page 42.

The explanation already given for the existence of a low level inversion formed by night cooling implies that ground frosts occur more frequently than air frosts, and, in general, low level districts are more susceptible to night frosts than the slightly higher ground. Furthermore, since cold and dense air tends to sink, valleys and hollows become particularly cold on clear calm nights.

Fog

On most cold clear nights the dew point of the air decreases as some of the water vapour at very low levels is condensed and deposited as dew on the ground. But the rate of decrease of the dew point is usually less than that of the air temperature so if the cooling by radiation goes on long enough the air will become saturated, and continued cooling will produce condensation and cloud. Usually dense enough to restrict the visibility to less than 1,100 yds. (1 km.), such cloud is better described as *radiation fog*.

The initial depth of a radiation fog is critically dependent on the degree of turbulence in the air. In very calm conditions the condensation may be confined to a very shallow layer on the ground and the resultant *ground fog* may be only a foot or so deep. But only a slight increase in the stirring motion in the air is enough to spread the cooling up through a hundred feet or more and visibility deteriorates. Not infrequently a sharp increase in turbulence occurs just after dawn when heat from the sun is just strong enough to stir up the air at low levels but not sufficient to warm the air appreciably; it is, therefore, not at all unusual for radiation fog to form suddenly just after dawn.

The clearance of radiation fog is usually effected by one of three mechanisms:

1 The raising of the temperature of the air to above the saturation point by solar insolation.
2 The arrival of a drier airstream.

3 The lifting of the fog into low stratus as a result of an increase in wind and low level turbulence.

In the absence or failure of such mechanisms the fog will persist throughout the day, and if the subsequent night is also calm and cloudless the fog will tend to deepen as a result of further nocturnal radiation from the top of the fog out through the usually crystal clear air above.

Fog of other types

Night cooling is not the only generator of cloud at ground level. Hills and mountains may be high enough to reach into or right through an extensive layer of cloud and the cloud actually on the hillside is naturally known as *hill fog*. The same description can also apply to a fog formed as a result of the ascent of air up the mountainside, but the alternative name, *upslope fog*, is slightly more specific.

Another type of fog was described in Chapter 2 to illustrate condensation by cooling. In that illustration the fog reported at the Channel Isles was the end product of the cooling of warm moist air passing over a progressively colder surface. Naturally such fog can be called *sea fog* but if we merely wish to indicate that, unlike radiation fog, which forms *in situ*, a fog arrives from somewhere we can call it *advection fog*.

Sailors of polar oceans occasionally encounter *sea smoke*, or *steam fog*, as the sea surface steams into relatively cold air above it. In the British Isles we get an inkling of the process involved by the steaming from lakes and rivers in cold weather or from roads in sunshine after rain, but since such steam can persist or thicken only in rare conditions, steam fog is mainly of academic interest.

Smoke

In the densely populated industrial areas of the British Isles coal is burnt at the rate of about 10,000 tons per square mile per year, while for even small provincial towns the annual coal consumption is often as much as 500 tons per square mile. Over two million tons of soot from this burnt coal, together with an approximately equal amount of other atmospheric pollutants such as dust from roads and fields are deposited on our towns and countryside every year; London, Manchester and about 90 other towns get over 150 tons per square mile, and about 4 tons per square mile are deposited in the open country. In the interval between rising from and returning to ground level this particulate matter pollutes the atmosphere and restricts the visibility. Poor visibility must be expected when the pollution is dense, and this density is related not only to the proximity of the smoke source but also to the depth through which the smoke is distributed; a given amount of smoke spread through several thousand feet will restrict visibility far less than the same amount confined to a shallower layer of the atmosphere. It follows that smoke haze is particularly likely under low level inversions, for the conditions usually associated with such inversions inhibit the stirring up of the low level air to above the inversion top. Thus an inversion acts as a sort of lid on whatever smoke is being injected into the air from below, and in winter time if this lid is less than 1,000 ft. the concentration of smoke in very large towns can sometimes limit visibility to less than 1,100 yds.—the conventional visibility criterion for defining fog.

The density of smoke is also related to the wind speed. The stronger the wind the quicker and the farther will the smoke be carried from its source in a given time. Light wind conditions tend to inflict dense smoke and poor visibility close to a smoke source, whereas fresh winds carry and diffuse the smoke to form relatively slight haze over a large downwind zone. Intermediate conditions in which the wind is just sufficient to transport a smoke pall horizontally without being able to stir it well up into the atmosphere can be particularly troublesome to meteorologists and aviators. It is not uncommon for a pall to move slowly about the countryside reducing visibility to about 1 mile over several counties at a time, and while such a reduction of visibility is hardly noticeable in towns, the country hiker would lose his fine view of the landscape and an inexperienced pilot in the air would probably lose himself in such poor visibility.

About half of the smoke in our atmosphere is emitted by domestic fires, and from visibility records kept in or near large towns we can detect the effect of our national winter habits. The domestic chore of lighting a fire at about 8 a.m. or 9 a.m. is shown by the marked tendency for town visibility to decrease to a minimum at about 9 a.m. During the afternoon, when whatever heat there is from the sun tends to increase low level turbulence and to divert attention from the hearth, visibility is at its best—especially between 2 p.m. and 3 p.m., but comes the evening with renewed stoking of the fire and visibility is once more at a minimum between 8 p.m. and 9 p.m. Finally the nation sleeps, the fires go out and the atmosphere is at its cleanest between about 3 a.m. and 4 a.m. Of course, this cycle of events is often distorted by overriding changes in the general meteorological situation, but this relationship between urban visibility and domestic smoke is close enough to expose our Sunday habit of getting up late—the Sunday visibility is at its lowest at about 10 a.m., one hour later than the weekday minimum.

The same domestic fires that produce the smoke contribute to keeping ground level slightly warmer in the town than in the country. Sometimes this warmth produces weak convection just sufficient to keep the smoke up to roof top level but not strong enough to change radically the dominating inversion. In such conditions the smoke forms a layer of yellow or brown cloud sometimes called high fog but once described more aptly by Dr Scorer as "*fumulus.*"

In meteorological practice the word "fog" denotes visibility of less than 1,100 yds. (1 km.) regardless of the cause of the obscurity, but, to be more specific, *water fog* is used to describe fog due to condensation of water vapour, *smoke fog* is applied in its obvious sense, and for describing a combination of the two types *smog* seems to have entered our language in the past few years.

Visibility observations

Although both horizontal and vertical visibility are of considerable importance in aviation, adequate and systematic techniques are not yet available for measuring or forecasting the vertical visibility and, unless otherwise stated, visibility reports or forecasts refer only to the horizontal visibility as seen by an observer on the ground. This visibility is defined as the greatest distance at which objects are recognisable by an average observer, the object being such as would be easily identified in a clear atmosphere. At a few stations photo-electric methods are employed to attain consistency in observation but the more common and reasonably adequate method is for the observer to use a carefully mapped set of objects or lights on which to base his estimations.

As for most other meteorological elements, many of the terms used to describe the visibility are rigidly defined. Here is the appropriate table for aviation procedures:

Description	*Visibility*	*Symbols used on weather charts*
Dense fog	less than 55 yds. (50 m.)	≡ See note below
Fog	55–220 yds. (50–200 m.)	
Slight fog	220–1,100 yds. (200–1,000 m.)	
Mist (due mainly to water drops)	1,100–2,200 yds. (1–2 km.)	=
Haze (due mainly to smoke or dust)		∞ or ∞
Poor visibility	$1\frac{1}{4}$–$2\frac{1}{2}$ miles (2–4 km.)	
Moderate visibility	$2\frac{1}{2}$–$6\frac{1}{4}$ miles (4–10 km.)	
Either may be described as Slight mist *or* Slight haze		
Good visibility	$6\frac{1}{4}$–25 miles (10–40 km.)	

Note.—Several variations of the fog symbol illustrated above are used to chart some of the characteristics of the fog. For example, the symbol ≡| means that the fog has become thinner during the preceding hour and the sky is discernible through the top, while ≡≡ denotes fog in patches.

The terms used in bulletins issued for the general public via the British Broadcasting Corporation (B.B.C.) are:

Description	*Visibility*
Dense fog	Less than 50 yards
Fog	50–200 yards
Mist	200–1,100 yards

CHAPTER 5

Warm Fronts and Cold Fronts

To introduce yet another means of causing air to ascend and cloud to form let us glance quickly back at the trajectories drawn in Figure 1.9, p. 13. By 06 GMT 9 November 1949 evolution of the current pressure systems had contrived to sandwich warm air (*A*) between two colder masses (*B* and *C*). Figure 5.1, presenting a more detailed view of the sandwich, reveals how much warmer and moister is the air from the Azores than the masses from farther north; over south-west England temperatures and dew points, marked at the left of each station circle, are over 50° F. while in the preceding cold air they are mainly in the forties. The division between the cold and warm air is noticeable enough to justify a specially marked boundary. On coloured charts this particular type of boundary is drawn as a red line, and on black and white charts it takes the internationally agreed form used in Figure 5.1. To meteorologists and aviators throughout the world such a line drawn on a weather map means that cold air is being closely followed by warm, and, for brevity, the phenomenon is called a *warm front*.

One of the most significant features of a warm front is the tendency for the warm air literally to overtake the cold; in the illustrated example the warm airstream from the west-south-west appeared to climb up over the preceding cold air, and to visualise the three dimensional structure we can refer to Figure 5.2. Moving somewhat faster than the *surface front* (i.e. the ground level position of the front), the warm air appeared to flow up an imaginary sloping surface—the *frontal surface*—separating the warm and cold air masses. Naturally as it ascended the warm moist air was cooled by expansion and cloud was readily produced by condensation. Augmenting the actual meteorological information available with judicious guessing it was possible to construct a schematic cross-section of cloud associated with this particular front; it is included in Figure 5.2. The cross-section reveals that about 400 miles ahead of the front (the surface front) the frontal cloud was high and cold—freezing in fact. The excess of water vapour here produced ice crystals rather than liquid water drops, and the white wispy clouds

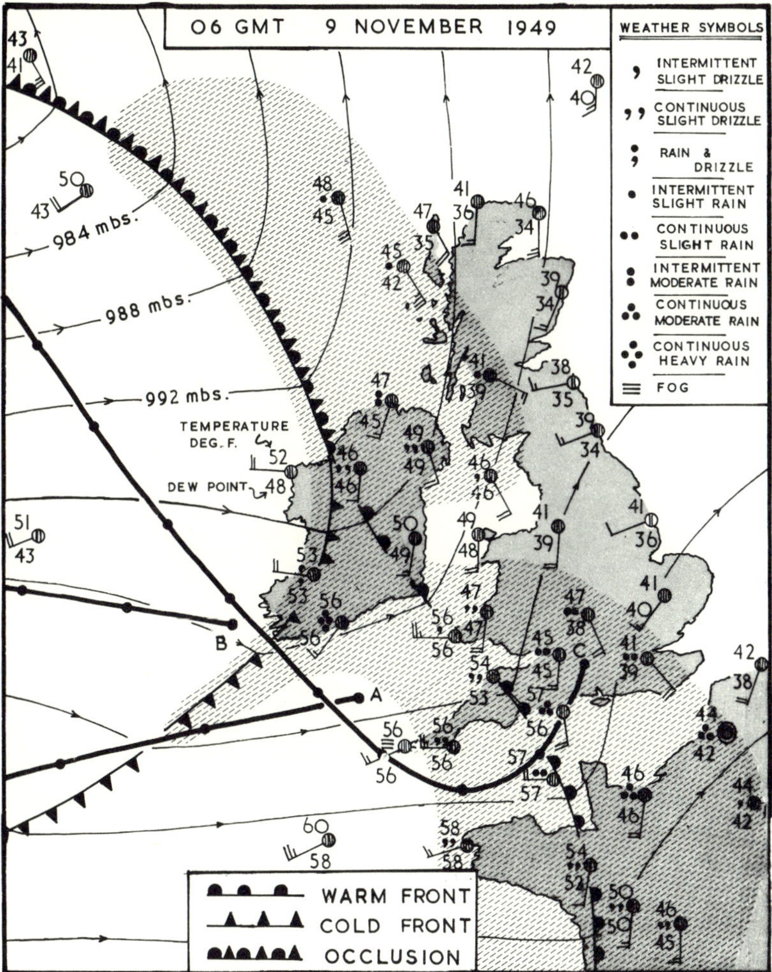

Fig. 5.1. The weather map shows warm and cold frontal features associated with the temperature contrasts between cold air from near Iceland (trajectory *C*) warm air from the Azores (*A*) and cold air from the west-north-west (*B*). Note: Temperatures are now plotted in ° C.

visible in this region were easily identifiable as cirrus (typified by Plate 3). These wisps owed their elongated comma shape to an increase of wind with height. After forming in the moist air, the ice crystals fell slowly and evaporated in the drier air below. But the wind speed at the level of cloud formation was much stronger than

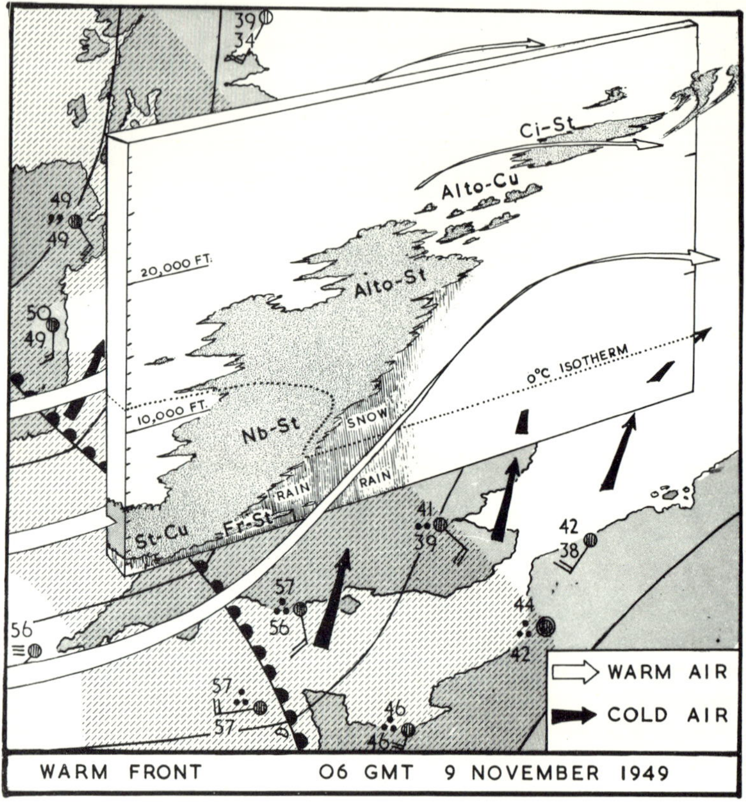

Fig. 5.2. Cross-section of the warm front.

that just below, so during the descent of about 3,000 ft. or so the tails of the cirrus wisps lagged far behind their quickly moving tufted tops.

The general movement of the cirrus as a whole showed the high level wind direction to be quite different from that at low levels. The low level geostrophic wind was south-west while the cirrus moved from the north-west; in other words, the wind veered with

Plate 3 CIRRUS UNCINUS *R. K. Pilsbury*

Wisps of cirrus cloud often presage the approach of a warm front, especially when the amount of cirrus tends to increase. The cirrus clouds illustrated acquired hooked shapes as the ice crystals forming the clouds fell slowly from a strong wind stream at high levels into a weaker flow several thousand feet below.

height, and this is another of the characteristics of a warm front. We shall see later that it is a natural result of the juxtaposition of the warm and the cold air.

Closer to the front the upward motion and the moisture content of the warm air sufficed to produce a milky white veil of cirrostratus. Evidently this was still ice crystal cloud, for a halo like that of Plate 4 was just discernible and it is crystals of ice formed delicately and precisely in the high atmosphere that can bend the sun's (or moon's) rays to form this characteristic pattern.

Towards the west the presence of altocumulus indicated that some sort of convective or irregular motion was superimposed on the slow rise of the warm air, but apart from this hiatus the cloud continued to thicken and lower towards the front. Soon the sun was barely visible through the altostratus, and now the absence of a halo denoted that, despite its sub-zero temperature, this cloud was

Plate 4 CIRROSTRATUS *R. S. Scorer*

A halo can usually be seen around the sun when the sky is covered with cirrostratus. On most occasions the halo is faint and may not be noticed unless the eyes are shaded from the sun itself by a patch of cloud or the observer's hand. The halo is very faintly coloured. Often there is a somewhat more colourful tangential arc at the top of the main halo, and occasionally other rings and arcs appear.

composed mostly of liquid water drops. Supercooled water drops, as they are called, are not uncommon in the atmosphere; at temperatures between 0° C. and about − 40° C., such drops do not turn to ice unless they are provided with suitable nuclei, such as mineral dust particles, on which to freeze.

Within a 150-mile belt ahead of the front condensation was sufficient to produce not only a thick layer of nimbostratus but also a downpour of rain which began to moisten the air at low levels. This moistening, coupled with low level turbulence in the gradually strengthening wind, favoured the formation of low fractostratus just ahead of the front.

Behind the front there was little or no upward motion in the air at medium and high levels. Cloud in the *warm sector* between the warm and cold fronts comprised a cover of stratocumulus formed by low level turbulence, but, with the warm air being very moist, even this

Plate 5 ALTOCUMULUS *R. K. Pilsbury*

The more or less regularly arranged elements of cloud are associated with gentle convection and wind shear in the cloud layer.

smaller scale vertical motion was sufficient to produce excessive condensation leading to rain or drizzle.

Although, in south-west England, the passage of the imaginary line denoting the front was not accompanied by a cessation of rain or a sharp change in the appearance of the cloud when viewed from below, the advent of the air from the Azores was plainly marked by a change in wind direction; the approximately southerly winds gave way to a flow from the west-south-west. The associated trough in the pressure pattern also contributed to the detection of the front. As the trough accompanied the front across the countryside the atmospheric pressure automatically recorded by barographs decreased at first, then remained fairly steady after the front had passed. About 300 miles ahead of the front pressure falls were about 0·3 mb. per hour but within the rain belt decreases of just over 1 mb. per hour were recorded at several stations.

Since the weather history just related is characteristic of warm frontal phenomena, it will be helpful to list the features described for future reference.

Plate 6 ALTOSTRATUS *R. S. Scorer*

Patches of fractostratus are seen in this picture below the grey sheet of altostratus through which the sun is barely visible. Such a sky as this often heralds the onset of rain ahead of a warm front.

WARM FRONTAL CHARACTERISTICS

Well ahead of the warm front

1 Cirrus increases in amount.
2 Movement of cirrus may reveal a wind veer with height.
3 A halo may be visible in the cirrostratus.
4 Pressure begins to fall and the surface wind backs.

Closer to the front

1 Medium cloud thickens and lowers.
2 The rainbelt arrives.
3 Patches of ragged low cloud may form.
4 Wind gradually increases in speed.
5 Dew points begin to rise in the rain.
6 Pressure fall becomes appreciable.

At the passage of the front

1 Surface wind veers.

2 Pressure ceases to fall and becomes steady.
3 Temperature and dew points increase.
4 Rain may ease off or be replaced by drizzle.

But remember that the front described was specially selected for demonstrating warm frontal characteristics. Other warm fronts may be broadly similar but they are almost certain to differ in detail according to the prevailing situation; some of the characteristics listed above may be missing, and local or temporary events may be superimposed on the broad frontal system. Even in our specially selected front we can detect anomalies in the frontal régime. Notice the 06 GMT temperature (57° F.) and dew point (56° F.) at Portland Bill on the south coast of England. Such warmth and moisture seemed representative of the warm air mass, yet the wind direction indicated that this air mass had not yet arrived. The apparent inconsistency was a local effect due to the moistening over the English Channel of a very shallow layer just ahead of the warm front. This shallow layer soon lost much of its warmth and moisture on moving away from the coast over relatively cold dry land, whereas the genuine warm air mass, which was warm and moist through some considerable depth, retained high temperatures and dew points throughout its passage across the country.

Farther to the north another anomaly—the absence of rain at Anglesey and Dublin—can serve to remind us that the concept of warm air climbing up over the cold may perhaps be too simple to account for some of the frontal phenomena we observe. Nevertheless the concept is a justifiable basis on which to build our ideas of warm frontal structure, and, rather than dwell upon the modifications which may or may not occur, it would be wiser to pass on to another type of front.

The cold front

By convention a cold front is marked on a weather chart either by a blue line or by the symbol shown in Figure 5.1. It is easy to guess that this type of front denotes the boundary between warm air and a following cold air mass. But a cold front is not simply a warm front in reverse—in fact it is not a simple phenomenon at all.

The chart in Figure 5.1 shows a cold front drawn between the air which moved along trajectory *B* and the warmer air, *A*, from the

Azores. Once again meteorological ground level and upper air observations interspersed with a little guesswork have been used to construct a pictorial cross-section of the cloud. There it is in Figure 5.3. By comparison with the warm frontal structure, it is not so easy to visualise an imaginary sloping surface separating the

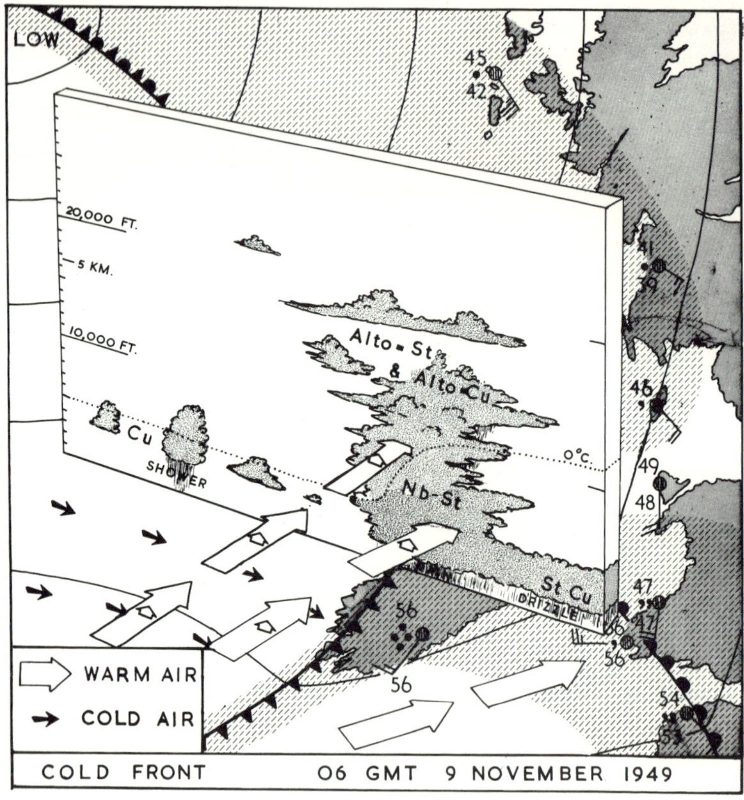

Fig. 5.3. Cross-section of the cold front.

warm from the cold air. But if we do try to fit such a surface to the rear of the frontal cloud we see that it is considerably steeper than the warm frontal surface, and here, in the cold frontal régime, the advancing cold air seems to act as a wedge prising up the warm air ahead. The resulting condensation produced a band of nimbostratus and rain fairly close to the ground level position of the front.

At medium levels the presence of altocumulus suggested that

Plate 7 ALTOCUMULUS CASTELLANUS *R. S. Scorer*

Convective instability is sometimes produced within an extensive layer of slowly rising air. Such instability is often confined to medium levels and is indicated by the presence of altocumulus castellanus. Because the updraughts associated with the individual clouds are usually weak and confined to medium levels, this type of convection is not normally suitable for thermal soaring. Occasionally altocumulus castellanus tends to form in straight lines as shown on this photograph, but in some situations, particularly those associated with hot summertime depressions which form over Europe, medium level instability produces convection cloud over such extensive regions that the cloud mass looks more like altostratus from below. Sometimes this type of medium level cloud is many thousands of feet deep and it is then likely to produce prolonged showers or thunderstorms.

convection currents were interwoven with the broad scale lifting of the warm air, but because the structural details of cold fronts can vary from one cold front to another, and because these details are seldom fully revealed by routine meteorological observing networks, the precise form and significance of this medium level convection is open to speculation.

A better understood feature of the cold front is the variation of wind direction with height. Figure 5.3 shows how the wind backed with height just behind the cold front, and the next chapter will tell the reason why.

It is apparent that the cold front was accompanied by a decrease in temperature and dew point, a trough in the isobars and a surface wind veer. As soon as the cold frontal rain had passed, a change in the pattern of cloud became evident; no longer was the low level turbulence or moisture sufficient to maintain a cover of stratocumulus; clouds in the cold air were formed in convection currents rising from the relatively warm sea and in some of the convection clouds water drops grew large enough to fall out as showers of rain. Later in the day convection also occurred over Ireland, Wales and much of England as the cold air invaded the countryside. The ensuing rain showers washed some of the smoke and dust particles in the air down to the ground and thereby helped to improve the visibility.

Obviously a cold front is followed rather than preceded by its principal features, so the characteristics listed below comprise a guide to recognising rather than predicting the passage of a cold front.

COLD FRONTAL CHARACTERISTICS

Ahead of the cold front

1 Warm sector cloud—probably stratocumulus or stratus—possibly drizzle.
2 Precipitation close to the front.
3 Pressure falls.

At the passage of the cold front

1 Surface wind veers.
2 Temperature and dew points decrease.
3 Cloud cover breaks up.
4 Pressure rises after falling.
5 Precipitation.

At some cold fronts the line marking these changes is so definite and the surface winds are so strong that the effect is called a *line squall.*

Behind the cold front

1 Pressure rises.
2 Visibility improves after precipitation ceases.

Frontal systems

The warm and cold fronts depicted in Figure 5.1 did not suddenly come into being on the morning of 9 November. These moving boundaries between warm and cold air had a fairly recognisable history. At 00 GMT 8 November they were discernible as two curved spokes emanating from a depression south of Greenland—

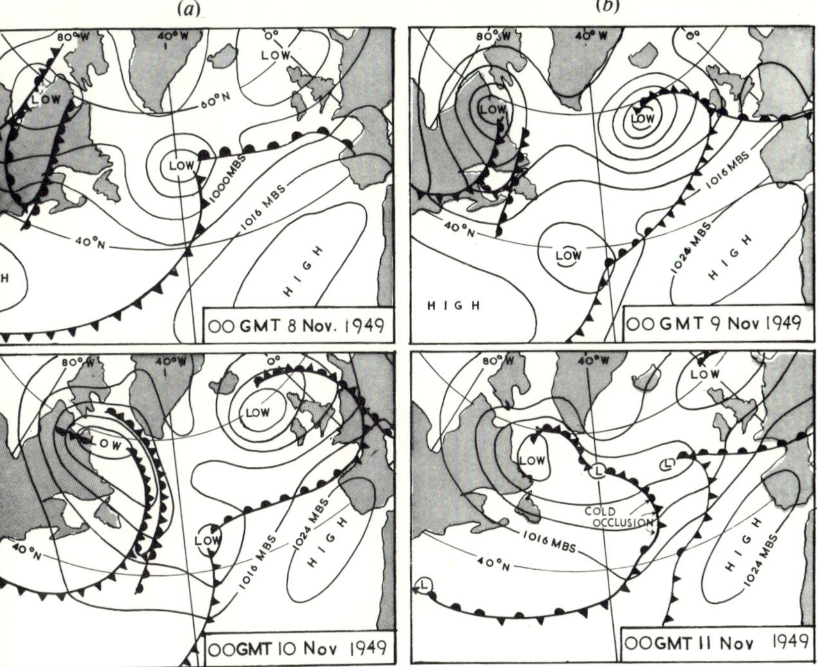

Fig. 5.4. In the illustrated sequence of events a depression south of Greenland moved quickly north-eastwards while a secondary depression developed well to the south-west. In the region of Labrador two occlusions were brought close together and by 00 GMT 11 November weather observations did not justify more than a single line to represent this part of the frontal system.

as illustrated in Figure 5.4*a*. Twenty-four hours later (Figure 5.4*b*) the warm front had just reached Ireland and had the cold front hard on its heels. With the warm air rising at both the warm and the cold front, the warm sector was narrowing hour by hour and the cold front was steadily catching up with the warm. Farther in towards the centre of the depression the two fronts had already coalesced to form an *ocelusion.* On black and white charts the occlusion is marked as the obvious combination of the warm and cold front symbols while for coloured maps a purple line is used.

While the warm and cold fronts associated with the depression south of Iceland at 00 GMT 9 November were occluding, another secondary depression was twisting the tail of the cold front into a similar warm and cold frontal pattern some 1,300 miles to the south-west. With its associated warm and cold fronts beginning to occlude, this developing depression moved, like its predecessor, towards the British Isles, and by 00 GMT 11 November the cold front exhibited another kink in its tail betraying the birth of yet another low pressure centre in this particular family of depressions.

Families of between 2 and about 10 depressions linked by fronts are common features of temperate latitude weather systems. Only two or three depressions of a particular family may be evident at any one time, but as the older depressions fill up so new low pressure centres appear, each in turn developing on the cold front trailing from its predecessor. The young depressions with their wide open warm sectors usually deepen and move quickly, while, at the other end of the family tree, it is not unusual for the older occlusions to be concertinaed into a broad band as their associated depressions slow down and fill up.

The first three charts of Figure 5.4 show two occlusions being brought closer together as they crossed Labrador. By 00 GMT 11 November these two fronts were depicted on the chart as a single line—not because the occlusions had coalesced but because the actual weather observations did not justify a more analytical representation of this part of the frontal system. Although frontal changes in pressure, temperature, dew point, wind and cloud did occur within a very broad belt of cloudy weather associated with the occlusions, nowhere were the changes sharp enough to delineate clear cut fronts; the single occlusion on the chart was more of a reminder of the history and existence of the broad region of cloudy weather which had moved eastwards out over the Atlantic.

Another change in representing this frontal system is apparent between latitudes 44° N. and 52° N. In this region the converging occlusions together with the occluding warm and cold fronts were drawn on the chart for 00 GMT 11 November as one front—*a cold occlusion*—which is the name given to occlusions whose cold frontal characteristics are more evident than the warm frontal components. Figure 5.5 illustrates the basic temperature distributions associated with a cold occlusion and its converse, a *warm occlusion*.

Occlusion weather

Basically the occlusion is a warm front followed immediately by a cold front, but we have noted that occlusions are often old fronts harboured in slow moving depressions and their characteristics (which do not necessarily include equal shares of warm and cold frontal features) become blurred with age. This is not to say that occlusions are unimportant; some of the most prolonged rain or snow over England has been associated with almost stationary occlusions lying across the country with a low pressure system to the

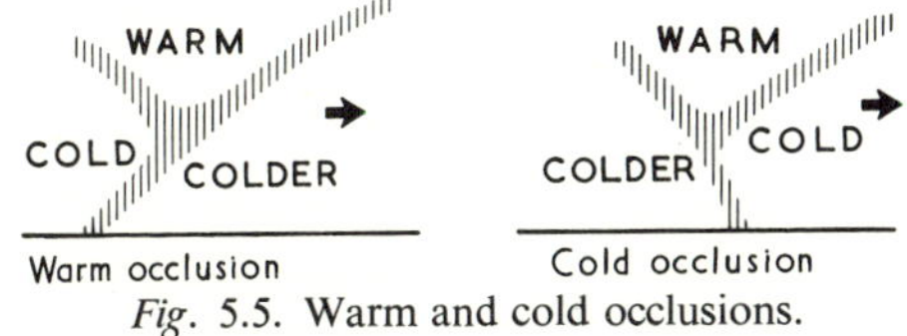

Fig. 5.5. Warm and cold occlusions.

south; furthermore, the warm or cold frontal features of an occlusion are sometimes rejuvenated by temperature changes on one or both sides of the front. Thus occlusions may be associated with anything between broad cloudy belts with diffuse frontal changes and weather patterns which resemble either warm or cold frontal systems.

One of the practical difficulties in depicting or discussing fronts is that, for convenience, we try to use a few definite words and symbols to represent systems which are not well defined. The word "occlusion" is often inadequate to convey more than a rough idea of the frontal systems to which it is applied; in fact, Canadian meteorologists have supplemented the frontal nomenclature with the word "*trowal*" (trough of warm air aloft) which they find useful in describing some of the North American weather systems.

CHAPTER 6

Jet Streams and Pressure Changes

The concept of geostrophic force is applicable to the flow of air not only at low levels but also throughout the troposphere and to some height up into the stratosphere. A chart of the atmospheric pressure at, say, 20,000 ft. above M.S.L. represents the instantaneous wind flow at that level; the wind blows more or less along the high level isobars with a speed proportional to the pressure gradient just as it does at lower levels. The pressure patterns at any two levels are

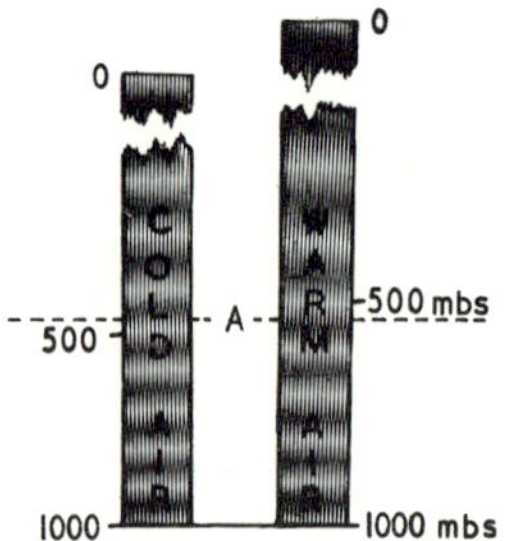

Fig. 6.1 The pressure decrease with height in warm air is less than that in cold air.

rarely identical, but they are linked together by the distribution of temperature in the air between the two levels. To see how this link is forged let us consider the two columns of air of equal weight but different temperatures resting on the ground, as shown in Figure 6.1. Since the columns are of equal weight they will produce equal pressures at ground level, but, with dissimilar temperatures, the columns will not be of equal height; the top of the column of cold dense air will be lower than that of the warm column, and it follows that at, say, level *A* in the figure, the barometric pressure in the warm column is greater than that at the same level in the cold air.

Therefore, the pressure gradient at *A* will produce a geostrophic wind blowing between the two columns, the sense of direction being into the diagram for the northern hemisphere. Such a wind is called a *thermal wind.*

Extension of the argument shows that, if the barometric pressure at M.S.L. is uniform throughout a large area over which an uneven temperature distribution exists, then the thermal winds will blow between warm and cold air in the same manner that geostrophic winds blow between high and low pressures; on the weather map, the thermal winds north of the Equator blow anticlockwise around pools of cold air and clockwise around warm air masses with speeds proportional to the temperature gradient. Thus we can visualise

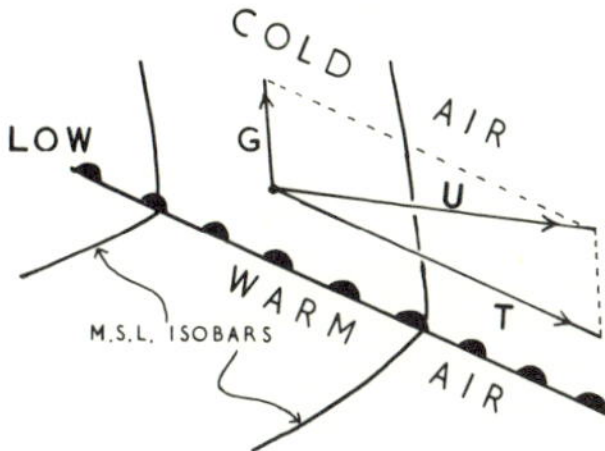

Fig. 6.2. Just ahead of the warm front the geostrophic wind appropriate to the M.S.L. isobars is represented by the vector *G*. If the thermal wind between M.S.L. and, say, the 30,000-ft. level is represented by *T*, then *U* (the vector sum of *G* and *T*) will represent the wind at 30,000 ft.

thermal winds as blowing along well-defined fronts: the greater the temperature contrast between the warm and the cold air the stronger will be the thermal wind.

Although this thermal wind concept is useful, it is to some extent imaginary; well defined fronts are normally associated with distinct pressure gradients rather than uniform pressure at M.S.L. (i.e. they are associated with windy rather than calm conditions at low levels) and the real geostrophic winds at high levels are obtained by superimposing the thermal wind on the low level flow. For example, if the thermal wind between M.S.L. and 30,000 ft. associated with the warm front in Figure 6.2 is represented by the vector *T* while the geostrophic wind appropriate to the M.S.L. isobars is represented by *G*, then the actual geostrophic wind at 30,000 ft. will be represented by the vector *U* (the vector sum of *G* and *T*).

Without experience or a comprehensive set of meteorological observations it is naturally difficult to estimate thermal winds with accuracy but even a very rough and ready application of the principle adds interest and understanding to the weather systems we observe and the forecasts we hear in everyday life. Applying the principle to a frontal depression we derive a high level flow pattern (Figure 6.3) consistent with the upper wind characteristics of the frontal system already described in Chapter 5; the wind direction veers with height ahead of the warm front, and behind the cold front the high level wind is backed from the low level geostrophic direction.

Those who want to put some figures into the method can use the formula:

Thermal wind speed per 1,000 ft. depth of air = 1 knot per °C. per 100 miles (very approximately)

This means that if, say, the mean temperature of a 10,000 ft. layer of air changes at the rate of 2° C. per 100 miles between regions of

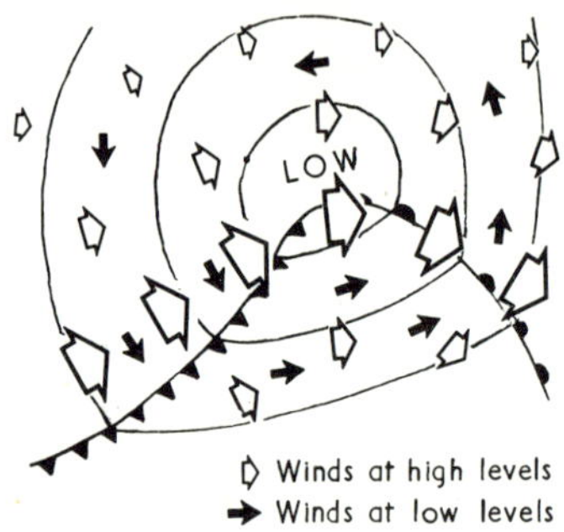

Fig. 6.3. The high level (20,000–40,000 ft.) flow over an active frontal depression usually includes a channel of strong winds blowing more or less parallel to the warm and cold fronts.

warm and cold air then the thermal wind strength appropriate to this 10,000 ft. layer will be

$$10 \times 2 = 20 \text{ knots}$$

High level winds can be very strong in the vicinity of fronts; considering a layer from, say, 2,000 ft. to 32,000 ft., a mean temperature change of 5° C. per 100 miles (which is not an excessive temperature gradient across an active warm or cold frontal zone) leads to a thermal wind for the 30,000 ft. layer of

$$30 \times 5 = 150 \text{ knots}$$

The wind at the upper level is the vector sum of this 150-knot thermal wind and the geostrophic wind applicable to the 2,000 ft. level.

In the stratosphere the horizontal temperature gradients are usually opposite in direction to those of the tropospheric systems. This is consistent with the tropopause in a warm air mass being higher than that in a cold airstream. Figure 2.1, on page 19, shows the effect; in the stratosphere the air over the Equator is colder than that over the poles, and similarly the stratosphere over a warm sector is colder than that on the cold side of the lower level fronts. The thermal wind, therefore, increases with height to a maximum at or near the tropopause and then, as a result of the reversal of the horizontal temperature gradient, decreases with height in the stratosphere.

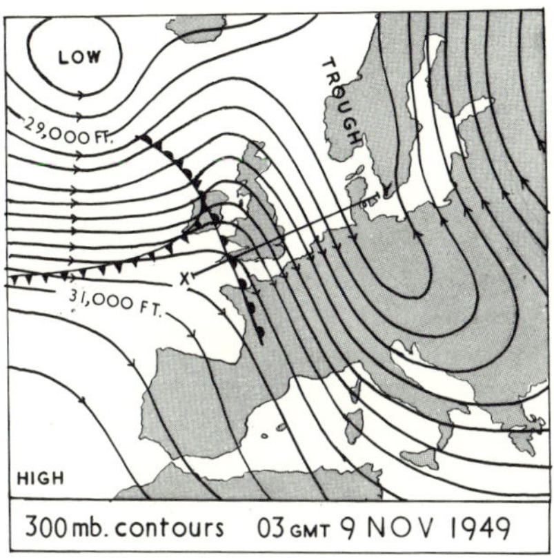

Fig. 6.4*a*. In most meteorological practices it is expedient to draw pressure contour maps to represent flow patterns aloft. For many practical purposes such maps can be viewed as pressure maps; the chart shown here depicts particularly strong winds at about 30,000 ft. approximately parallel to the warm and cold fronts. The cross-section (across *XY*) of wind speeds sketched in Fig. 6.4*b* reveals the strongest winds to be concentrated within some form of imaginary tube. Such a tube of strong winds is called a jet stream.

A corollary from this reasoning is that winds associated with a well marked front are liable to be particularly strong in a channel near the tropopause and more or less parallel to the front. Such channels of strong winds at high levels are often evidenced by both actual wind measurements and high level pressure maps. Figures 6.4*a* and *b* show a high level pressure map and a wind component cross-section for 03 GMT 9 November 1949. This type of wind distribution, which can be described as a tube rather than a channel of strong winds, is common enough to have earned the special name, *jet stream*.

A jet stream is not a writhing river of air perpetually encircling the globe; it is simply a well marked concentration of particularly strong winds formed as one of the by-products of strong horizontal temperature gradients in the troposphere. Jet streams come and go in a variety of shapes and sizes; over the British Isles jet streams of 100–200 knots over a length of between 200 and 800 miles are not uncommon; over the U.S.A. longer, meandering jet streams often stretch from the Rockies to the Atlantic seaboard, and over Japan

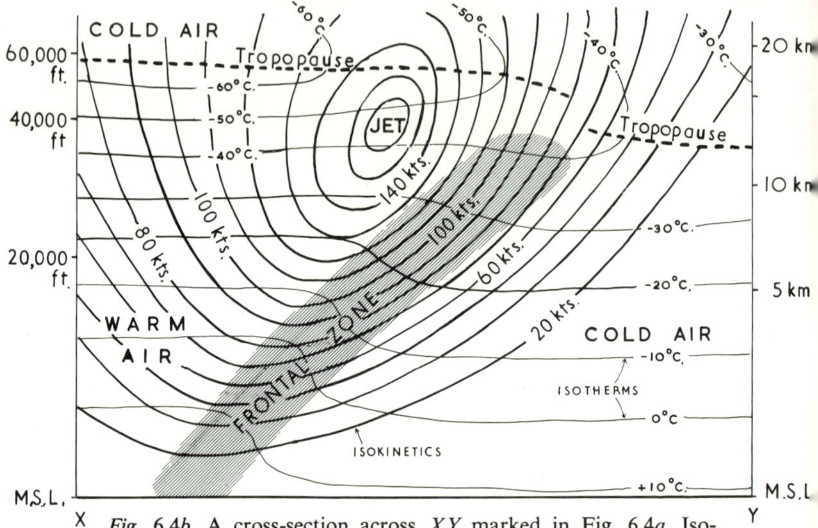

Fig. 6.4*b*. A cross-section across *XY* marked in Fig. 6.4*a*. Isotherms show the temperature distribution across the warm front, while *isokinetics* around the jet stream denote the wind speed components parallel to the front (out of the diagram). The height scale is condensed at high levels to facilitate illustration.

and New Zealand conditions are sometimes favourable for the development of 300-knot winds in the jet stream core.

Pressure changes

When the barometric pressure falls the water content of the tissues in the human body tends to increase, and the consequent swelling of these tissues may subject sensitive arthritic joints to some pain, but without such an unfortunate indicator as this, our bodies do not normally detect pressure changes occurring in the atmosphere.

Such changes are usually slow—often less than half a millibar per hour. Certain phenomena, such as tornadoes and some thunderstorms, can produce very sudden, localised pressure changes, but in most meteorological contexts a pressure fall of about 3 mbs. per hour is considered to be rapid—such a rate of fall would normally be indicative of the speedy approach of a vigorous depression.

Small though they are, these pressure changes would scarcely occur at all if the airflow were exactly geostrophic. Suppose that part of a M.S.L. pressure pattern were like that drawn in Figure 6.5.

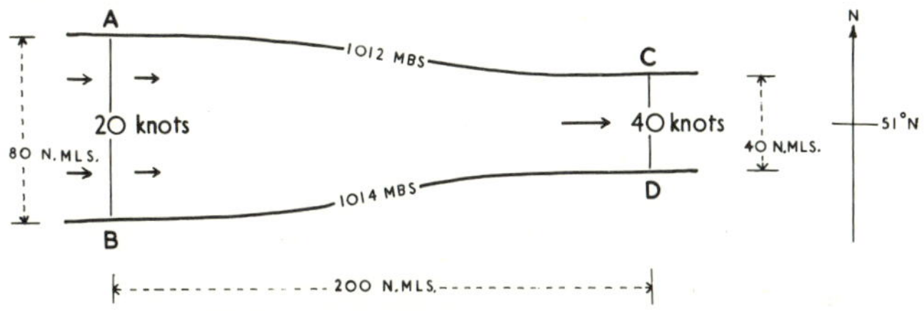

Fig. 6.5. An example of the balance between geostrophic flow into and out of a region. A more complete relationship between the geostrophic wind speed and the distances between isobars is included in notes at the end of this chapter.

If the actual wind were exactly geostrophic then (since the distance *AB* is twice *CD*) air will flow across *AB* into the region *ABCD* at half the speed of the flow across *CD*, but, with the inflow being twice the width of the outflow, the rate at which air pours across *AB* into the region will be balanced exactly by the rate of outflow across *CD*, and if a balance is maintained at all heights, the total amount of air over the region *ABCD* will remain constant and the barometric pressure will not change.

Because the geostrophic force changes with latitude and with the temperature of the air, pressure changes can be produced in a geostrophic flow which is directed towards the north or the south or which is warmed or cooled. But usually such pressure changes are negligibly small, and to account for the changes commonly observed we must recognise that broad scale wind systems are often not exactly geostrophic. Only slight differences between the actual wind speed and the geostrophic speed are necessary to produce significant pressure changes; in the situation shown in Figure 6.5 the wind speed of the outflow across *CD* need be increased by only one knot (from 40 to 41 knots) at all heights to reduce the M.S.L. pressure in the region *ABCD* at a rate of more than 3 mbs. per hour. In understanding the pressure changes associated with the development and movement of depressions and anticyclones, it is, therefore, essential to be aware of the existence of the forces which slightly upset the broad balance between geostrophic and pressure gradient forces.

Low level turbulence

One of the small but noticeable forces which accounts for differences between the geostrophic and ground level winds is associated with low level turbulence. This turbulence (which may range from a gentle stirring motion through a depth of a few hundred feet in light winds to a vigorous eddy motion up to 3,000–5,000 ft. in strong winds) is tantamount to a frictional force retarding the airstream; it prevents the low level winds from attaining the full geostrophic speed, and, because any reduction in wind speed means a reduction in the geostrophic force, the directions of these low level winds are slightly across the isobars towards low pressure. Very close to ground level, where the effect is usually most marked, the "surface wind" is often about 30 degrees back from the isobars and about two-thirds of the speed of the geostrophic wind. In routine meteorological messages the "surface wind" is taken to be that blowing at 33 ft. (10 m.) above an open site such as an airfield, and the reason for not choosing a lower level is that winds within a few feet of ground level are sometimes so affected by small local obstacles and the nature of the ground that they do not represent the general surface wind in the neighbourhood.

It is not difficult to perceive that the overall effect of low level turbulence is to produce a slight inflow of air at low levels towards the centres of depressions and a slight outflow from high pressure regions.

The cyclostrophic force

Another small but nonetheless significant force often exerted on air in motion is called the *cyclostrophic force* but it sounds less formidable when referred to as the centrifugal force tending to throw air off at a tangent to whatever curved track it happens to be following. A steady wind flow between the isobars drawn in Figure 6.6*a*, for example, can only be maintained when the wind speed is such that the pressure gradient force is counterbalanced by the sum of the geostrophic and cyclostrophic forces, both of which act at right angles to the direction of movement of the air. Therefore, the geostrophic force is less than that needed to maintain a geostrophic wind between straight but similarly spaced isobars—therefore the wind speed around depressions is somewhat less than the geostrophic speed.

By a similar argument it can be shown that anticyclonic curvature, such as that depicted in Figure 6.6*b*, produces wind speeds slightly

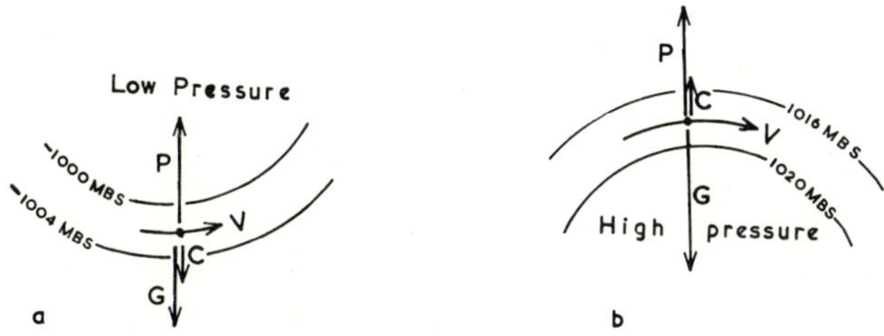

Fig. 6.6. When air flows along cyclonically curved isobars (*a*) the pressure gradient force is balanced by the sum of the geostrophic force and a centrifugal force. Therefore the geostrophic force need not be as great as that required for simple geostrophic flow and the wind speed is less than the geostrophic speed. For anti-cyclonic curvature (*b*) the centrifugal force is added to the pressure gradient force and the wind must be stronger than the geostrophic speed to maintain a balance between the pressure gradient and centrifugal force in one direction and the geostrophic force in the other.

in excess of the geostrophic values, but this effect is not normally noticeable in the centre of a high pressure region where the pressure gradient is weak.

As a result of the cyclostrophic force, air flowing along a path of variable curvature tends to slow down when entering a cyclonic bend and speed up at the beginning of an anticyclonic curve, and such variations in speed contribute to pressure changes; if the amount of air entering one side of a region is greater at all levels than that streaming out through the other side then the net accumulation of air within the region will be registered as a rise in the atmospheric pressure.

The wind computed by taking the cyclostrophic force as well as the pressure gradient and geostrophic forces into account is called the *gradient wind*—it is, of course, a more accurate representation of the true wind speed than the geostrophic wind, especially near the centres of intense depressions and in any curved sections of jet streams.

Wind speed changes

When a pressure gradient changes the geostrophic wind also tends to change but there is a slight lag before the wind speed attains its new value. The temporary lack of balance between the pressure gradient and the geostrophic force allows the air to move slightly across the isobars, towards high pressure if the pressure gradient slackens and towards low pressure in a tightening isobaric pattern. This lack of balance, however, may be more than temporary if the pressure gradient changes steadily for some hours or progressively for hundreds of miles in the direction of the general flow—as it does in the entrance and exit of many a jet stream. Therefore, we must add accelerations and decelerations to the forces which can cause slight but significant deviations from the geostrophic wind.

Convergence and divergence

In most weather situations, the combined effect of the subsidiary forces just mentioned are extremely difficult to calculate or measure

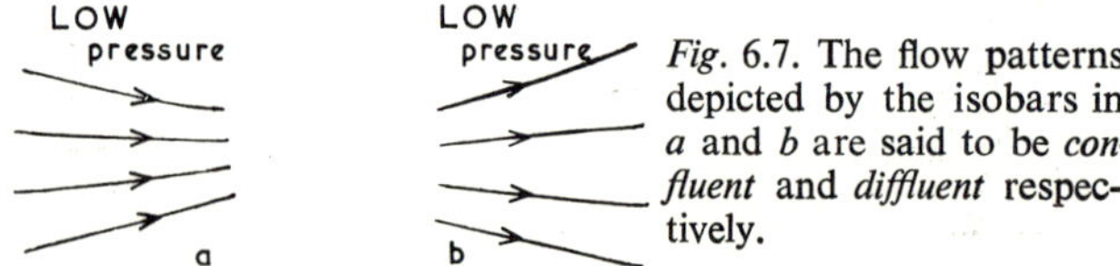

Fig. 6.7. The flow patterns depicted by the isobars in *a* and *b* are said to be *confluent* and *diffluent* respectively.

directly. The total effect is usually to produce a net inflow of air towards some regions and an outflow from others. Such inflow is usually called *convergence*, while *divergence* is another name for net outflow.

Convergence (or divergence) in the atmosphere is not necessarily associated with converging (or diverging) isobars and to avoid ambiguity the pressure patterns typified by Figures 6.7*a* and *b* are described as *confluent* and *diffluent* respectively.

In many weather situations convergence at some levels and divergence at others nearly but not quite cancel out each other's contributions to pressure changes at M.S.L., and this is a point to keep in mind when studying the development of depressions.

GEOSTROPHIC AND GRADIENT WIND SPEEDS

(The following notes and tables are included in this chapter for readers who wish to study more details of the method of measuring geostrophic and gradient winds. It is not essential, however, to study these details before passing on to the next chapter.)

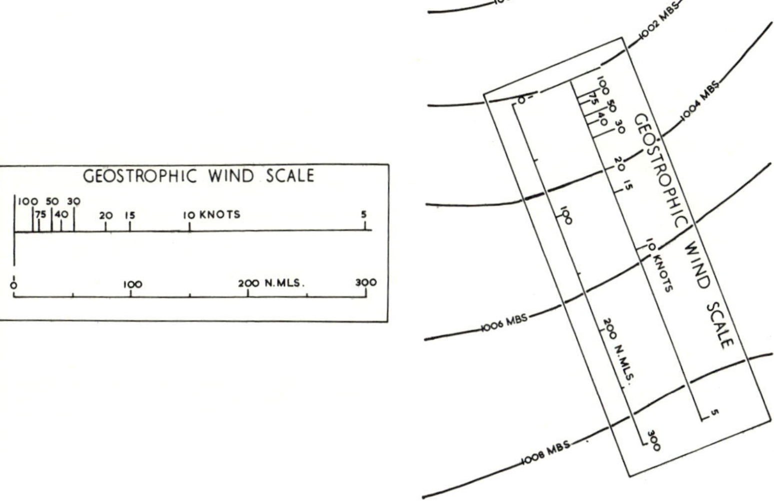

Fig. 6.8. A wind scale etched on perspex is laid on the pressure maps to measure the geostrophic wind. The illustrated scale is applicable to latitude 50°.

The formula for calculating the geostrophic wind speed is:

$$\text{geostrophic wind speed in knots} = 2068 \times \frac{G \times (273 + T)}{P \times \text{sine } L}$$

where G = the horizontal pressure gradient (mbs. per naut. mile)
T = the air temperature (° C.)
P = the pressure (mbs.)
L = the latitude (degrees)

Because the factor $(273 + T)/P$ for M.S.L. varies only slightly with changes of pressure and temperature the meteorologist can apply the formula to his weather map in the following form:

$$\text{geostrophic wind speed in knots} = \frac{1176}{D \times \text{sine } L}$$

where D = the distance in nautical miles between consecutive 2 mb. isobars on the M.S.L. pressure map.

Although this formula strictly applies to air at a pressure of 1013·2 mbs. with temperature of 15° C. (59° F.), it is approximately correct for a wide range of M.S.L. temperatures and pressures and is used to derive the following table.

GEOSTROPHIC WIND SPEED (KNOTS)

Latitude (deg.)	*Distances (naut. miles) between consecutive* 2 *mb. isobars*									
	20	30	40	50	60	80	100	200	300 n.mls.	
10°	340	226	170	135	113	85	68	34	23	knots
30°	118	78	59	47	39	29	24	12	8	knots
50°	77	51	38	31	26	19	15	8	5	knots
70°	63	42	31	25	21	16	13	6	4	knots
90°	59	39	29	24	20	15	12	6	4	knots

For any particular latitude a scale can be constructed to measure geostrophic wind speeds directly from a pressure chart; a *geostrophic wind scale* for isobars at 2 mb. intervals at latitude 50° is sketched in Figure 6.8.

The gradient wind

The wind speed obtained by taking the cyclostrophic force as well as the pressure gradient and geostrophic forces into account is called the *gradient wind.* The table on page 73 indicates the relationship between the gradient and geostrophic wind speeds at latitude 50° for various radii of curvature of the trajectory of the air.

The dashes denote combinations of geostrophic wind speeds and radii of curvature not normally encountered in the atmosphere.

Radius of curvature of trajectory (naut. miles)	*Geostrophic wind speed (knots)*				
	20	40	60	80	100
	Gradient wind speed (knots)				
Cyclonic					
250	17	31	42	52	62
200	17	30	40	49	58
150	16	28	37	45	53
100	15	25	33	40	47
50	12	20	28	34	40
Anticyclonic					
200	40	—	—	—	—
400	23	79	—	—	—
600	22	51	119	—	—
800	21	47	80	158	—
1000	21	45	74	111	198

CHAPTER 7

Insight into Depressions

Like many other natural phenomena, a frontal depression is a highly complex product of a few elementary processes each of which is not difficult to understand; the real difficulty is to unravel the pattern in which these processes are knitted into a complete depression with warm and cold fronts. Because of this difficulty we shall not attempt to delve too deeply into the intimate life history of a depression, but we can at least note the important factors in *frontogenesis* (the birth of recognisable fronts) and *cyclogenesis* (the development of depressions).

Forewarned that frontal theory is neither simple to expound nor easy to assimilate in a few brief paragraphs, let us consider the state of affairs represented in Figure 7.1*a* by the *diffluent* (diverging) M.S.L. isobars spanning a broad transition zone between warm and cold air. The isotherms drawn represent a plan view of mean temperatures up through the troposphere. With the geostrophic winds being strong for closely packed isobars and light for the weaker pressure gradients, it is apparent that the transition zone between the warm and cold air will be gradually reduced in width (Figure 7.1*b*). At this stage the transition zone is not necessarily associated with well marked frontal effects, but the increasing horizontal temperature gradient is necessarily accompanied by significant changes in the thermal winds, and, applying the principle outlined in the last chapter, it is possible to deduce that the upper level winds must now follow the pattern depicted in Figure 7.1*b*. Recalling the cyclostrophic effect also described in Chapter 6, we can deduce that somewhere in the region where the upper air flow changes from a cyclonically curved path to the straighter, faster flow there must be some divergence of air, i.e. more air flowing horizontally out of than into the region. Thus the barometric

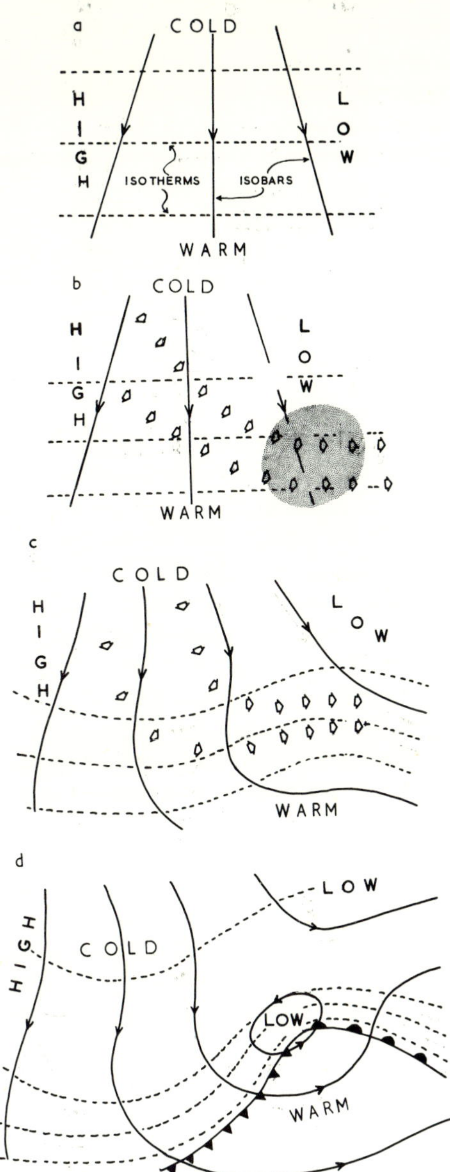

Fig. 7.1. The development of a frontal depression. Full lines denote M.S.L. isobars while dotted lines are isopleths of mean temperature from M.S.L. up to the tropopause. The broad arrows indicate winds at high levels.

pressure decreases in the area shaded in Figure 7.1*b*. The initial effect of this falling pressure is a distortion of the isobars (Figure 7.1*c*) and a temporary influx of air at low levels towards the region of falling pressure (the isallobaric low). It has been discovered that in developing frontal depressions this convergence of air at low levels very nearly compensates for the outflow aloft. The upper level divergence alone could produce a very large fall of pressure while the low level convergence alone could account for a very large rise in pressure, and the pressure fall actually observed at M.S.L. is the small difference between these opposing high and low level effects.

Because it is the winds which transport the warm and cold air from place to place changes in the wind flow resulting from the pressure fall lead to distortion in the shape of the isotherms. Soon the temperature gradient is intensified and the narrow thermal transition zone becomes bent into the shape sketched in Figure 7.1*c*. Observations show that this distortion leads to a change in the upper wind pattern such that the upper level divergence is increased and displaced downstream of its original position and the stage is set for the pressure fall to progress approximately in the direction of the upper winds. This is also the stage to let nature work out what happens next, and the subsequent events usually entail the low level inflow and high level outflow being linked by ascending motion in the warm air particularly near the centre of the depression and over the developing frontal zones indicated by the steep temperature gradients in Figure 7.1*d*. Such ascent is slow—often a mere 100–500 ft. per hour—but persistent enough to produce the frontal clouds. To try to work this out ourselves would lead to entanglement with thermal wind, cyclostrophic, isallobaric and latent heat effects at least, and the intractable problem would be to assess how much of each of these effects would be simultaneously operative at all times throughout the whole depression.

But our tentative prying does at least help to rationalize thoughts on the development of these frontal depressions. We may now appreciate that:

1 a horizontal temperature gradient cannot intensify indefinitely without creating a disturbance in the pressure system;
2 the disturbance is self-accelerating, and once created it develops rapidly;
3 the accompanying distortion of the isotherms includes a tightening

of the thermal gradient and the formation of a warm sector in the depression;

4 the fall of pressure is propagated (i.e. the depression moves) in approximately the direction of the high level winds over the depression centre.

5 Since these effects depend to some extent on the presence of strong thermal winds they tend to die out when the warm sector is eventually squeezed out of the depression; in other words depressions usually become less active when the warm and cold fronts occlude.

Even only a partial understanding or acceptance of these points shows the frontal depression to be, not a mysterious freak awaiting explanation, but a natural though intricate sequence of mundane events. Because the self-accelerating development starts at some critical stage in the initial tightening of the thermal gradient, it is extremely difficult to predict precisely where and when a new depression will form, but the forecaster equipped with a comprehensive set of pressure and temperature charts can usually delineate the regions in which conditions are broadly favourable for cyclogenesis. Both experience and theoretical reasoning suggest the tail ends of pre-existing cold fronts as likely birthplaces for new depressions—hence the family pattern. Figure 7.2 shows this cold front pattern and two other types of cyclogenetic regions, the second of which is of particular interest. Referred to as a *warm front wave* or a *warm front breakaway depression*, it is often a short-lived, one or two day affair which develops suddenly, ripples quickly down the frontal zone away from the main depression, and often produces an inordinate amount of rainfall for such a small disturbance.

It is natural that some regions of the world make better birthplaces for depressions than others; the general favourability of a region depends on the distribution of land and sea, the effect of mountain barriers, the ocean currents which largely control the sea temperatures, and the very broad scale global wind systems. The eastern seaboard of North America happens to be a favourable zone; so does the Norwegian Sea and the Mediterranean (though not so much in the summer). Fronts which originate in these regions are sometimes called the *Polar*, *Arctic* and *Mediterranean fronts* respectively, while some of the air masses either side of them are given such labels as *polar maritime* (to denote cold air from over the sea), or *arctic* (even colder) or *tropical continental* (warm from the land). Convenient though these names may sometimes be, they can

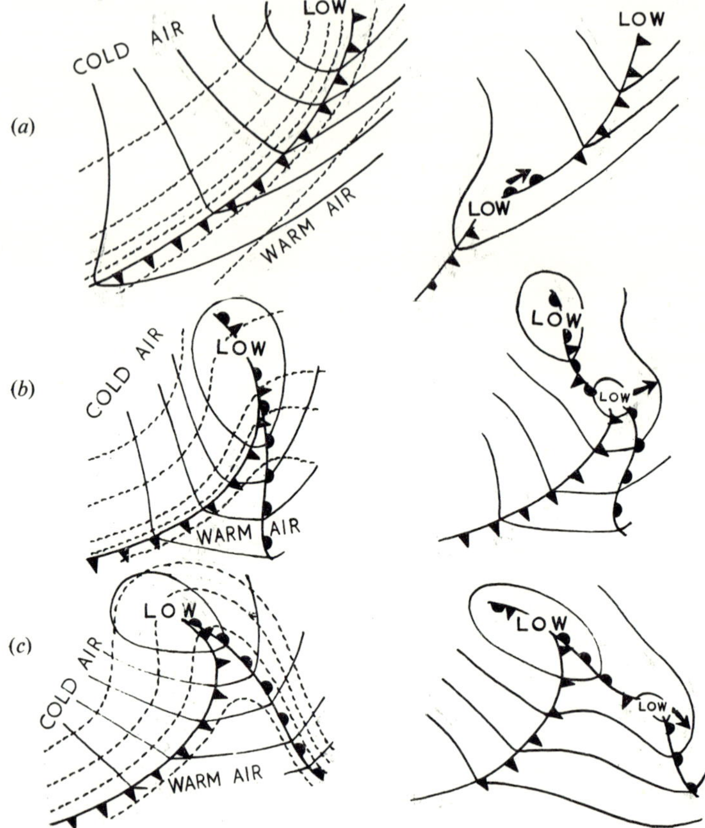

Fig. 7.2. Dotted lines indicate the shape of the isotherms in relation to the M.S.L. isobars. The situation depicted at the left in Fig. 7.2*a* is favourable for the development of a secondary low on the cold front, as shown on the right. Fig. 7.2*b* illustrates a typical secondary development at the tip of the warm sector, and 7.2*c* depicts a warm front breakaway depression.

surreptitiously instil in the unwary the misleading idea that a front is some sort of perfectly elastic membrane always and for evermore separating discrete masses of air drawn from a few exclusive sources. This idea may be of some use in very elementary tuition but it is not conducive to a mature and practical understanding of frontal weather systems as they actually are and as they are depicted. Fronts drawn on weather charts can be considered as convenient markers with which to track the frontal type of temperature and weather patterns we have been discussing in this chapter, and it is often a matter of opinion and usage whether or not a particular temperature gradient or a set of weather changes is worth calling a front. Doubt is occasionally expressed by using such terms as *pseudo-front* or *trough*; the first name is sometimes, but not often, applied to weather patterns similar but not easily traceable to frontal motions, and because fronts are usually associated with troughs of low pressure the word "trough" is sometimes used to describe frontal types of phenomena. *Upper front* is another term whose use should be regarded with some suspicion; it is intended to refer to frontal changes above but not at ground level (and such changes are sometimes associated with the effects of large mountain barriers), but, in practice, it is occasionally applied to fronts whose structure is not clear.

Figure 5.4 on page 59 shows a pair of cold fronts becoming almost parallel to each other off the Bay of Biscay. There is no reason why fronts should not become parallel at times, and when they do so the pattern is sometimes referred to as a *double frontal structure*, but this term is also applied to a single frontal zone in which noticeable frontal changes occur along two distinct lines. In practice this ambiguity is of little consequence because of the difficulty in distinguishing between a single broad frontal zone and two narrow zones close together.

Polar lows

Not all temperate latitude depressions are associated with the frontal patterns typified by the examples just described; in cold showery airstreams from the north it is not unusual to find a small depression (of about 50–100 miles in diameter) moving southwards. This small depression is often accompanied by showers of rain or snow and occasionally has what appears to be a cold front extending outwards from the low pressure centre across the broad northerly airstream towards high pressure. Such a depression as this is called a *polar low*, and from the forecasting point of view it is a troublesome phenomenon; it can develop suddenly, it is usually too small to be tracked through a coarse network of observations (such as that over the sea) yet it is often active enough to produce appreciable rain or snow in what might otherwise be a cold airstream with scattered showers and bright periods.

Polar lows are also liable to develop over inland seas, such as the Mediterranean and the Black Sea when cold showery airstreams sweep across their shores from the north in winter.

Thermal depressions

It is often argued that because warm air is lighter than cold there is a tendency for warm regions to become areas of low pressure. This argument is not strictly correct but the conclusions can be confirmed by the observed fact that depressions do tend to develop over land masses which become much hotter than their neighbouring seas. A depression over the Iberian Peninsula is a common feature of the weather map from about May to September and even over England a small depression superimposed on the general isobaric pattern can sometimes be detected on a hot summer's day. Such depressions as these are called *thermal depressions* (or *thermal lows*) and they are not normally associated with fronts.

Thundery depressions

Thermal lows over France are not uncommonly associated with upper wind and temperature distributions which lead to the formation of widespread thunderstorms at medium and high cloud levels. Sometimes these thunderstorms drift slowly northwards across the English Channel and over southern and central England. Low pressure cells of this type are usually non-frontal and are called *thundery depressions*. Slow moving thundery depressions are common summer-time features of the weather of Central Europe; spells of fine hot weather are liable to be interrupted by periods of thundery rain lasting as much as several days at a time.

Low pressure and frontal terminology

We have now mentioned a number of terms relating to fronts and depressions, and, together with one or two others, they are listed on the next three pages for future reference.

Name	*Representation on weather charts*		*Remarks*	*Schematic memory aids*
	On coloured charts	On black and white charts		
Warm front	Continuous red line		Warm air closely following cold, the cold air being on the same side of the black symbolic line as the semicircles	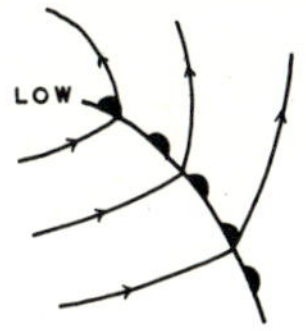
Cold front	Continuous blue line		Cold air closely following warm, the warm air being on the same side of the black symbolic line as the spikes	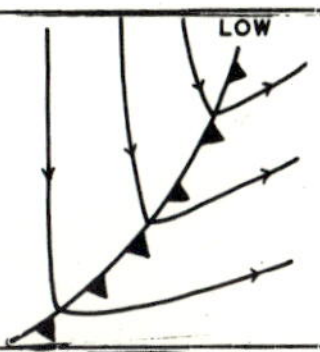
Occlusion	Continuous purple line		Coalescence of a warm and cold front	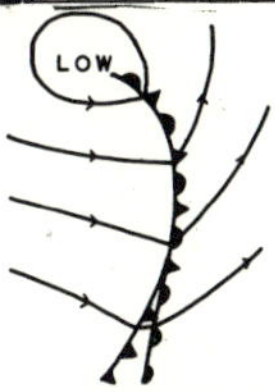
Warm occlusion	Continuous thin red line behind a thin purple line		Occlusion in which warm frontal features predominate	
Cold occlusion	Continuous thin blue line behind a thin purple line		Occlusion in which cold frontal features predominate	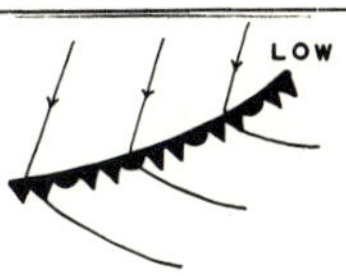
Stationary or quasi-stationary front	Continuous purple line for an occlusion		Such a front usually lies along or almost parallel to the isobars, or in a col	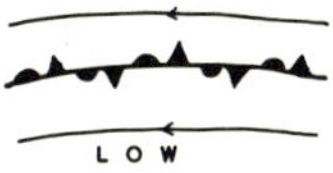
	Alternate red and blue lines joined to make a continuous line for simpler fronts			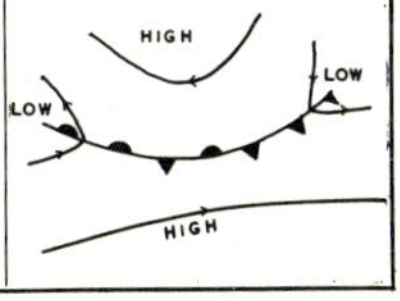

Trough	Indicated by the isobaric pattern	Strictly means trough of low pressure, but sometimes used to refer vaguely to frontal phenomena	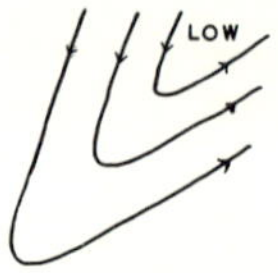
Frontal depression		Depression necessarily associated with fronts	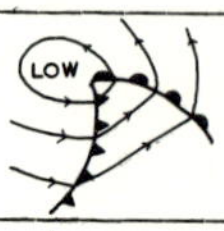
Family of depressions	Indicated by the isobaric and frontal patterns	Sequence of depressions linked by a common frontal system	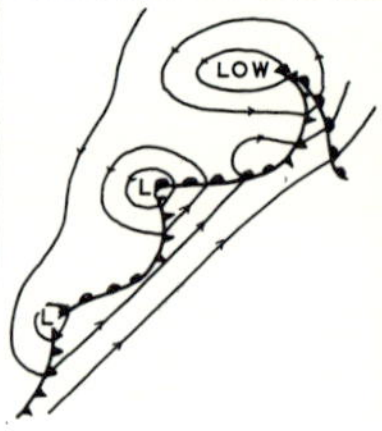
Warm front breakaway depression (or warm front wave)		Kink in the warm front likely to move quickly with or without a small secondary depression	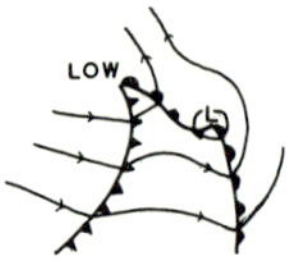
Wave on the cold front		Kink in the cold front which may or may not presage the development of a secondary depression	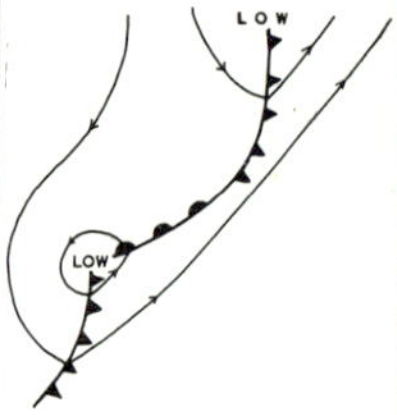
Back bent occlusion	Same as other occlusions	Occlusion approaching from the rear of its associated depression	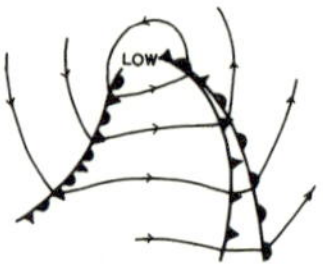
Polar low	Indicated by the isobaric pattern	Small depression in cold northerly airstream	
Trowal	Blue strokes and shorter red ticks in the pattern shown in the next column 	Used by Canadians to denote trough of warm air aloft	

Upper fronts	Broken line of appropriate colour	Appropriate symbols in outline	These names are not in frequent use in the British Isles. Intended for referring to upper air phenomena only, in practice their interpretation is often doubtful
Frontogenesis	Corrugated lines of appropriate colour	Warm Cold	Development or intensification of a front. But these symbols are not in frequent use
Frontolysis	Short strokes across the front of the same colour as the front itself	Short strokes across the front	Weakening of a front. Symbolic representation not in frequent use
Instability line	Zigzag blue line		Line of convection phenomena similar in many effects to a cold front
Line squall	No linear representation but this symbol marks places on the weather map where the squall has been observed		A sudden temporary increase of wind, often to gale force, and sharp, usually frontal changes
Pseudo-occlusion	Thin purple chain line		Often indicates some doubt in this part of the weather pattern analysis
Double frontal structure Secondary cold front	Similar to basic representation but two lines instead of one		Frontal changes likely to occur in two phases The second of a pair of parallel cold fronts

Hurricanes

Etymologically the word hurricane means a strong wind but in meteorological practice the name is usually applied to the intense depressions which normally approach (and sometimes reach) the Carribean or United States of America from a south-easterly direction before turning northwards towards the middle of the North Atlantic. This intense non-frontal depression (whose counterpart in the China Seas is called a *typhoon*) is usually represented by more or less circular isobars. The centre of the low pressure (or *eye of the storm*) is often almost calm, but at a radius of between 40 and 80 nautical miles the speed of the wind around the centre is at a maximum—often more than 100 knots.

CHAPTER 8

Anticyclones

Although the word cyclone is often thought of as referring only to strong winds, by definition it can be applied to the circulatory wind flow around any depression and, because the wind flows in the opposite direction around high pressure centres, the word anticyclone is a logical synonym for a region of high pressure.

An anticyclone is the antithesis of a depression in more than just wind direction. Reversing the tentative argument used in Chapter 7 to discuss cyclogenesis, we may be able to guess that:

1 the building up of high pressure systems (*anticyclogenesis*) is favoured by the weakening of a thermal gradient in a confluent pressure pattern—and the meaning of this phrase is illustrated in Figure 8.1;

2 the interaction between the high and low level winds is such as to weaken the thermal gradient even more;

3 because of this weakening and because pressure changes depend to some extent on the presence of an appreciable thermal gradient, the development of a high pressure system is likely to be a decelerating process;

4 convergence (inflow of air) occurs at high levels over anticyclones while divergence (outflow) takes place at low levels, the two effects being linked by a slow downward motion (*subsidence*) of the air in between;

5 surface winds are generally light in an anticyclone (but there is no reason why they cannot be strong on the outskirts of the high pressure region);

6 well marked fronts are not likely in anticyclones.

As with the study of cyclogenesis, it is difficult to assess with accuracy the magnitudes of the elementary processes which lead to the observed effects. But whether we can prove the six points listed above to our own satisfaction or not, they do represent the way nature seems to work, and they do promote an understanding of the behaviour of anticyclones.

Warm and cold anticyclones

Illustrated in Figure 8.1 are two regions favourable for anticyclogenesis. The principal difference between them is that one is on the warm side of the front and the other is in the cold air, and when a

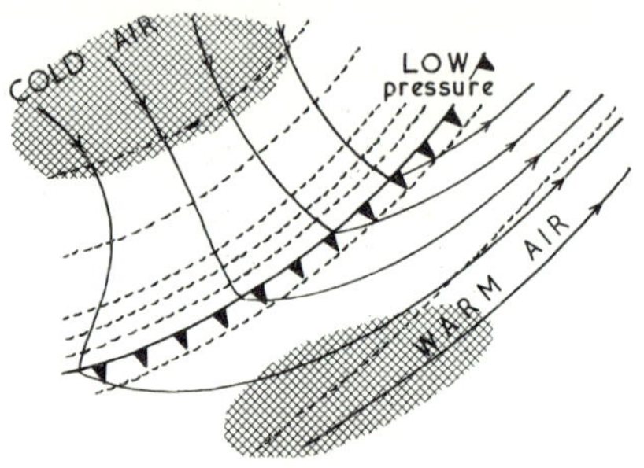

Fig. 8.1. The pressure and isotherm (dotted lines) pattern shown above is conducive to anticyclogenesis in the shaded areas.

high pressure centre develops it can be called a *warm anticyclone* or a *cold anticyclone* according to whether it contains warm or cold air. The distinction is not without some significance; the thermal wind principle caps the two types of anticyclone with dissimilar winds at high levels. The upper winds are liable to increase with height over (and especially towards the cold side of) a warm anticyclone, while cold anticyclones are noted more for light winds aloft.

Another distinction between the two types concerns their persistence. By weakening the thermal gradients in its vicinity, an anticyclone tends to inhibit further pressure changes, so that, once formed, a high pressure system tends to block the development and progress of the more active depressions, but the temperature and pressure structure of a cold anticyclone forms a much less efficient block than that of a warm high pressure cell. Therefore, while a warm high pressure system may persist for days, weeks, or even months, a cold anticyclone is more often seen as a relatively flexible and mobile feature of the weather map. This is not to say that cold anticyclones are never persistent; they do in fact persist for long winter spells inland over large continents, but not without some

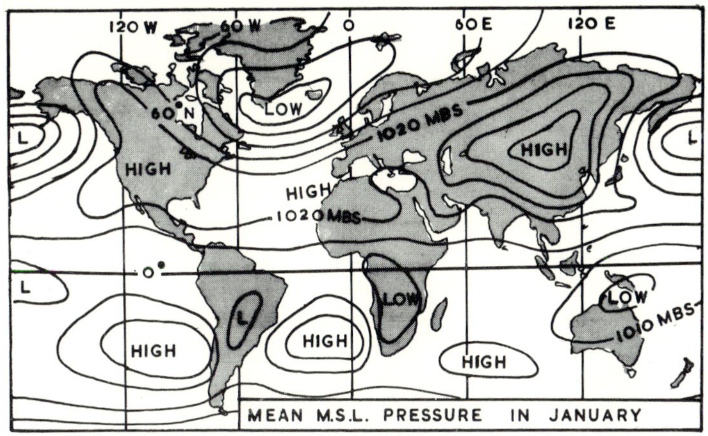

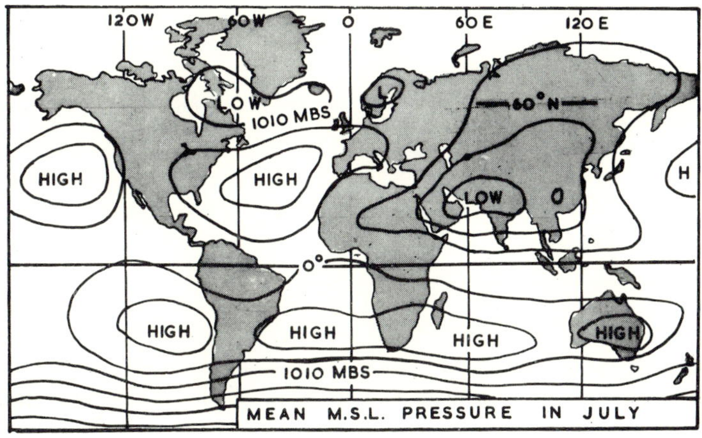

Fig. 8.2. Mean M.S.L. pressure in January and July.

fluctuations; a cold winter anticyclone such as the Siberian high is liable to suffer more low pressure incursions than a warm system such as the Azores anticyclone. Figure 8.2, comprising average M.S.L. pressure maps for January and July, shows both the winter tendency for high pressure to prevail inland over large continents and the general tendency for high pressure regions to predominate over the oceans in two subtropical belts which migrate northwards in our summer season and back towards the south in the winter months.

The effects of subsidence

Subsidence of air in an anticyclone is a very slow process—so slow that it is practically impossible to measure the downward airspeeds directly. However, rates of descent of the air have been inferred from various meteorological observations, and investigations have revealed the order of magnitude of the downward speeds likely in well developed anticyclones. The following table gives some guidance on the rate of subsidence in anticyclones over the British Isles.

RATE OF DESCENT OF AIR IN WELL DEVELOPED ANTICYCLONES

Height above M.S.L.	*Average over 6-hour period*	*Average over 36-hour period*
5,000 ft. (1,500 m.)	100 ft./hr. (30 m./hr.)	50 ft./hr. (15 m./hr.)
10,000 ft. (3,000 m.)	300 ft./hr. (90 m./hr.)	100 ft./hr. (30 m./hr.)
15,000 ft. (4,500 m.)	450 ft./hr. (135 m./hr.)	150 ft./hr. (45 m./hr.)
20,000 ft. (6,000 m.)	400 ft./hr. (120 m./hr.)	100 ft./hr. (30 m./hr.)

Slow though it is, subsidence is the vital link in the chain of events that leads to anticyclonic weather. The subsiding air is compressed and warmed—at the saturated or dry adiabatic lapse rate according to whether it is or is not saturated with water vapour. Thus unsaturated subsiding air becomes appreciably warmer while its relative humidity decreases. A simple calculation shows that the temperature of unsaturated air subsiding at, say, 200 ft./hr. will increase by 3·6° C. in 6 hours. Taking the saturated adiabatic lapse rate as 1·5° C. per 1,000 ft. we can also calculate that the same amount of subsidence would raise the temperature of cloudy air by only 1·8° C.—assuming the cloud contains enough moisture to maintain the saturation. Therefore, if subsidence operates on a region containing a layer of cloud, a temperature inversion is likely to be established as the air just above the cloud top is warmed by descent more than the air in the cloud itself.

If this layer of cloud persists during the night and if, as is usually the case, the sky above it is clear, then the top of the cloud will cool by nocturnal radiation, just as the ground cools under cloudless night skies. So the inversion of temperature above the cloud top will be accentuated, and the cooling by radiation at the cloud top can easily counteract the warming by subsidence. Unfortunately, the outcome is not decided by these two factors alone; the issue is confused by a convective motion within the cloud layer, by the dryness of the air just above, and by the motion and humidity of the air near cloud base. Rather than attempt to unravel the relevant processes we shall note and discuss the observed results.

Considering, for the moment, only medium and high cloud we can note that of the well developed anticyclones over the British Isles:

60% contain no medium or high cloud
30% contain very patchy medium or high cloud
10% contain altostratus

Obviously anticyclonic subsidence is moderately efficient at dissipating medium and high level cloud, although the occasional presence of altostratus does indicate the proximity of more effective frontal régimes on some occasions.

Dealing now with low cloud only, weather records reveal that of these anticyclones over Britain:

2% contain fog
17% contain no low cloud
64% contain stratocumulus
17% contain cumulus

The fog is, of course, radiation fog formed as a consequence of nocturnal cooling in light or calm winds under cloudless skies.

By far the majority of the anticyclones with stratocumulus occur during the winter months of the year. The stratocumulus sheets are often very variable in horizontal extent and, being dependent on the state of balance or unbalance between several factors already mentioned, the stratocumulus is liable to form or disperse somewhat erratically. Occasionally, however, the strato-cumulus persists and covers the sky for one, or perhaps several days, and deserves its name of *anticyclonic gloom.*

In 17% of the anticyclones conditions at low levels were suitable for convection and cumulus; in fact in many a summer-time anti-cyclone the actual lapse rate of temperature from ground level up to the base of the anticyclonic inversion is often about the same as the dry adiabatic lapse rate and, as we shall see in a later chapter on convection, such a state is favourable for the development of both thermal and turbulent vertical currents. The height to which the vertical currents will reach is limited to the height of the base of the inversion. Of our British anticyclones:

20% confine convection or turbulent motion to below 3,000 ft. or less

65% confine convection or turbulent motion to below 3,000–6,000 ft.

15% permit some convection to about heights of over 6,000 ft.

The effectiveness of the inversion depends to some extent on how intense it is and in this context we can note that the rise in temperature from the base to the top of the inversion is about

3–6° C. in 25% of the anticyclones
½–3° C. in 50% of the anticyclones

In the remaining 25% the effect of subsidence and distribution of cloud is sufficient to modify the temperature aloft but not to create a definite inversion. When a subsidence inversion does form, however, it is usually confined to a shallow layer of air—about 500–1,500 ft. deep.

As mentioned in Chapter 4, an inversion acts as a sort of lid on smoke injected into the atmosphere from below, and the lower the height of this lid the poorer will be the visibility. Persistent smoke haze in or near industrial and built-up areas is, therefore, common in anticyclonic conditions. With an inversion base at about 3,000 ft. visibility at ground level is often restricted to 1–3 miles over extensive areas in smoke drifting from such sources as London or Manchester, and although such a restriction is hardly noticeable to the man in the street it does make map reading difficult from a glider.

Transient ridges of high pressure

Since anticyclones and subsidence go hand in hand we can expect high pressure to be a clue to subsidence at work, and weather records for the British Isles show that for M.S.L. pressures of:

less than 1000 mbs. there is a 1 : 100 chance of persistent subsidence
1000–1020 mbs. there is a 1 : 15 chance of persistent subsidence
1020-1040 mbs. there is a 1 : 10 chance of persistent subsidence
over 1040 mbs. there is a a 1 : 4 chance of persistent subsidence

If these chances of subsidence seem rather low we should remember that they refer to *persistent* subsidence likely to be associated with a few days at least of anticyclonic weather and not to temporary transient effects.

It may be argued that the rate of rise of pressure should be a better guide to subsidence and anticyclonic development but if we enquire the chances of subsidence for various pressure changes over 3-hour periods (the conventional period of time for routine observations of pressure tendencies) we find that for a pressure rise of:

over 4 mbs. in 3 hours there is practically no chance of persistent subsidence
2–4 mbs. in 3 hours there is a 1 : 20 chance of persistent subsidence
0–2 mbs. in 3 hours there is a 1 : 10 chance of persistent subsidence
while for a pressure *fall* of
0–2 mbs. in 3 hours there is a 1 : 10 chance of persistent subsidence

The explanation of this apparent paradox that rapid pressure rises are not good indicators of persistent subsidence is that such rises are associated more with the movement of pressure systems than with the actual formation of an anticyclone. The pressure at a place in the path of an active depression falls quickly as the depression approaches and rises quickly after it has passed, but experience shows that the rapid rise is likely to be short lived; it soon gives way to a fall ahead of the next low pressure system in the family of depressions. Thus the ridges of high pressure between two active depressions is often as mobile as the depressions themselves. It must not be inferred that all ridges are mere passengers in trains of successive depressions;

the point being made here is that rapid pressure rises usually denote small transient ridges of high pressure while the slower but more persistent pressure rises are better predictors of more durable anticyclones.

Anticyclonic spells over Britain

Investigation into the incidence of anticyclonic spells of weather over the British Isles have revealed several interesting features which are best noted by studying the actual statistics. The left hand side of the table opposite shows the approximate monthly number of anticyclonic spells of various durations which occurred in 50 years of British weather. The right hand side of the table denotes the percentage frequency of airstream directions accompanying these spells; for example, in the 50 Januaries investigated there were 16 anticyclonic spells of between ½ and 1 week, 12 of between 1 and 2 weeks, 7 of 2–3 weeks and 1 of over 3 weeks. Of the total of these January anticyclones 36% were in such a position that they brought air from the continent, 37% brought mild air from the Atlantic, 12% brought cold air from the Atlantic, and the remaining 15% were situated over or so close to the British Isles that the wind was light or calm over most of Britain.

One of the most striking features illustrated in the table is the contrast between the months of August and September; August had only one 2–3 week anticyclonic spell in 50 years compared with 12 in September. The contrast between June and July is almost as sharp. Obviously May, June and September each provided more anticyclonic weather than the months of July or August.

A feature common to July, August and September is the tendency for anticyclonic spells in these months to bring warm airstreams to the British Isles from the Atlantic. Such airstreams are likely to be moist and are therefore somewhat more favourable to cloud formation than the drier airstreams from the Continent. Nearly a third of the May anticyclones bring rather dry air from the Continent towards the Atlantic and it is not at all unusual for the British Isles to enjoy a spell of fine sunny weather with easterly winds in this spring month. The continental air associated with 43% of the December anticyclonic spells, on the other hand, is likely to be cold and fairly dry. By making these plausible premises that continental air is likely to be warm and dry in the summer and cold and dry in the winter, that

Number of anticyclonic spells over Britain in 50 years					Percentage frequency of airstream sources			
Month	*Duration of spell*				*Air from the Continent*	*Warm or mild air from the Atlantic*	*Cold or cool air from the Atlantic*	*Air almost stagnant over Britain*
	½–1 *wk.*	1–2 *wks.*	2–3 *wks.*	*Longer than 3 weeks*				
Jan	16	12	7	1	36	37	12	15
Feb	16	12	8	1	33	29	15	23
Mar	18	17	2	1	32	30	17	21
Apr	16	15	2	2	23	28	27	22
May	15	18	5	2	32	25	27	16
June	17	22	5	1	22	32	30	16
July	14	17	0	0	15	42	23	20
Aug	18	12	1	0	22	37	18	23
Sept	16	14	12	3	29	32	18	21
Oct	18	15	5	1	37	23	20	20
Nov	21	16	5	0	35	30	16	19
Dec	16	17	3	1	43	33	8	16

moist air is likely to be cloudier than drier air, and by remembering the direction of circulation of winds around an anticyclone, the table above can be used to make a number of other deductions on the monthly features of anticyclonic spells in Britain. We may even be tempted to use the statistics as a basis for making a long range forecast, but the relationship between past records and future weather is a matter for speculation, so if we do hazard a guess that next May or June will include a finer spell of anticyclonic weather than July or August we should regard such a forecast more as a fascinating gamble than a scientific prediction.

CHAPTER 9

Charting the Weather

When consulting a professional meteorologist or listening to his forecast it is helpful to have some knowledge of the organisation on which he depends. The provision of a meteorological service starts with routine observations made at internationally agreed times at a large number of observing stations throughout the world, and, with meteorology being of particular importance in aviation, most countries maintain the majority of their observing stations at airfields. This usually results in an uneven distribution throughout the countryside, but each country has to strike a compromise between economy and meteorological requirements. Of the 200 or so observing stations at airfields and other selected sites in the British Isles about a third are concentrated into the eastern half of England while the network over such regions as the Scottish Highlands, the Welsh mountains and south-west England is relatively coarse.

Meteorological events over the oceans are just as important as those over land, and it is fortunate that routine observations are made voluntarily on hundreds of ships at sea throughout the world. To supplement these ship reports special ocean weather ships maintain station at a number of selected positions, eight of which are in the North Atlantic.

Augmenting the land and sea reports are observations made from aircraft on operations ranging from transatlantic flights to specially organised meteorological reconnaissance missions, and although these aircraft observations can seldom be made with the same regularity as those made on land or at sea, they do play a valuable part in building up a three dimensional picture of the actual weather systems.

The agreed times for making routine observations from land

stations and ships are 00, 03, 06 . . . . 18 and 21 hours GMT daily, but some stations record hourly, or even half-hourly, observations.

The elements observed

The routine observations made at ground stations and on ships usually include a number, if not all, of the following items:

Surface wind direction Surface wind speed Visibility Present weather Recent weather Cloud amounts Cloud bases Cloud types	Of particular interest in aviation	All relevant to the analysis of the current weather systems
Air temperature Dew point	Of particular interest in fog prediction	
Barometric pressure (M.S.L.)	For compiling pressure charts	
Barometric change in past 3 hours		
Amount of rainfall at land stations between 09 and 21 GMT, or between 21 and 09 GMT State of the ground (or sea) Maximum air temperature between 09 and 21 GMT, or Minimum air temperature between 21 and 09 GMT Minimum grass temperature between 21 and 09 GMT Total amount of sunshine at land stations during preceding day		Of interest in making climatological studies rather than short range forecasting

Radio-sonde observations

As mentioned in Chapter 2, an apparatus called a radio-sonde is used to measure temperature and humidity in the air aloft. Carried upwards at about 1,200 ft./min. by a gas-filled balloon, this instrument automatically transmits, in the form of radio signals, temperatures and humidities up to about 60,000–80,000 ft. and, while the ascent is in progress, upper winds are determined by tracking the balloon with radar. At present these radio-sonde ascents are made regularly at 00 GMT and 12 GMT at ocean weather ships and at selected meteorological stations in most well developed countries. The United Kingdom radio-sonde stations are situated at Lerwick (in the Shetlands), Stornoway (in the Hebrides), Shanwell (near Dundee), Aldergrove (near Belfast), Aughton (near Liverpool), Hemsby (near Great Yarmouth), Crawley (Surrey) and Camborne (Cornwall).

Pilot balloons

A cheaper but more restricted method of determining the winds aloft is to track the ascent of a small gas-filled balloon with the aid of a theodolite. The height of the balloon at any time is determined either by filling the balloon to such a size that it rises at a pre-computed rate, or from measurements of the angular elevation of the balloon and the apparent length (measured by a scale in the optical system of the theodolite) of a paper and thread tail suspended from the balloon itself. Visible through the theodolite as a pinpoint of reflected sunlight, a *pilot balloon* can be tracked to many thousands of feet on a fine, clear day, and on clear nights a balloon carrying a candle lantern can be detected up to a few thousand feet. But these balloons cannot, of course, be seen through cloud and the methods used to calculate their height are subject to various inaccuracies. So, with the development of the more efficient radio-sonde techniques and with the growing interest in fast, high level flying, the use of pilot balloons has declined in a number of countries since the Second World War.

Atmospherics

A stroke of lightning is an electrical discharge which emits radio waves on a wide band of wavelengths. Nuisance though they may be when heard as crackling atmospherics on ordinary radio receivers, these radio waves do enable the lightning to be located by radio direction finding techniques. The British Meteorological Office maintains six direction finding stations: Leuchars, Hemsby, Camborne, Long Kesh in Northern Ireland, Malta and Gibraltar. Operators equipped with very long wave direction finding radios at these stations are linked by radio and land line for ten minutes in every hour to a controller who determines the position of the lightning flashes from the bearings reported by the operators. Reasonably accurate up to distances of about 1,500 miles from the British Isles, this technique yields hourly reports (known as *SFLOCS*) on the position of thundery outbreaks over Europe, the Mediterranean and the eastern half of the North Atlantic.

Radar and precipitation

The ultra-short waves used in radar are reflected not only by solid objects such as aircraft but also by agglomerations of raindrops or snow flakes. Areas of rain or snow are seen as bright patches on the radar screen and by watching the movement of these patches it is sometimes possible to predict with reasonable accuracy the onset or end of precipitation during the next hour or two. Unfortunately, this method of prediction sounds easier to apply than it really is. Radar echoes are not always easy to interpret with confidence; at close range echoes from small rain clouds are sometimes obscured by local radar reflections; as the range is increased the reduction in the penetrative power of the radar beam impairs the radar view, and because radar waves usually travel in straight lines the rain clouds in the troposphere are seldom detected at ranges greater than about 90 miles. Some atmospheric conditions, especially low level inversions, cause the radar beam to become curved and the effective range is often increased, but at the same time this refraction of the beam also adds difficulties to interpretation of the echoes.

Light rain or drizzle cannot normally be detected by radar operating on the commonly used 10 cm. wavelength, but even when the raindrops are numerous and large enough to produce strong echoes the forecasting problem remains to predict not only the movement of the rain area but also how the area will change in size and shape as it moves.

Radar is used as an aid to local forecasting in the London area and at some airfields meteorologists receive reports from operators of the local radar landing aids, but the main meteorological use of radar in the British Isles is for research rather than for routine forecasting.

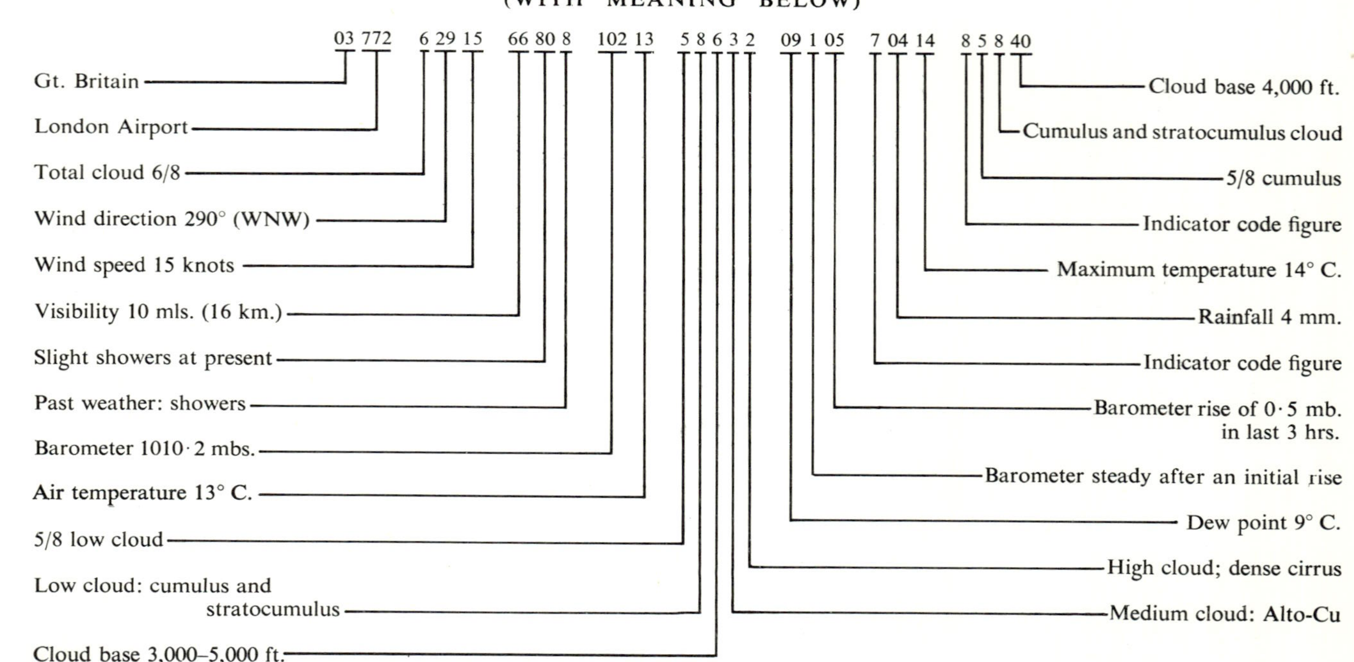
CODED WEATHER MESSAGE
(WITH MEANING BELOW)
03 772 6 29 15 66 80 8 102 13 5 8 6 3 2 09 1 05 7 04 14 8 5 8 40
Gt. Britain
London Airport
Total cloud 6/8
Wind direction 290° (WNW)
Wind speed 15 knots
Visibility 10 mls. (16 km.)
Slight showers at present
Past weather: showers
Barometer 1010·2 mbs.
Air temperature 13° C.
5/8 low cloud
Low cloud: cumulus and stratocumulus
Cloud base 3,000–5,000 ft.
Cloud base 4,000 ft.
Cumulus and stratocumulus cloud
5/8 cumulus
Indicator code figure
Maximum temperature 14° C.
Rainfall 4 mm.
Indicator code figure
Barometer rise of 0·5 mb. in last 3 hrs.
Barometer steady after an initial rise
Dew point 9° C.
High cloud; dense cirrus
Medium cloud: Alto-Cu

Communications and codes

Meteorological observations lose much of their value to weather forecasting after they are a few hours old, and to minimise delay in the collection and dissemination of these observations, meteorological communications are co-ordinated on a world wide basis.

From a communications centre at Bracknell, Berkshire, teleprinter lines radiate to group centres from which more teleprinter lines radiate to the observing stations in the British Isles. This organisation enables the hourly observations from stations in the British Isles to be made available to a forecaster at the communications centre at about 10 minutes past each hour, and to a forecaster at an airfield at about 20 minutes later. Similar land line or radio networks exist in most countries and the hubs of these national networks are themselves linked by radio or teleprinter. At most stations in Britain sufficient information is received via the international communications network to construct a chart of the weather over Europe and much of the North Atlantic within about 3 hours of the observations being made.

A speedy exchange of information would be impossible if every observer sent out a detailed report in his own language. So an international code or shorthand is used. Each report is translated into a few groups of five figures according to a system which at first sight may appear complicated. However, this international code is an invaluable device for packing copious information into a brief internationally understood message (as evidenced by the example opposite) and practised meteorologists talk and think in terms of it.

The weather map

At most forecasting offices plotters transpose the incoming coded weather messages on to large charts and, since it usually takes nearly 3 hours to obtain and plot the weather from mid-Atlantic to Russia and from Iceland to North Africa, it is perhaps convenient that the large area charts are usually plotted at 3-hourly intervals—for 00, 03, 06 . . . 21 hours GMT. Naturally the area mapped, the scale of the charts and the frequency with which they are plotted are selected to meet the requirements of each particular office, but the plotting systems are determined by international

Item	*Colour in red and black system*	*Position relative to "station circle"*	*Units*	*Remarks*
Barometric pressure	Black	Top right	mbs. and tenths of mbs.	Last three figures only
Barometric tendency	Red for falling pressure, black for rising pressure	Right	mbs. and tenths of mbs. during last 3 hours	Usually two figures (occasionally three) followed by a symbol suggestive of type of tendency e.g. ✓ means falling at first then rising.
Temperature	Black	Top left	° F. in some English speaking countries ° C. elsewhere	°C. is now used in the United Kingdom
Dew point	Red	Bottom left	do.	do.
Surface wind direction	Black	Straight line to station circle	—	Calm denoted by a circle around the station circle
Surface wind speed	Black	Feathers on wind direction line	10 knots per full feather	
Present weather	Black	Left	—	Selection of symbols shown on page 102
Past weather	Red	Bottom right	—	Usually denotes weather in past 3 or 6 hours occasionally supplemented by a black symbol relating to weather in past hour.

Item	*Colour in red and black system*	*Position relative to "station circle"*	*Units*	*Remarks*
Visibility	Red	Left of present weather	Hundreds of metres up to 5,000 m. then km. plus 50, e.g. 60 = 10 km.	Two figures
Total cloud amount	Black	Vertical strokes and short horizontal stroke in in station circle	Vertical stroke =2/8 of sky cover, short horizontal stroke = 1/8	⨂ means sky obscured (by fog or smoke)
Type of low cloud	Black	Beneath the station circle	—	Selection of symbols shown on page 103
Low cloud amount	Black	Beneath low cloud symbol	Eighths of sky covered	One figure at left of oblique stroke
Low cloud height	Black	Beneath low cloud symbol	Hundreds of feet	Two figures at right of oblique stroke
Medium cloud	Black	Above station circle	Amount and height occasionally denoted below cloud symbol	Selection of symbols shown on page 103
High cloud	Red	Above medium cloud	—	Selection of symbols shown on page 103

agreement. As with the codes, the object is to condense a large amount of information into a compact form. The main features of the system used in British meteorological practice are listed in the table on pages 100 and 101 and typified by Figure 9.1 which shows the plotted version of the coded weather message described on page 98.

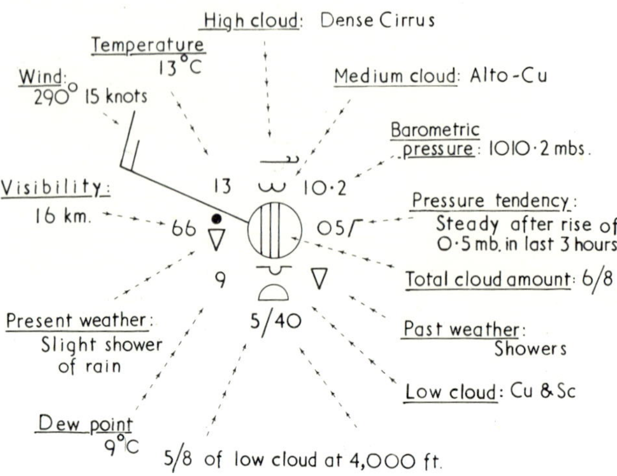

Fig. 9.1. Plotted version of the coded weather observation on page 98.

PRINCIPAL WEATHER SYMBOLS

Drizzle	Rain shower
Rain	Fog
Sleet	Mist
Snow	Smoke haze
Hail	Thunderstorm

Subclassifications of precipitation are denoted by arrangements and modifications of the type shown below.

- Intermittent slight rain
- Continuous slight rain
- Intermittent moderate rain
- Continuous moderate rain

Intermittent heavy rain

Continuous heavy rain

Slight snow shower

Moderate or heavy rain showers

SELECTION OF CLOUD TYPES

Low cloud	*Medium cloud*
Cumulus humilis	Thin Alto-St
CuNim calvus	Thick Alto-St
St-cu	Alto-Cu
Stratus	Ac and As
CuNim capillatus	Ac Castellanus

High cloud

Ci ("mares' tails")

Ci (associated with CuNim)

Ci (in bands)

Ci-St

Ci-cu

The forecaster's task

While the weather map is being plotted other assistants are usually at work drawing graphs showing the winds, temperatures and humidities as determined by the radio-sonde ascents and processing data for the construction of pressure maps at various levels in the atmosphere and charts to determine the thermal winds (described in Chapter 6).

Very briefly, the weather forecaster's task is to analyse the plotted and processed weather observations into a coherent but continuously changing three dimensional picture and to predict the subsequent developments. In tackling this formidable task he draws isobars, fronts and very occasionally *isallobars* (isopleths of pressure changes) on the weather maps. He calls these weather maps *synoptic charts* while the instantaneous weather pictures they portray are referred to as *synoptic situations*. A suitably graduated *geostrophic scale* is often used to measure geostrophic wind speeds at points of special interest on the pressure maps and the forecaster's routine often includes a study of "thermal" charts which relate to thermal winds and not to thermals in the gliding sense.

The forecaster's scientific ability is required not to make intricate calculations on a routine basis but to analyse complex atmospheric processes into elementary and more easily understandable components whose relative significance in any particular circumstances may (with experience) be assessed in the light of current features and trends in the synoptic situation.

One of the principal tasks of the forecasters at the Central Forecasting Office (C.F.O.), located at the communications centre, is to predict the movement and development of the pressure systems at M.S.L. and at several upper levels up to just above the tropopause for 24 and 36 hours ahead. These forecast pressure charts and the reasoning behind them are used as a framework on which to make forecasts of the weather itself and it is these forecasts which are illustrated on television screens, broadcast at intervals by the B.B.C. and presented in divers forms by the daily press.

For use as background information, descriptions and coded forms of the forecast pressure maps prepared at C.F.O. are included in the messages transmitted from the communications centre to group centres where the forecaster's duties often include the preparation of detailed regional forecasts for about 6 to 18 hours ahead and aviation forecasts for specified routes. Usually a regional forecast is passed on to the group's satellite stations to be issued to aviators by forecasters who keep a watch on the local weather and the local trend as indicated by current observations within their zone of interest.

Thus the forecasting organisation is to some extent pyramidal; responsibilities are telescoped along roughly the same channels as the national communications network. The whole system, however, is flexible enough to cater for the wide variety of operational requirements throughout the country. London Airport, for example, with a large forecasting staff provided with copious information of direct interest to international aviation, can function as an independent forecasting unit, whereas at the public enquiry office in London duty forecasters are sometimes so busy answering enquiries that they must rely on a steady flow from C.F.O. of forecasts ranging from the forecast pressure charts to such forecasts as the risk of ice forming on electrified railway lines in the south of London.

CHAPTER 10

Airflow at Low Levels

As in most aspects of gliding, actual experience is the best guide to efficient hill soaring, but as a prelude to acquiring such experience or as an aid to interpreting experience already accrued it is instructive to ponder a while on the distribution of horizontal and vertical speeds of the air flowing up and over a long hill ridge. As a basis for discussion we can consider the aerodynamically simple case of a uniform airstream blowing across a circular shaped ridge as shown in Figure 10.1*a*. By neglecting the effect of friction and by assuming (to satisfy the mathematical pundits) the air to be unsaturated with a

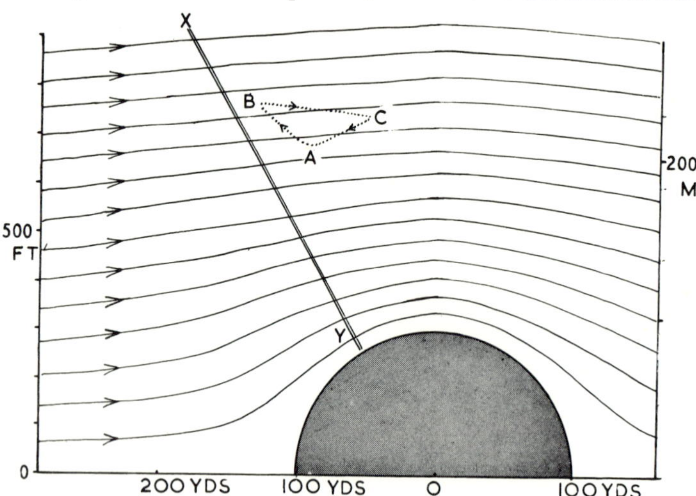

Fig. 10.1*a*. Streamlines in an "idealised" flow across a hemispherically shaped ridge. In this particular flow maximum hill soaring heights would be obtained along the line *XY*. *ABC* represents a flight path along which lift would be obtained on *AB* of the upwind section. The sectors *BC* and *CA*, however, are outside the zone of "lift" in this illustration.

dry adiabatic temperature lapse rate, the horizontal and vertical speeds of the air at any point can be calculated without much difficulty. Application of the relevant formulae to a 20-knot airstream blowing towards a ridge 300 ft. high yields the vertical and horizontal velocity distributions shown in Figure 10.1*b*. There are three features of special interest in the vertical speed pattern: the

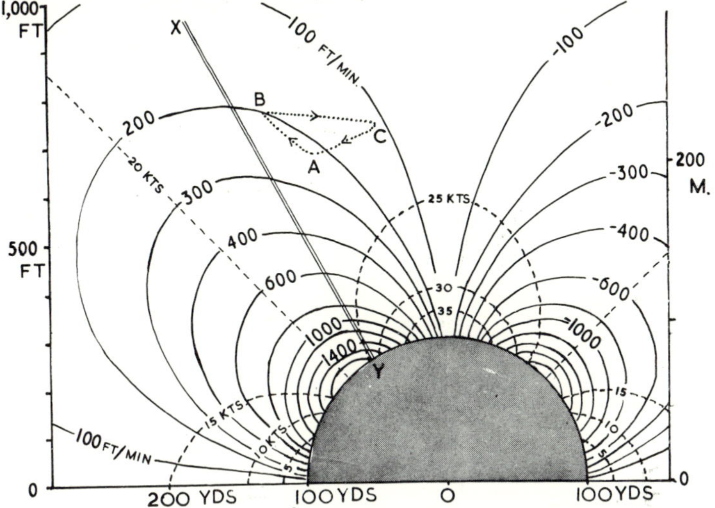

Fig. 10.1*b*. The vertical and horizontal wind speed components of a 20-knot "idealised" flow of the form illustrated in Fig. 10.1*a* are shown by the full and broken lines respectively. Negative values on the full lines in lee of the ridge denote downdraught strengths.

orientation of the vertical velocity zones, the general variation of lift well above and upwind of the hill and the more pronounced variation close to the hill surface. Allowing 200 ft./min. for the sinking speed of his glider, a pilot in this hypothetical situation could soar up to about 800 ft. above the flat ground level and to maintain this maximum altitude he would need to keep about 150 yds. upwind of the hill crest. If he can fly the glider with a sinking speed of 150 ft./min. relative to the air then he can either gain an extra 100 ft. of height or widen the up- and downwind extent of his soaring flight. If he flies too far downwind towards the hill crest he is liable to emerge quickly from the zone of indicated lift, and, unless the gliding angle of his aircraft is atrociously steep, he will not re-enter this zone until he turns and flies upwind again. Figure 10.1 illustrates a flight path which would show this effect of indicated lift during upwind flight (*AB*) and sink on the downwind leg (*BC*).

Compared to the vertical speed pattern the horizontal velocity distribution shown in Figure 10.1*b* is of secondary importance, but we should at least note that at the hill crest the surface wind is much greater than that of the flow some distance upstream and decreases with height above the hill crest, while at the foot of the hill the wind is light and increases with height. These effects, which are characteristic of many an airflow over hills of various shapes and sizes, must be borne in mind when contemplating launching or landing at hill sites.

Of course, the circular ridge profile and uniform airflow used as a basis for discussion do represent an oversimplification of the actual

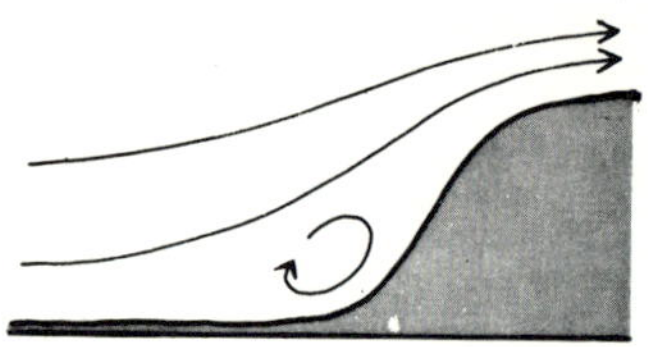

Fig. 10.2. A "bolster" eddy on a steep windward escarpment.

hill soaring conditions likely to be encountered, but we can reason out some of the modifications necessary to obtain more realism. The surface friction effect likely to retard all winds close to the ground must be superimposed on the smooth flow depicted in Figure 10.1. This surface friction effect is greater over wooded hill slopes than over comparatively smooth grass or snow-covered ridges —wooded slopes therefore tend to be poor generators of hill lift.

The effect of the steepness of the hill slope is difficult to assess. Obviously hill lift is likely to be weak over gentle slopes, but too steep an escarpment is liable to induce windward eddies in a position such as that shown in Figure 10.2. The steep escarpment may also lead to eddies on the leeward side of the ridge, and in Figure 10.3 the windsocks emphasising the eddy flow pattern are not mere figments of hypothetical argument; such a discrepancy between two adjacent windsocks was actually observed at Camphill, Derbyshire, on a July afternoon in 1954. Set up some 50 ft. from the top of Bradwell Edge, these windsocks (one at 12 ft., the other at 6 ft., above the ground) evinced just such an eddy as that depicted in the figure.

There does appear to be a slight tendency at least for such eddies per 1,000 ft., whereas when a dry adiabatic lapse rate prevails the eddies seem to be inhibited by more general desultory turbulence.

There is no set of simple rules for guessing or predicting when or

Fig. 10.3. Eddies on a leeward slope.

precisely whereabouts large eddies will form. But merely realising that they do exist and that they are mostly unpredictable should prompt caution in launching or landing, and while there is no adequate substitute for hill soaring tuition in the air, it is enlightening to use a few minutes of non-gliding weather or of a winter's evening to make speculative pencil sketches of the probable streamlines or eddies in the airflow across ridges of various shapes, artistic intuition being all that is usually required to make the sketches broadly correct.

It is usually easy to guess the principal effects on hill lift of gulleys and other irregularities in an escarpment although it may surprise

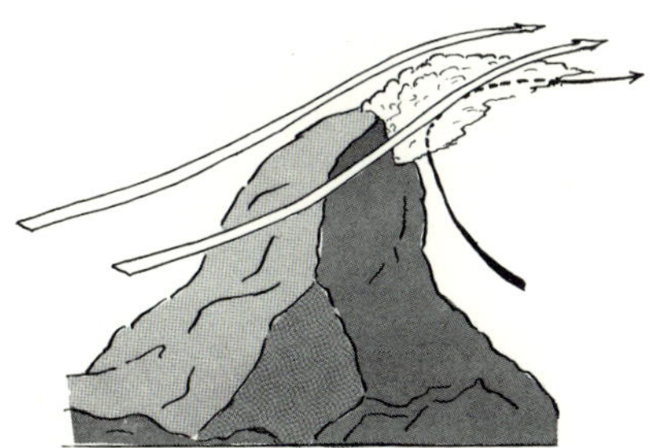

Fig. 10.4. The shape of the streamlines past a high mountain peak is sometimes betrayed by the "smoking mountain" cloud streaming from the peak. This cloud forms in the air which is drawn up the leeward slopes before joining the main airstream.

the inexperienced pilot to learn that upward vertical currents are sometimes found on the leeward slopes of isolated mountain peaks; when this leeward air is relatively moist it may produce a cloud appearing to stream from the mountain peak, as illustrated in Figure 10.4.

Hill lift can also be complicated by heating or cooling of the ground and by lee wave phenomena which are the subject of Chapter 16, but before enlarging on these complications it would be as well to forestall possible confusion between vertical air motion and the meaning of "lift" and "sink" in gliding language. In this book the speeds of vertical currents always refer to actual air movement while "lift" and "sink" will be used to accord with the motion of a medium performance glider, i.e. unless otherwise stated, lift equals the vertical speed of upcurrents minus about 180 ft./min.

The wind gradient and gustiness

A potential danger in the gliding approach to landing is the usual increase of wind with height from ground level up to at least a height of about 150 ft. During the final landing leg into wind this *wind gradient*, as it is commonly called, has the effect of reducing the airspeed of a glider whose actual momentum changes but slowly as the aircraft descends into decreasing headwinds. Failure to make allowance for this effect can result in an inelegant approach and a heavy, possibly expensive, landing especially as the wind gradient is often most pronounced within a few feet of the ground. The wind gradient also calls for considerable prudence in making turns at low levels; in a steeply banked turn the low wing may well be in an airflow a few knots slower than that at the level of the upper wing and the dangers of this type of situation can easily be figured out by any glider pilot.

In light or moderate winds the wind gradient itself usually deserves attention without being unduly worrying, but in a stronger flow the danger of stalling in a lull during an approach into wind is seriously increased by gusts and lulls in the winds at low levels.

In this particular paragraph the "average" is considered to apply to periods of between a few minutes and about half an hour, while gusts and lulls refer to the noticeable variations which last for between a few seconds and about half a minute. During these gusts and lulls the surface wind speed over flat sites is likely to increase or decrease momentarily by as much as 70% of the average wind speed; a 15-knot surface wind is likely to include gusts to about 25 knots and lulls in which the wind speed drops to 5 knots.

Katabatic winds

Because the cooling of air by nocturnal radiation is greatest at ground level, a feature of hilly terrain on practically calm, clear nights is that the air close to the hill slopes becomes cooler and denser than air at the same level over the adjacent valleys. Therefore, this hill slope air tends to slide down into the valleys and in doing so creates a *katabatic* wind. Down gentle slopes of small hills these winds are often light and merely add to the difficulties of interpreting surface wind observations, but large escarpments and long steep valleys can produce fresh katabatic breezes. Snow-covered slopes or glaciers are particularly prone to katabatic winds and on such slopes the cooling of air at the snow or ice surface frequently makes downslope winds liable to persist during both night and day—such a persistent katabatic flow has the alternative name, *glacier wind.*

Not infrequently the onset of a katabatic flow is sudden, only a few minutes elapsing between the existence of light or practically calm winds and the forceful arrival of a definite wind down the hillside. This katabatic wind is normally confined to a shallow layer, often less than 500 ft. deep. In an investigation into katabatic flow down a steep 42-degree slope in the Innsbruck range of mountains pilot balloons were used to measure winds at various distances from the mountainside. Typical of the results are the observations tabled below.

Katabatic winds for a steep (42-degree) escarpment in the Innsbruck range of mountains

Distance in yards perpendicularly away from the slope	5	10	15	20	25	30	35	40	50	100	110
Wind speed in knots down the slope	2	3	4	4	5	5	5	4	4	$\frac{1}{2}$	0

These tabulated observations portray only weak downslope winds but even a strong katabatic flow has similar features in that the flow extends to only a short distance away from the slope and the maximum wind speed is at about a quarter of this distance from the hillside.

Obviously, katabatic winds do not constitute soaring conditions but the glider pilot should include them in his stock of meteorological knowledge in order to interpret local wind observations and to supplement his general ideas of mountain airflow.

Anabatic winds

Of more direct concern to the soaring pilot are the winds urged upwards along hill slopes by daytime insolation. The mechanism is practically the converse of the katabatic variety; heating from the sun is communicated via the ground to air close to a hill slope quicker than it is to the air at the same level over the adjacent lowland, and the associated density variation produces a wind (an *anabatic* wind) up the hillside. This anabatic flow is usually confined to a shallow layer on the hill slope but not quite as shallow as its katabatic counterpart. Measurements of anabatic upslope winds over the steep 42-degree slope already mentioned in the last section produced a set of observations tabled below.

Anabatic winds for a steep (42-degree) escarpment in the Innsbruck range of mountains

Distance in yards perpendicularly away from the slope	5	10	15	20	25	30	35	40	50	100	120
Wind in knots up the slope	5	6	7	7	8	8	8	7	7	5	5
Vertical component in ft./min. of wind velocity	300	380	450	490	510	510	500	480	450	320	300

These measurements accord with other observations and with theoretical studies which show the distribution of anabatic winds to be like that illustrated in Figure 10.5. The primary factors governing the depth (D) of the flow are the gradient of the escarpment and the temperature lapse rate of the air over the adjoining lowland. Broadly speaking, gentle slopes and temperature lapse rates close to the D.A.L.R. are both favourable for deeper than average anabatic wind layers, while steep slopes and inversions tend to limit the upslope winds to a shallow layer. But the anabatic wind speed is related to the hill gradient, the temperature lapse rate and the rate of insolation in such a way that appreciable lift is often confined to shallow rather than deep anabatic layers. In order to get the most lift out of upslope winds a pilot must often fly very close (within a few wing spans) of the mountainside and, naturally, in such a position he must be particularly alert.

Occasionally anabatic winds attain speeds of over 20 knots, yielding a vertical component of about 1,500 ft./min. or more on a 45-degree slope, but all too often the general anabatic soaring conditions along a mountain range are marginal and some experience

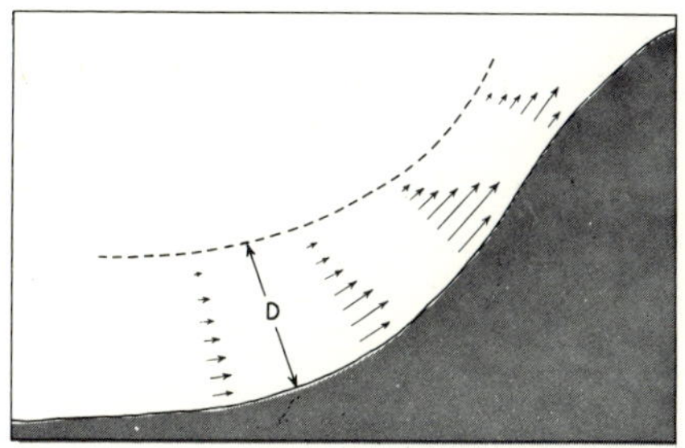

Fig. 10.5. Anabatic flow.

is needed first to assess where and when to seek the best lift and secondly to avoid flying into newly formed cloud clinging to the slope or into the mountainside itself. The upward flow is usually strongest on the sections of the slope directly facing the sun; bare rock which is readily heated by direct sunshine is a good generator of anabatic flow while poor lift or even sink may be found over a neighbouring surface of snow. Cloud cover needs watching as anabatic winds are very quick to decline when the mountain slope becomes shaded by cloud. Sudden cloud formation in the upslope flow itself presents another hazard to anabatic soaring; the anabatic phenomenon is not exempt from the rule that ascent of air leads to cooling, and condensation if the air contains sufficient moisture. Furthermore, over mountainous terrain parcels of air follow such tortuous paths and have such divers histories that it is unwise to reckon on one single condensation level being appropriate to a large region; the condensation level in one valley may be quite different at times from that in the next, and it is dangerous to forget this fact when learning to fly in truly mountainous terrain such as the Swiss, Austrian or French Alps where anabatic soaring is widely practised.

Mountain and valley winds

A valley can be considered to comprise three sloping surfaces, two steep mountain escarpments and the valley floor between them. All of these three slopes can generate ana- or katabatic winds and the interplay between these winds often produces a recognisable daily sequence of events. Before sunrise the predominant katabatic flow takes the form of a steady wind (sometimes known as Bergwind) down the valley. Soon after sunrise anabatic winds (Hangaufwinde) begin to flow up the steep escarpments flanking the valley and these upslope winds gradually intensify during the morning. By midday the anabatic flow up the valley has become well established and during the afternoon this up valley wind increases at the expense of the mountain slope winds which gradually weaken. By late afternoon the up valley wind predominates, but comes the evening and the katabatic flow down the mountain slopes (Hangabwinde) sets in and this wind persists for a while until the nocturnal cooling is sufficient to restore the early morning flow down the valley. Naturally the details of diurnal changes vary but the broad features of the sequence of events (illustrated in Figure 10.6) are often recognisable in wide and deep valleys. Experience suggests that the precise shape of the valley cross-section or the inclination of the valley floor are of little consequence, but the sequence is primarily a fair weather phenomenon and is best observed in deep and wide valleys such as those in the Swiss Alps.

It is not surprising that wind directions in mountainous terrain are often bewildering in their variability in place and in time (and we have not included the effects of lee waves or convection yet), but it is helpful to make a note of the salient features of ana- and katabatic winds and to remember that such phenomena are products primarily of daytime insolation and nocturnal radiation. The greater the low level heating or cooling the firmer will be the establishment of up- or downslope winds—while generally overcast or windy conditions over a mountainous region will minimise diurnal temperature changes and preclude all ana- and katabatic flow except possibly the more persistent glacier winds.

One of the complications which can and does arise in the study of mountain airflow is the interaction between the valley winds in two valleys leading to the same mountain pass. Usually the insolation (or nocturnal radiation) in one of the valleys differs from that in the other (for example, a valley opening out towards the Equator will be heated by the sun more than a valley open towards higher

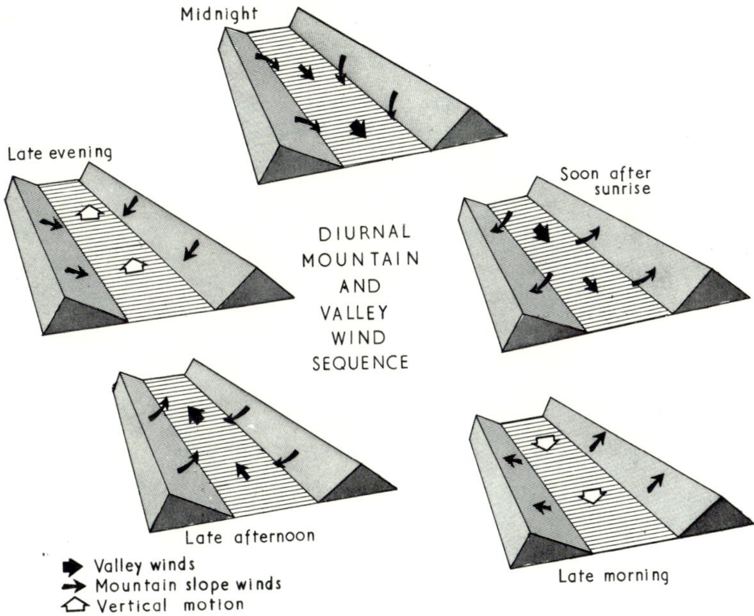

Fig. 10.6. Mountain and valley wind sequence.

latitudes) and, of course, the valleys do not normally have the same dimensions. The result of these differences is that ana- and katabatic effects on one side of the pass are much greater than those produced on the other, and occasionally the anabatic wind of one valley spills over the pass into the upper reaches of the adjoining valley, which thereby experiences downslope flow both by night due to its own kataflow and by day due to this superabundant development of the anaflow on the other side of the pass. One of the localities in which this anomalous valley wind is observed is the windshed between

Engadine and Bergell in Switzerland, and from this locality the phenomenon has acquired the name, the *Maloja* wind.

Foehn winds

Some airstreams which flow across a mountain range are experienced as conspicuously warm and dry winds in the leeward lowlands. Winds of this type have earned special names, such as the *Chinook* in North America, the *Kachchan* in Ceylon and the

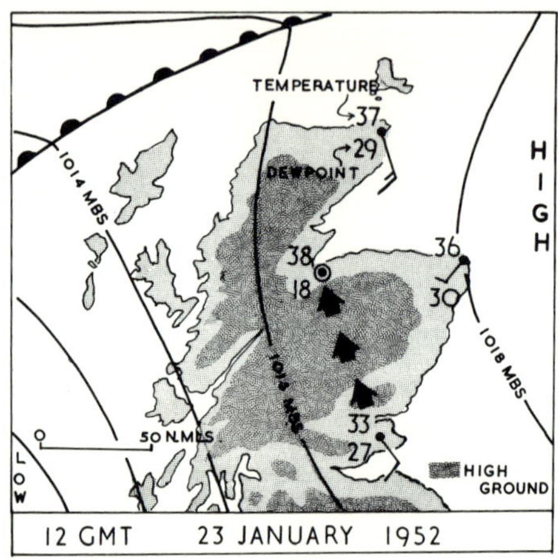

Fig. 10.7*a*. An example of a foehn effect in Scotland producing relatively warm and dry air in lee of the high ground. On this occasion rain was encountered by the pilot of a powered aircraft over the high ground itself.

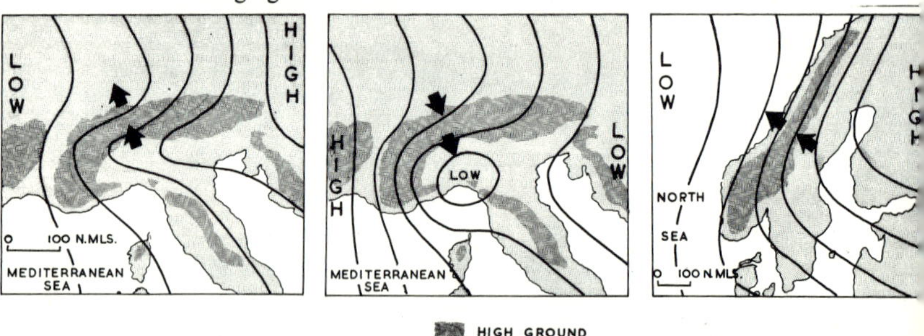

Fig. 10.7*b*. In mountainous regions the low level wind flow is often across rather than along the M.S.L. isobars. The M.S.L. pressure system illustrated usually produces foehn winds in the directions of the broad arrows.

Zonda in Argentina, but they are all of a class known as *foehn winds*. Leaving their warmth and dryness to be explained in Chapter 12, let us take a look at Figure 10.7 which shows some of the pressure patterns commonly associated with foehn winds in Scotland, Norway, Switzerland and Italy. In mountainous regions such as these the adjustment of barometric pressure readings to M.S.L. yields artificial pressure gradients which do not bear a simple relationship with the broad low level wind flow, but accumulated experience shows that these types of synoptic situations usually produce foehn winds blowing in the direction of the broad arrows.

Shallow low level temperature inversions over an extensive sheltered valley can persist for between an hour or two and many days, according to the current synoptic situations, and occasionally foehn winds flow over the top of the inversion and warm only the small hills which happen to stick up out of the shallow pool of stagnant cold air. Appropriately enough, such hills are called *foehn islands*.

Local winds

Winds which happen to have conspicuous characteristics in any particular district are often known by local names. The *mistral* is a cold northerly wind which is channelled down the Rhône Valley between the French Alps and the Central Massif of France; the Dalmatian coast is sometimes subjected to an unpleasantly cold north-easterly wind known as the *bora*; the *buran* is the name given to a cold north-easterly over Russia and Siberia and when this wind whips up drifting snow to form a blizzard it is called a *purga*.

Winds conspicuous for their warmth include the easterly *leveche* in Spain, the *leste* in Madeira and the *khamsin* which, blowing from the Sahara in advance of a low pressure system, is often unpleasantly hot and dry by the time it reaches Egypt. Occasionally it is strong enough to stir up sandstorms, especially at the leading edge of the hot air.

CHAPTER 11

Sea Breezes

On a sunny day the temperature at the surface of a land area rises more quickly than that of an adjoining sea surface, the sea being heated to a greater depth than the land. Therefore, in calm, light or possibly moderate winds, the air over land is heated more quickly than that over the sea, and if the sea air is colder than that over the land then the horizontal temperature gradient across the coastline is intensified.

In Chapter 7 we noted that the tightening of a horizontal temperature gradient is liable to spark off a pressure and wind disturbance which intensifies rapidly once the tightening has reached some critical but ill-defined stage. We also noted the difficulty in

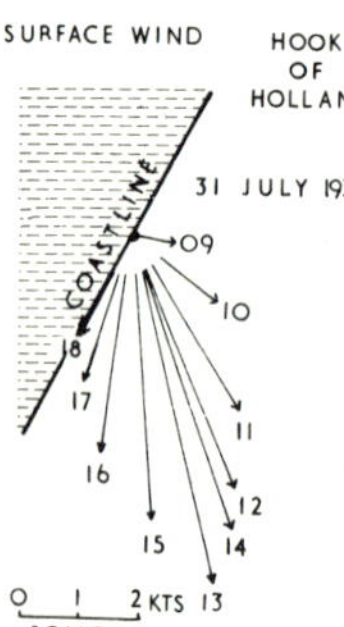

Fig. 11.1. Typical variation of wind near the coast during a day favourable for sea breezes.

dissecting these elementary but intricately interwoven processes which lead to fronts and frontal depressions. The study of sea breezes is beset with the same type of difficulty and so the following paragraphs describe rather than explain the significant sea breeze characteristics.

An early consequence of the differential heating of air across the coastline is a slight rise of pressure over land at a height of about

3,000 ft. or above accompanied by an almost imperceptible seaward flow of air at about the same level. As a result of this upper air movement the M.S.L. pressure over land decreases very slightly and air at low levels flows inland from the sea. At first this landward flow, called the sea breeze, blows almost directly across the coast but as the M.S.L. pressure inland continues to fall (still only slightly) the sea breeze increases in strength and begins to veer. At the coast it is

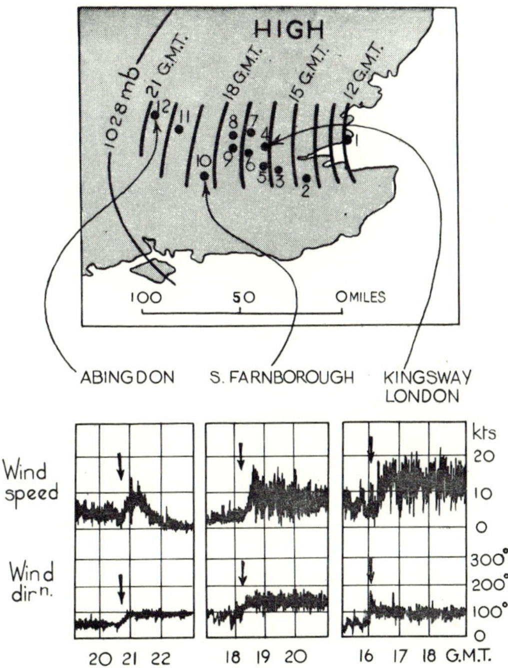

Fig. 11.2. Observations from the meteorological offices labelled 1–12 and named in the text were used to plot the hourly isochrones of the position of the sea breeze front which advanced inland from the Thames estuary. The autographic records illustrate the changes in wind speed and direction at the passage of the front.

often at its strongest and is directed at about 30–50 degrees to the coastline by mid-afternoon, but from then on the speed decreases although the direction continues to veer until by late afternoon the breeze is almost along the coast as illustrated in Figure 11.1.

The distance inland to which the sea breeze penetrates depends on the duration and strength of the sunshine, on the height to which the heat from the sun is distributed, on the direction and strength of the superimposed general wind flow and on the sea temperature. In the tropics sea breezes are felt at distances up to about 150 miles inland from the shore; in temperate latitudes about 50 miles is considered a

SEA BREEZE ACROSS LONDON, 1 JULY 1949

Ref. in Fig. 11.2	*Place*	*Time of arrival of sea breeze GMT*	*Wind direction in degrees and speed in knots*		*Highest gust in knots*	*Air tempera-ture in deg. F.*		*Relati humidi*	
			B	A	A	B	A	B	/
1	Shoeburyness	1130	080/1	130/7	8	64	63	56	6
2	West Malling	1530	060/7	060/14	—	75	70	46	6
3	Biggin Hill	1550	030/2	060/10	—	76	69	40	6
4	Kingsway	1605	030/6	090/12	23	76	72	46	6
5	Croydon	1610	030/4	060/10	18	78	73	38	6
6	Kew	1640	050/6	100/15	22	77	72	37	5
7	Hendon	1650	050/6	100/8	—	77	72	35	5
8	Northolt	1725	040/10	100/13	—	77	71	36	5
9	London Airport	1730	030/6	080/15	20	79	71	34	5
10	South Farnborough	1810	070/3	120/9	20	77	69	40	6
11	Benson	1950	360/6	060/10	—	—	—	—	-
12	Abingdon	2040	060/4	100/8	16	—	—	—	-

B = Before arrival of the sea breeze
A = After arrival of the sea breeze

deep penetration, but this is only a rough guide. On a hot July day in 1949 a sea breeze from the Thames estuary was detected as far inland as Abingdon, about 100 miles from the coast. Figure 11.2 shows isochrones marking the leading edge of the sea breeze as it passed meteorological observing stations in southern England, and the items given on page 120 are extracts from observations recorded at twelve of these stations.

Before the arrival of the sea breeze winds were light and mostly north-easterly, but the air from the sea spread inland with a slightly stronger flow from between 060 and 130 degrees, and at those stations equipped with pressure tube anemometers the rapidity of this change and the gustiness of the sea breeze were well marked on the autographic wind records—parts of which are reproduced in Figure 11.2. Abrupt changes were also registered in the measurements of temperature and humidity, and it was apparent that the transition

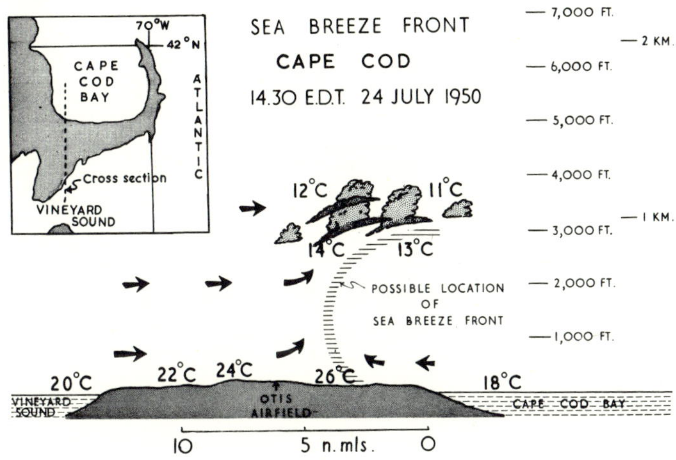

Fig. 11.3. The temperatures and airflow characteristics in this illustration were obtained during a local investigation of this particular sea breeze phenomenon.

zone between the cool moist sea air and the dry air inland was very narrow. In fact this transition zone was frontal in that it comprised a horizontal temperature gradient which, after an initially gradual tightening, had triggered off a self-accelerating process which tightened the temperature gradient even more and persisted for a while—even after the original cause (in this case differential heating) had virtually disappeared. Thus the *sea breeze front* can be considered as a shallow ephemeral species of cold front. Warm inland air rises ahead of the wedgelike advance of cool air from the sea and, if the inland air is not too dry, the ascending air is marked by a line of cloud, usually cumiliform. (More will be said about the rôle of sea breezes in convection in Chapter 14.) Evidently some ascent also takes place close to the front in the cool moist sea air for, on occasions, this ascent of air is marked by cloud with a peculiar, vertically striated form resembling a tattered translucent curtain.

Another form of sea breeze frontal cloud is shown in Figure 11.3, which illustrates how the ascent of air sandwiched between sea breezes flowing inland from opposite coasts of the Cape Cod

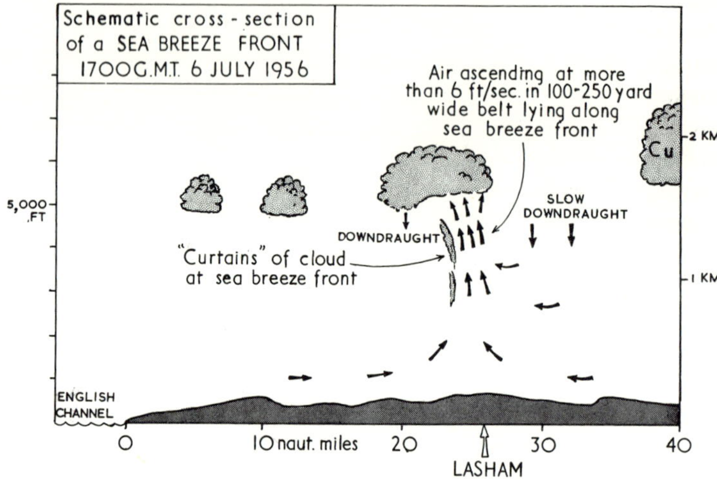

Fig. 11.4. In this cross-section of a sea breeze front the vertical motion and cloud structure are illustrated schematically and not to the horizontal scale indicated. The structure, which was first sketched by J. K. Mackenzie, is almost identical with that noted by E. A. Moore on 21 May 1958. On this latter occasion, however, sections of the front were marked by a visibility contrast rather than a distinctive cloud pattern.

peninsula produced a line of almost stationary lenticular clouds. A little later in the development of the sea breezes the onset of convection was indicated by cumulus clouds sprouting from the lenticular bars.

Whether marked by cloud or not the upward motion at the sea breeze front is occasionally strong enough for soaring flight. On 6 July 1956 J. K. Mackenzie soared in sea breeze lift for most of a late afternoon 3-hour flight in the neighbourhood of Lasham. With the sea breeze front orientated ENE–WSW and moving inland from the south coast at about 5 knots, lift, mostly 300–500 ft./min. but occasionally as strong as 1,500 ft./min., was located in a belt just north of the advancing air from the sea. The belt was a narrow one, only 100–250 yds. wide, but it was possible to climb to about 4,000 ft. provided the glider was flown straight along the landward side of the sea breeze front. Circling flight was tactically useless for soaring since downdraught existed immediately to the north (as sketched in Figure 11.4) and all but a thin slice of the cool sea air was void of lift. The thin, steeply inclined wafer of sea air which did rise was significant not for its weak lift but for its wisps of cloud which, having formed in the cool, moist, rising sea air, clearly marked the sea breeze frontal zone. With such a visible guide as this, soaring close to a sea breeze front resembles anabatic soaring, the wispy curtain of cloud taking the place of the mountain slope. Unlike the mountainside, of course, the cloud is liable to move and may disappear.

Between 6 p.m. and 8 p.m. on 21 May 1958 Aylett Moore was able to maintain height at about 3,300 ft. during a sea breeze soaring flight over the route Lasham–Winchester–Woking–Wisley. On several sections of the front he found a cloud and wind structure very similar to that reported by Mackenzie, but between these sections the sea breeze front was cloudless. Fortunately the pronounced haziness of the moist sea air (which probably included abundant smoke from Southampton and other large urban districts on the south coast) contrasted strongly with the cleaner air inland, and the sea breeze wall of haze could be followed even to the extent of discerning some indentations of about half a mile or so in the otherwise smooth north-north-west face of the front. During most of this flight lift was weak, only about 200 ft./min., and confined to within a belt not more than 150 yds. wide, but some pointers to the position of this narrow belt were provided not only by the haze and the wisps of cloud (about 200 yds. south of the best lift) but also by isolated smoke plumes which converged from the west-north-west in the land air and from the west-south-west in the sea air towards the sea breeze front.

Unfortunately for glider pilots, a sea breeze front is not always bordered with a curtain of cloud or a change in visibility, and it is likely that many an opportunity for sea breeze soaring goes unnoticed. As yet little experience has been accrued in locating a belt of sea breeze lift without visual aids in the form of cloud, haze or converging smoke plumes. Whether it is feasible to use the temperature, humidity and wind changes across a sea breeze front as signposts to the belt of lift is a matter for further exploration, offering ample scope for ingenuity in instrument design and flight technique. But we can at least be prepared for sea breeze soaring by remembering the salient features of the flight observations just described, by discerning the general weather conditions favourable for sea breezes, and by learning to detect the passage of a sea breeze front at the ground.

To glimpse both the force and fickleness of the sea breeze phenomenon let us look at the autographic wind, temperature and

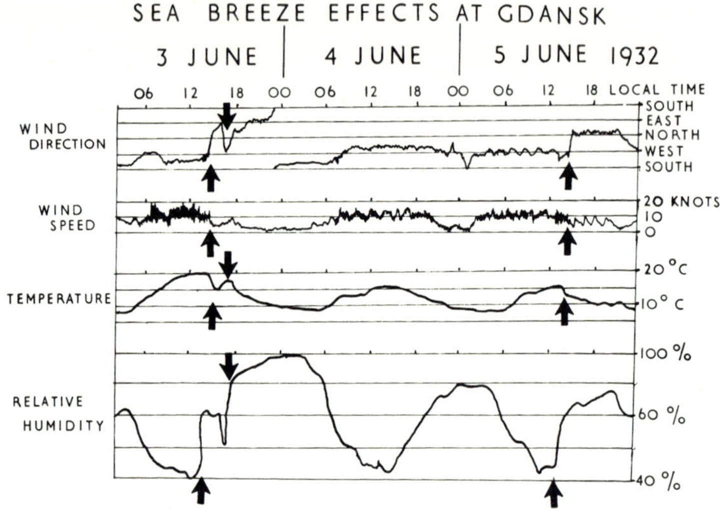

Fig. 11.5. Arrows indicate sea breeze effects on the autographic records.

humidity records for three days in June at Gdansk, on the coast of Poland. They are reproduced in Figure 11.5. During the mid-morning and early afternoon of the first day, 3 June, a gusty 12-knot west-south-westerly wind was maintained by the prevailing pressure gradient while bright sunshine produced an appreciable rise in temperature. This rise continued until, quite suddenly, at 1420 hrs. (local time), the sea breeze arrived from a north-easterly direction bringing with it cool and moist air from the Baltic. The recorded rise in humidity is even more abrupt than the temperature fall. A sea breeze is not necessarily stronger or more gusty than the winds inland and perhaps the light wind speed, of only 5 knots, in this sea air at Gdansk on 3 June was an indication that the sea breeze was not as firmly established as the autographic records suggested, for at 1620 hrs. wind, temperature and humidity changes marked the return of the inland air which persisted for an hour before the sea breeze set in once again with a repetition of its earlier effects.

During the night of 3–4 June the wind became practically calm and, of course, the indicated wind direction in such conditions is of little or no significance. A slight change of the general pressure pattern occurred during the night and when the wind speed did increase after dawn on 4 June it brought from a north-westerly direction air cool enough to reduce the rise in temperature which the

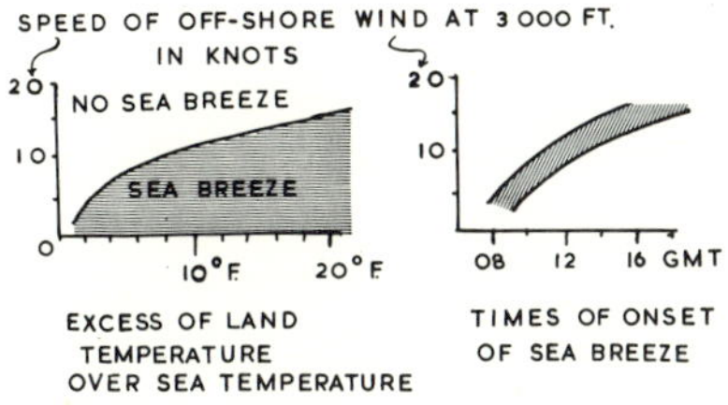

Fig. 11.6. When wind and temperature conditions are represented by points in the shaded section of the diagram on the left then a sea breeze is likely to reach Thorney Island some time in the interval indicated by the shaded band on the right.

day's sunshine would otherwise have produced. So on this second of the three days there was not enough inland heating to bring sea breeze to Gdansk.

After another night of light winds the morning and early afternoon of 5 June was characterised by 10-knot westerly winds, convection cloud and a temperature rise to 60° F. This early afternoon temperature was no higher than that attained on the previous day, yet at 1430 hrs. on 5 June the sea breeze from the north-north-east set in with very sharp changes in wind, temperature and humidity. Notice that during the sea breeze period, between 1430 hrs. and 2100 hrs., the wind speed showed four more or less regularly spaced oscillations between about 4 and 9 knots. Mathematical analysis has shown that wind speed pulsations such as these are not inconsistent with other more distinctive features of sea breeze phenomena, but it is practically impossible to predict just whether or not these pulsations will be significant or even discernible in any particular sea breeze. It is, in fact, often difficult in many temperate latitude countries to predict whether or not a sea breeze will occur at all on any particular day; who would have predicted with confidence the absence or advent of the sea breeze on the synoptically similar days, 4 June and 5 June at Gdansk?

In an attempt to devise simple rules for forecasting sea breeze phenomena a study was made at Thorney Island (whose position is effectively just inland from the south coast of England) of the

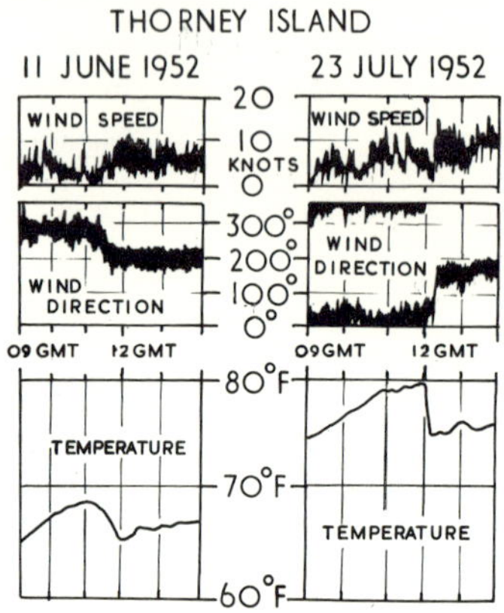

Fig. 11.7. Autographic records showing sea breeze effects on a day of shallow convection (11 June 1952) and deep convection (23 July 1952).

relationship between the temperature difference between land and sea and the local wind at 3,000 ft. with the sea breeze from the south coast. The results for off-shore 3,000 ft. wind directions are illustrated graphically in Figure 11.6, but these results should be interpreted with caution; they have been deduced only for Thorney Island and for the wind directions stated. Nevertheless, such a study as this does illustrate the relative power of horizontal temperature gradients and off-shore wind speeds in controlling sea breeze effects, and the same or a similar technique of investigation may well be applied to other stations in the course of acquiring more experience and understanding of sea breeze phenomena.

The Thorney Island study also suggested that the depth of inland convection is related to the abruptness with which the sea breeze sets in. Figure 11.7 shows a sudden change in wind direction and an abrupt fall in temperature as the sea breeze of 23 July 1952 replaced the inland air in which convection had distributed the sun's ground level heating up to 8,000 ft. This figure also shows the more gradual sea breeze changes associated with inland convection to only 4,000 ft. on 11 June 1952. These two examples accord with other observations that the arrival of a sea breeze is likely to be established suddenly (in about 10 minutes) on days of deep convection but gradually, with perhaps fluctuations over a period of 1 to 2 hours, when convection from the ground is limited (say, by anticyclonic subsidence) to a relatively shallow layer of the atmosphere.

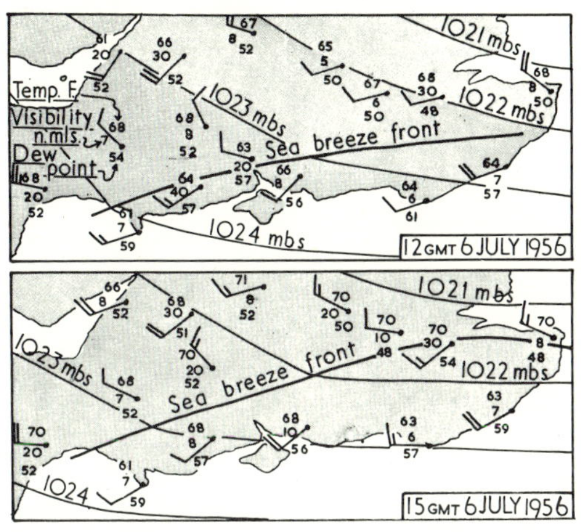

Fig. 11.8. Two of the hourly charts on 6 July 1956. Note that the visibilities are plotted in nautical miles. Each full feather of the wind arrows represents 10 knots.

The sea breeze soaring flights by Mackenzie and Aylett Moore were both made in airstreams favourable for convection from ground level up to between 7,000 and 10,000 ft. and it is instructive to examine in detail the weather records relevant to these flights.

On 6 July 1956 surface temperatures inland in southern England rose to about 69° F. (12° F. higher than the average July sea temperature in the middle of the English Channel) and cumulus at about 4,500 ft. with tops to 8,000 ft. formed in the westerly airstream which covered most of the British Isles. In Figure 11.8 the synoptic charts show wind and dew point differences between the inland and the sea breeze air but neither the sharpness nor the precise positions of the front can be deduced from these charts alone. A clearer indication of the sea breeze frontal progress can be gleaned from the autographic records copied in Figure 11.9 and the isochrones

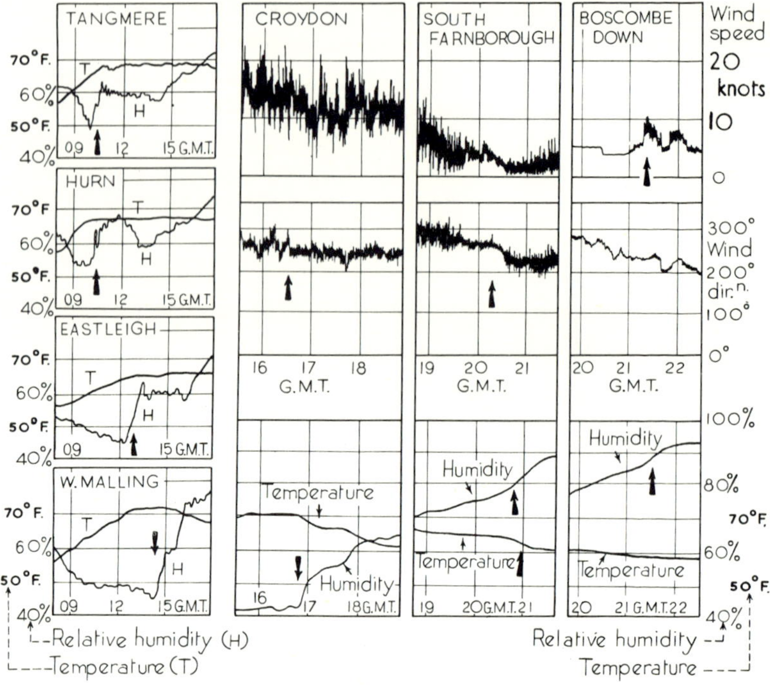

Fig. 11.9. Large arrows indicate sea breeze effects on the autographic records. The positions of the recording stations are marked on Fig. 11.10.

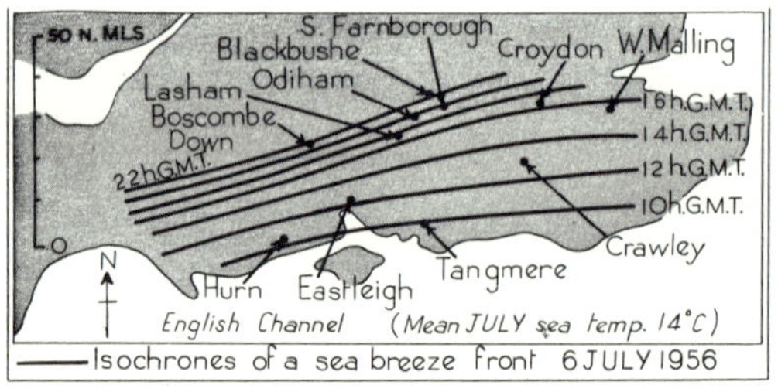

Fig. 11.10. Isochrones of the sea breeze front of 6 July 1956.

(Figure 11.10) of the sea breeze front have been determined from these records and other routine observations. Towards the limit of its penetration inland the front slowed down to a mere 1–2 knots but its movement and existence up to 2200 GMT was still consistent with recorded changes in wind direction and relative humidity at South Farnborough, the sudden increase in wind speed and rise in humidity at Boscombe Down and with the change in wind direction at Blackbushe. However, during the early evening the line of small cumulus associated with the sea breeze front appeared (at Lasham) to have its progress not only retarded but reversed and by 2030 GMT this cloud could be seen about 4 miles south of Lasham. Thus the front appeared to be in two places at once and the explanation of this double existence may well be linked to the observed tendency for some sea breeze fronts to progress inland in a series of pulsations rather than with a steady movement; on occasions the sea breeze frontal effects appear to decline in one belt while intensifying in another belt about half a mile or so farther inland.

Sometimes a sea breeze front in a general westerly or west-northwesterly airstream penetrates so far inland in the east of the country that it moves into the Thames estuary as a paradoxical sea breeze from the land. The sea breeze fronts are also likely to extend farther south-westwards than marked in Figure 11.10. A narrow belt of sea breeze lift may well have developed south of the coast before moving slowly north. It is very likely that some soaring flights over the sea have been sustained by off-shore sections of a sea breeze front, but when exploring such soaring conditions it is wise to remember that the lift in a well marked sea breeze front has often been observed to occur in a narrow belt sandwiched between broader zones of downdraught.

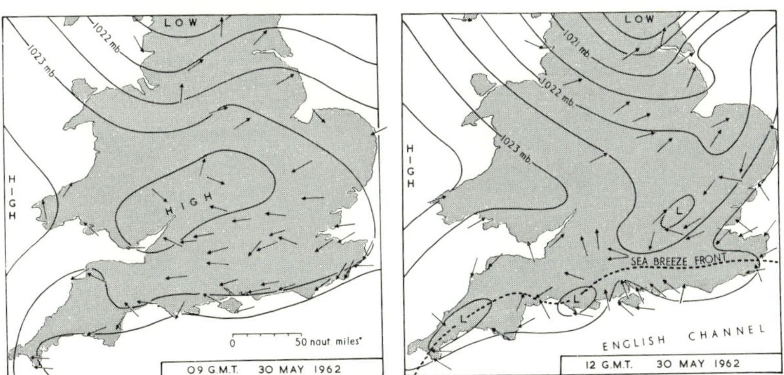

Fig. 11.11. M.s.l. pressure patterns and surface winds at 09 and 12 GMT on the day of the sea-breeze flight. Surface winds indicated by the arrows were mostly about five knots. Temperatures inland rose from about 9° C. to 15° C. during the morning.

Sea breeze in an easterly

On 30 May 1962 a long sea breeze front formed in a light easterly airstream over southern England.

Figure 11.11 shows the change of pressure pattern over England —from an anticyclone in the morning to a thermal low pressure system as temperatures inland rose to about 15° C. Surface winds, dew-points and observations from several glider pilots revealed the existence of the sea breeze front from about 10.30 GMT onwards. Figure 11.12 shows the extent of inland penetration by 21.00 GMT and Figure 11.13 illustrates the sharp rise in humidity, the wind changes and slight fall in temperature that marked the passage of the front.

I was fortunate enough to be at Lasham as the front approached. At 17.00 GMT thermal soaring conditions appeared to be on the wane, but to the south tattered wisps of cloud indicated the front.

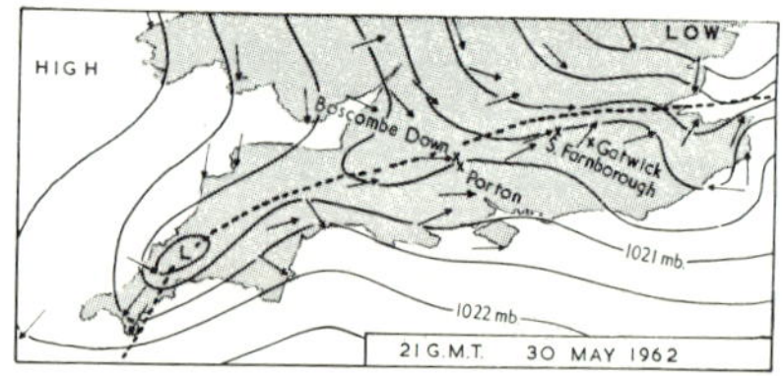

Fig. 11.12. The dotted line marks the sea-breeze front at 21 GMT.

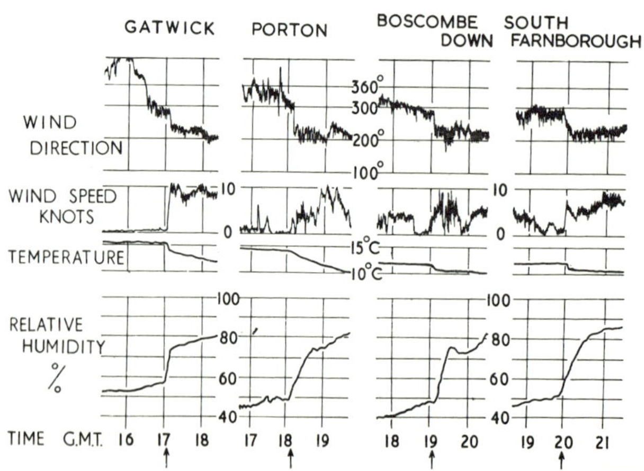

Fig. 11.13. Autographic records for stations whose locations are marked in Figure 11.12. Times of passage of the sea-breeze front are indicated by the arrows.

After being aerotowed to 2,000 ft. I headed south and soon located rising air. Two other gliders joined me and it soon became apparent that the air was rising smoothly up some sort of sloping surface, as depicted in the right-hand half of Figure 11.14.

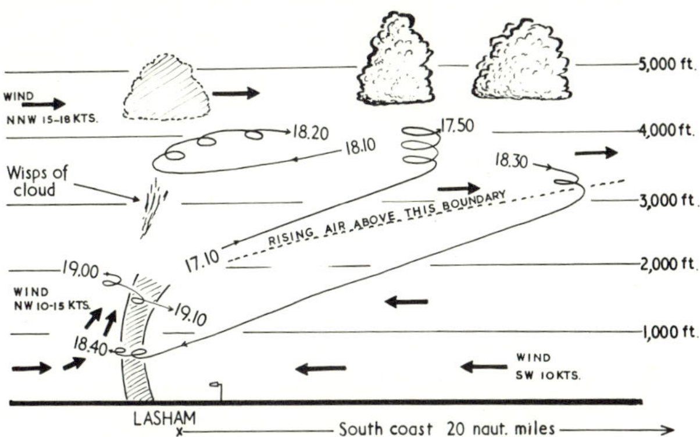

Fig. 11.14. A schematic cross-section of the sea-breeze wind and cloud structure on 30 May 1962 as revealed by gliding. The horizontal extent of the structure illustrated was about five miles, but the clouds and width of the shaded turbulent zone are not drawn to scale. Sections of the main features of the glider flight path are shown by the thin lines with times in GMT at intervals.

The timetable was:

GMT	
1710–1750	Initial climb
1750–1810	Exploring the extent of rising air
1810–1830	Flying north to the bar of cloud (shaded with dotted outline) and circling under this cloud as it drifted north
1830	Set course back to airfield
1840–1900	Climb during straight flight on east to west course.

The wisps of cloud appeared and disappeared just before the development of the bar of cloud above. The left-hand half of the picture was not apparent until the flight path had entered the narrow (100-metre wide) turbulent mixing zone between the land and sea air. The position of Lasham is marked in Figure 11.10.

The three of us flying above 2,500 ft. had no difficulty in remaining airborne in the NNW wind of 15–18 knots at our flying levels, but to the south of the airfield other pilots found no lift in the SW wind below.

The wisps of sea-breeze frontal cloud to the south had disappeared and isolated wisps had formed just north of the airfield. But these wisps soon disappeared and an east–west bar of cloud began to form at a slightly higher level. The lift under this freshly formed bar was strong but soon weakened as the cloud drifted towards the south and began to dissipate. On the descent back to Lasham there was no lift until the glider entered what was apparently a transition zone between the moist sea air and the flow from inland. This zone was very narrow—only about 100 metres wide—and noticeably turbulent. One half of a circle on the edge of the zone would be in smooth air, and on the other half the aircraft would be buffeted by the small scale turbulence. Immediately inland of this frontal zone there was a narrow band of lift. Figure 11.14 illustrates the main features of the sea breeze frontal structure on this occasion.

Secondary sea breeze fronts

Occasionally a day's autographic records or observations indicate the passage of two sea breeze fronts, a primary front in the late morning followed by a secondary sea breeze front during the afternoon, and the explanation of this double effect appears to be that, after veering at the passage of the primary front, winds near the coast gradually reverted to the earlier general direction, thereby restoring conditions suitable for sufficient differential heating across the coastline to create a second sea breeze front.

Pseudo sea breeze fronts

Viewed from above, an extensive layer of low stratus can aptly be described as a sea of cloud and if this "sea" happens to have a clear cut edge over a land mass it may even promote the development of a pseudo sea breeze front. On 29 April 1958 in the situation shown in Figure 11.15 a westerly airstream across England was moist enough to bring low stratus from over the Irish Sea into the Cheshire Plain and, with the Welsh mountains blocking the advance of the low cloud immediately to the south, the low cloud over the north-west Midlands was bounded by a fairly sharp edge south of which bright sunshine was able to warm the air at low levels sufficiently to produce small cumulus clouds. The low stratus was thick enough to prevent a rise in temperature in the area it covered and so conditions were ripe for a pseudo sea breeze front to develop and move southwards. In fact there appeared to be a double frontal effect which produced weather changes like those mentioned above, and it is quite feasible that the soaring conditions were somewhat similar to those found at genuine sea breeze fronts.

After crossing Ternhill between 1000 GMT and 1035 GMT the first pseudo sea breeze front seemed to weaken to the extent of becoming only just detectable as a slight temperature drop and deterioration in visibility at Shawbury just before 1100 GMT. The passage of the second pseudo front, however, was well marked by changes in wind direction, visibility and temperature at Ternhill between 1400 GMT and 1500 GMT and at Shawbury about an hour later.

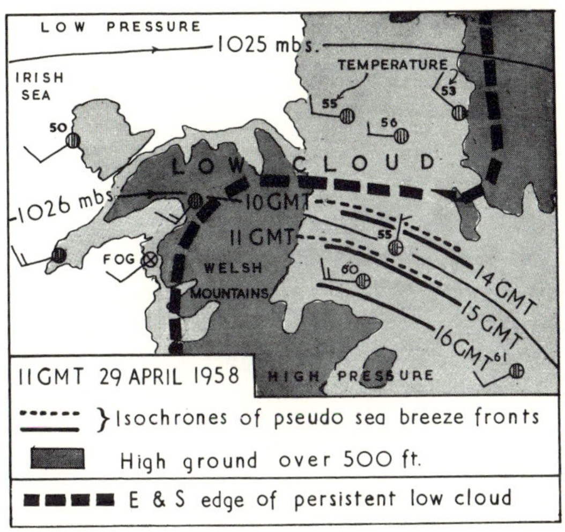

Fig. 11.15. Pseudo sea breeze fronts appeared to move southwards from the southern edge of a persistent low cloud cover. The two stations in the path of the pseudo sea breeze fronts are Ternhill and Shawbury.

Convection behind the sea breeze front

After the passage of a sea breeze front convection is liable to suffer at least a hiatus as the cool air arrives at low levels. However, if this damp sea breeze air is heated sufficiently for convection to be resumed the cumulus cloud base will be lower than that in the drier inland air.

Although large cumulus or even cumulonimbus clouds do occasionally form in the sea breeze air, it is more common to find poor thermal soaring conditions on the seaward side of a sea breeze front, especially when convergence at or just inland of the sea breeze front is sufficient to trigger off the formation of a band of cumulonimbus clouds.

CHAPTER 12

The Tephigram

For the pilot planning a cross-country flight a verbal description of the countryside and landmarks around him are inadequate; he needs a map on which can be measured distances and angles according to the rules of navigation. The meteorologist, also finding mere words inadequate, uses a sort of map on which to plan his concepts of certain atmospheric processes, but his map is called a tephigram and the lines on it are drawn in accordance with the rules of thermodynamics.

Without being absolutely essential, a familiarity with the tephigram is such a useful aid in tracing and understanding convection phenomena that it is worth spending a little time getting to know this particular thermodynamic diagram.

In meteorological literature the letter T is often used to denote air temperature while the Greek symbol Φ (phi) frequently stands for entropy—which can conveniently, though not with strict accuracy, be thought of as the potential heat energy of the air. Thus the T–Φ gram, usually written as tephigram, is a piece of graph paper having the two quantities temperature and entropy as axes. Hence the basic lines of a tephigram include vertical temperature lines (isotherms) marked in degrees centigrade and horizontal entropy lines—as illustrated in Figure 12.1.

For every pair of values of its temperature and entropy air has a particular pressure which can be calculated once and for all, so that it is possible to construct on the diagram lines of equal pressure. Because pressure is closely associated with altitude, these slightly curved isobars stretching from the top right to the bottom left of the tephigram give a rough indication of height above M.S.L. We may recall that pressure at M.S.L. is often about 1000 mbs.; the 10,000 ft.

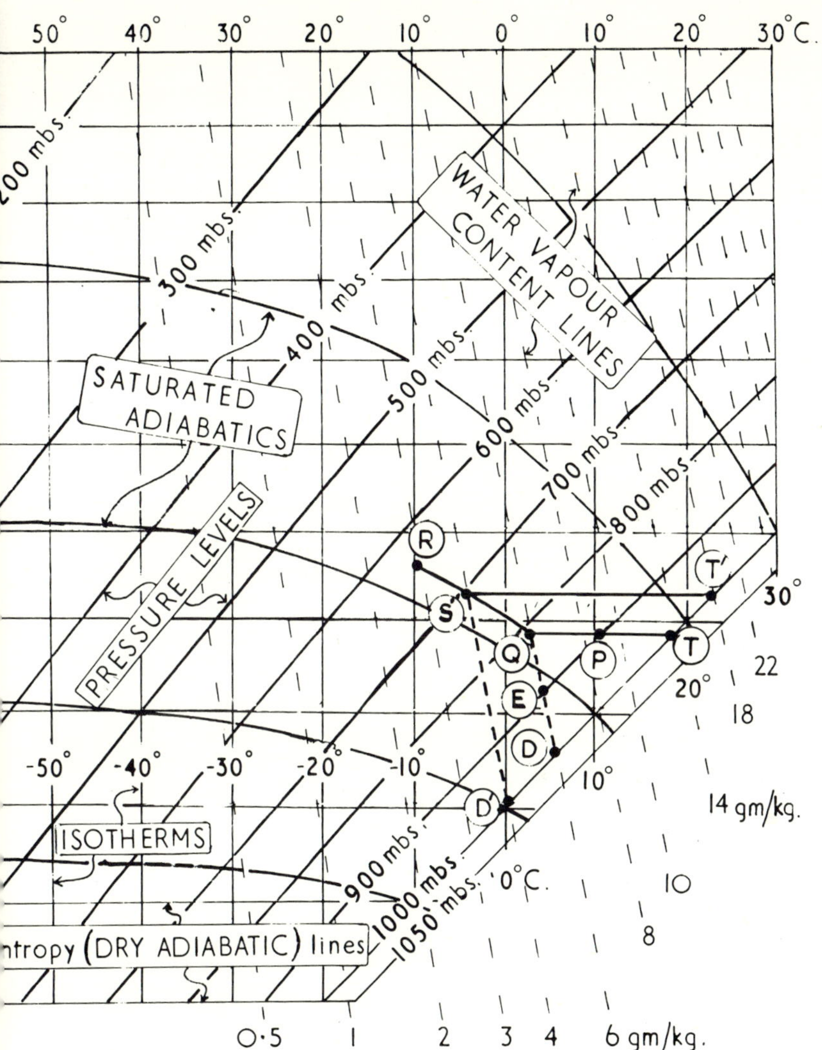

Fig. 12.1. The principal lines of a section of the tephigram are labelled, while the points *T*, *P*, *Q* . . . etc., in this diagram refer to examples of the use of the tephigram elaborated in the text.

(approx. 3,000 m.) pressure is roughly 700 mbs. and the 20,000 ft. (approx. 6,000 m.) pressure is about 500 mbs.

The pressure and temperature of a parcel of air can be represented by a dot marked on the tephigram; for a pressure of 1,000 mbs. and temperature of 19° C., for example, the point *T* in Figure 12.1 is the representative dot. Suppose this parcel of air rises to the 900 mb. pressure level without gaining or losing any of its heat either by radiation or by mixing with its surroundings. It will expand and cool adiabatically as the pressure decreases and the representative dot will trace out a line on the tephigram. It is one of the fundamental laws of thermodynamics that, for unsaturated air, this line will be parallel to the entropy lines; in other words it will be the straight horizontal line *TP* in Figure 12.1.

So far only unsaturated air has been considered, but it is possible for our parcel of air to contain invisible water vapour up to a certain limit which depends primarily on its temperature. The limit in this example is indicated by the value of the almost vertical pecked line running through the point *T*, the label 14 gm./kg. meaning that if the parcel contains 1 kg. of dry air then 14 gms. of water vapour would be required to saturate it. Saturation water vapour content lines for other pressures and temperatures are usually printed as pecked lines such as those shown in Figure 12.1 and their pattern underlines the statement made in Chapter 2 that the cooler the air the lower is its capacity to absorb water vapour.

If the parcel of air whose temperature is represented by point *T* contains, say, only 6 gms. of water vapour per kilogram of dry air then the point *D* at the same pressure level and on the 6 gm./kg. water vapour content line can be taken to represent the moisture content of the air. The temperature at *D*, 6° C., is then the dew point of the air and the relative humidity of the parcel is:

$$\frac{\text{actual water vapour content}}{\text{saturation water vapour content}} \times 100 = \frac{6}{14} \times 100 = 43\%$$

If this air, together with its 6 gms. of water vapour, rises again to the 900 mb. level the dot representing the dew point will move from *D* along the pecked line to *E* (no water vapour being added to or extracted from the parcel of air in the process) and, since the air remains unsaturated, its temperature will again fall to that denoted by point *P*.

Now let us see what happens if the parcel of moist air rises higher still. Its temperature dot will still follow a horizontal line but only as far as the point *Q* on the 6 gm./kg. water vapour content line. At this level (815 mbs. or about 5,800 ft.) saturation is attained and any subsequent fall of temperature during continued ascent will be at the saturated adiabatic lapse rate which is represented by the curved lines stretching from bottom right to top left in Figure 12.1. Thus from *Q* upwards the condensed excess moisture will be visible in the form of cloud and when the parcel of saturated air reaches the 640 mb. level its temperature will be represented by the point *R*. The tephigram shows that, at this stage, the parcel can contain only 3 gms. of water vapour per kilogram of dry air; the remaining 3 gm./kg. will be in some form of liquid or frozen water.

We are now in a position to relate these basic manœuvres on the

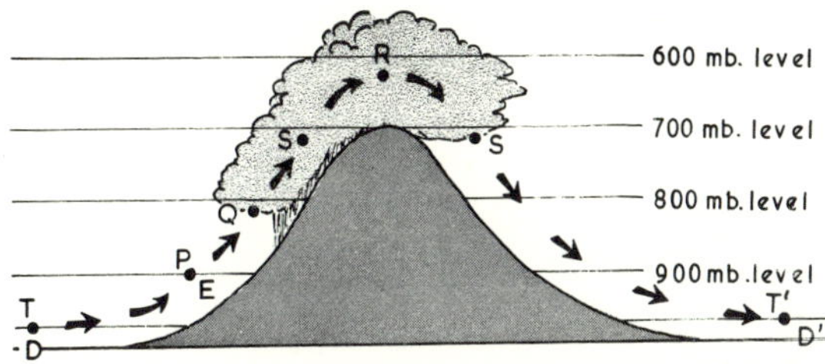

Fig. 12.2. In this illustration of the foehn effect the temperatures at points *T*, *P*, *Q* . . . etc. are represented by corresponding points marked on the tephigram in Figure 12.1, and the whole process is described in the text.

tephigram to actual weather phenomena and it is an instructive exercise to use the tephigram to study the foehn effect, wherein air flowing across a mountain range is forced to rise and form cloud which precipitates rain or snow on the mountain before the air descends into the leeward lowland as a comparatively warm dry wind. The history of the parcel of moist air already described with the aid of Figure 12.1 is typical of the first stage of the foehn effect illustrated by the streamline *TPQR* in Figure 12.2. During its ascent to about 12,000 ft. (the 640 mb. level) cloud is formed at about 5,800 ft. and the temperature at the top is indicated by the point *R* on the tephigram. Now suppose that 2 gms. of the water content per kilogram of dry air falls out in the form of snow (the temperature being below 0° C.). Only 4 gm./kg. of the water content will be left, so that, during its descent, the parcel becomes unsaturated on passing point *S*, on the 4 gm./kg. water vapour content line. Therefore, the subsequent descent will be along the dry adiabatic to the point *T′*. Meanwhile the dew point will move along the 4 gm./kg. pecked line to *D′*. Thus the air will be warmer and drier than it was on the windward side of the range.

Stability on the tephigram

Suppose the temperature up through a layer of unsaturated air is represented by the line *ABCD* in Figure 12.3*a* and that some agency moved a parcel of this air adiabatically upwards from say the level at *B* to that at *C*. Dry adiabatic cooling would reduce the temperature of the parcel to that represented by point *X*, so that, at its new level,

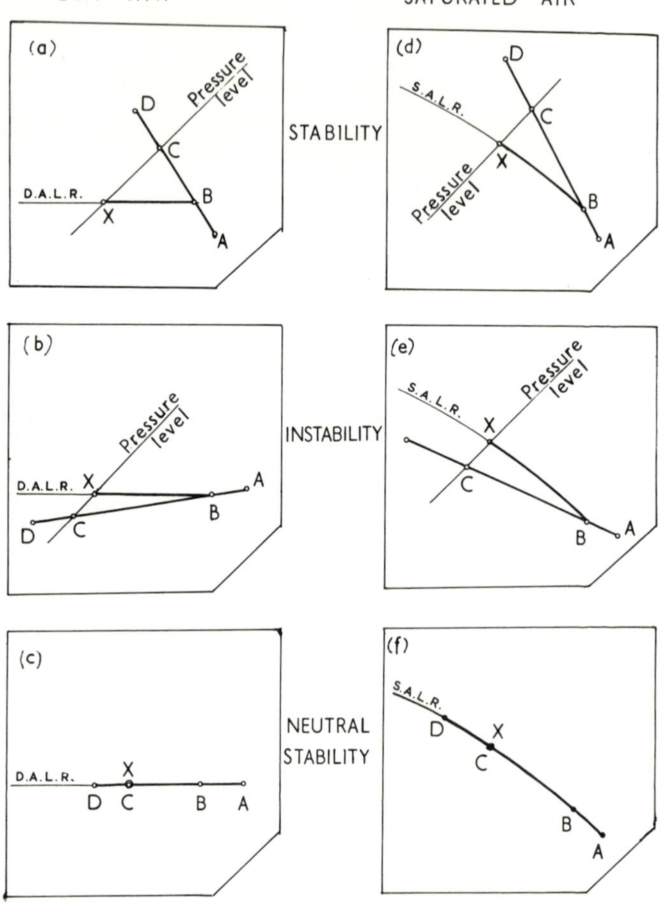

Fig. 12.3. For many practical purposes a schematic representation of the shape of the tephigram is sufficient to map the theoretical reasoning behind various thermodynamic processes. Here, with environment temperatures represented by curves *ABCD* and displacements of air by *BX*, the tephigram is used to illustrate the concept of stability elaborated in the text.

the parcel would be cooler and denser than its surroundings. It would, therefore, tend to sink back to its original level. Similarly the buoyancy forces would tend to resist an adiabatic downward displacement of the parcel of air to levels below *B*, and because of its tendency to inhibit internal vertical motion the layer *ABCD* would be called a convectively *stable* layer.

The line *ABCD* in Figure 12.3*b*, however, represents a layer in which an upward movement of a parcel from, say, *B* to *X* would be accelerated as a result of the buoyancy of the displaced parcel with respect to its cooler surroundings. Similarly, a downward displacement, once started, would tend to increase as the descending parcel became progressively colder than its environment. In this case the layer with the vertical temperature distribution *ABCD* is known as a convectively *unstable* layer; it tends to amplify whatever internal vertical displacements occur. The lapse rate represented by *ABCD* is also referred to as being *superadiabatic*.

If the temperature lapse rate through a layer of unsaturated air actually is the D.A.L.R.—as represented by *ABCD* in Figure 12.3*c*, then internal vertical motion will be neither amplified nor damped by buoyancy forces and the stability of the layer would be neutral. Sometimes such a layer is called an adiabatic layer.

The stability of layers of saturated air can be considered in a similar way, and Figures 12.3*d*, *e* and *f* illustrate stability, instability and neutral stability in saturated layers. The principal problem of atmospheric convection is threefold; how do layers of the atmosphere get into unstable states, what triggers off the vertical motion of parcels of air within an unstable layer, and what forms do the convection currents take?

Convection in shallow layers

First a brief note on convection in shallow layers of air at levels too high to be seriously influenced by very small features of the countryside. Without elaborating unnecessarily on the precise mechanisms illustrated in Figure 12.4, it is easily conceivable that widespread ascent of air (like that associated with frontogenesis) can lead to the formation of instability in shallow layers of air. When these layers are too high to be seriously influenced by very small scale ground effects, it is natural that the convective motions should occur in more or less regular cellular patterns, and indeed such patterns are often discernible in those altocumulus cloud systems commonly known as "mackerel skies." The vertical currents in such convective systems are slow, and they are mentioned here not for their soaring potential, but as an aid to interpreting some of the cloud patterns frequently observed. The depth and horizontal extent of the convective cells depend primarily on the depth of the unstable layer

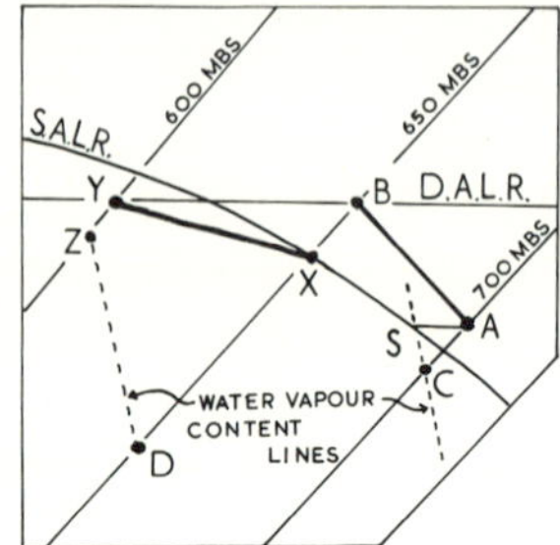

Fig. 12.4. Suppose the temperatures at the bottom and top of a layer of air are represented by *A* and *B* while *C* and *D* are the corresponding dew points. If the whole layer is lifted 50 mbs. then the temperature at the base will trace out the path *ASX* on the tephigram while the top will cool from *B* to *Y*. Thus the layer will become unstable as a result of the lifting.

and to a lesser extent on the wind distribution up through this layer. When a wind shear exists the cells may become aligned into billow-like rolls of cloud usually across the direction of the shear and the spacing between the axes of the rolls is about two and a half times the depth of the unstable layer.

Insolation on the tephigram

One of nature's methods of raising the temperature at the base of an airstream is by making the air flow over a progressively warmer land or sea surface (as described in Chapter 3), but a mechanism of much greater interest in gliding meteorology is insolation—heat from the sun. Passing through the troposphere almost without heating it, heat rays from the sun warm the ground which in turn warms the air close to it. If the air were quite still this process would soon lead to the development of a pronounced superadiabatic layer on the ground. But with such a layer being so unstable, any wind, however light, soon triggers off convection currents which carry some of the surface heat up into the atmosphere. Experience and a little reasoning show that, assuming this convective and turbulent stirring up of the air is an efficient method of distributing heat throughout the layer in which it acts, the temperature lapse rate of the layer will eventually become adiabatic. For example, an hour or two of the sun's heating may change the curve *TPQRS* (Figure 12.5) into curve T_1PQRS. After perhaps another hour the surface temperature, for this example, may be up to 10° C. and the curve would be transformed into *T′QRS*. If the ground level dew point of the air were represented by the point *D* then, at this stage, some of the parcels of air rising adiabatically from the ground to the level of *Q* would become saturated at the temperature *Q* at this level of 860 mbs. (about 4,500 ft.). Therefore, for any further ascent, no matter how small, the temperature of this parcel would fall at the saturated adiabatic lapse rate, depicted by *QXS*; the rising air would become warmer than its surroundings and would therefore be propelled farther upwards by its buoyancy. On passing the level *S* it would become colder than its environment and its ascent would

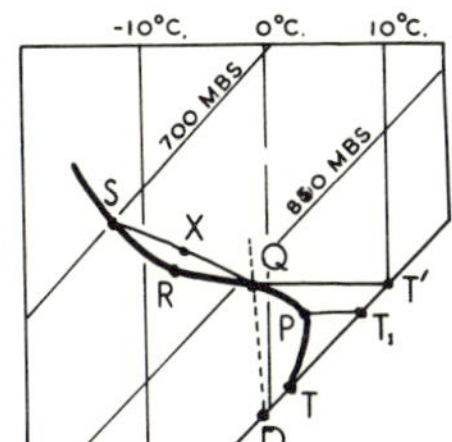

Fig. 12.5. Forecasting cumulus with the tephigram.

therefore be checked. Since this and other similarly rising parcels of air would be visible as cloud from the 860 mb. to about the 700 mb. level we could say that the *T–Φ* curve *T′QRS* and dew point *D* represent conditions favourable for the development of cumulus with a cloud base at 4,500 ft. and tops to about 10,000 ft., and although this inference assumes that the parcels of air ascend without mixing with their surroundings or without losing moisture by evaporation, this elementary reasoning forms an adequate basis for forecasting the approximate height of convection cloud over more or less flat countryside. Often the principal problem of predicting the likelihood of such convection cloud is to determine whether or not there will be enough effective insolation to transform the early morning *T–Φ* curve into one suitable for penetrative convection to occur; if *TPQRS* (Figure 12.5) represents the airstream temperatures at dawn, would the sun's heating during the day be sufficient to change the curve to *T′QRS*? This is a problem in which the use of the tephigram has a special advantage, for its design ensures that the heat received can be related directly to appropriate areas measured on the tephigram. Put into plain words, this means that the amount of heat needed to change the curve from *TPQRS* to T_1PQRS is proportional to the area TPT_1T; similarly area $T_1PQT'T_1$ is a measure of the heat required to effect the change from T_1PQRS to $T'QRS$. Meteorologists can estimate approximately how much of the sun's heat is likely to warm the surface air and many forecasters have insolation data for sunny days tabulated in units of areas on the tephigram. Some sample predictions illustrated in Figure 12.6 are

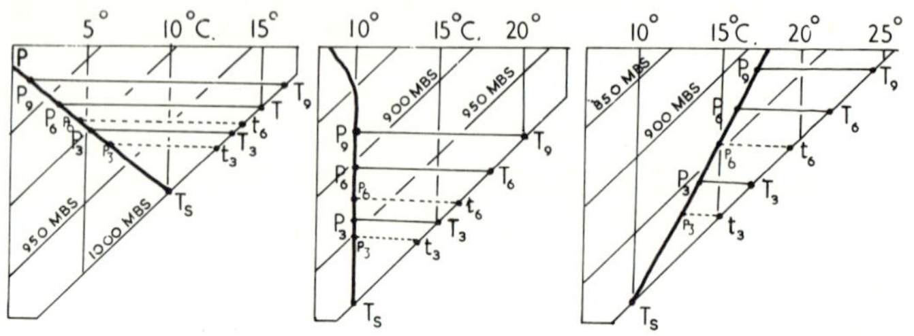

Fig. 12.6. Examples of the effect of insolation. If T_sP is the $T - \Phi$ curve at sunrise then insolation on a clear day will change the curve to

T_3P_3P	3 hours after sunrise	in mid-June
T_6P_6P	6 hours after sunrise	
T_9P_9P	9 hours after sunrise	
t_3p_3P	3 hours after sunrise	in mid-December
t_6p_6P	6 hours after sunrise	

for clear days in central England. Reductions in heating due to cloud cover are estimated by experience which suggests that thin layers of cloud, not more than 500 ft. thick, are likely to allow between 35% and 95% of the sun's heat to get through, while an extensive layer of cloud about 3,000 ft. thick may reduce the effective insolation to between 15% and 55% of the clear day quota.

To illustrate the value of predicting the approximate height to which convection currents will reach we can study the events of 2 August 1957 during the British National Gliding Championships at Lasham.

With the aid of a strut thermometer carried on a Tiger Moth to 5,000 ft. the temperature and cloud structure over Lasham at 0800 GMT on this August day were found to be that represented by the T–Φ curve and notes in Figure 12.7. Neither the haze layer, which was a by-product of earlier events, nor the low stratus, which formed as a result of nocturnal cooling, were dense enough to reduce the effective insolation by more than about 5% or 10% and the low cloud was soon dispersed by evaporation from the top and by convection currents from below—or, more colloquially, the stratus was soon "burnt off" by the sun. After the dispersal of this low cloud the air temperature at the Stevenson screen level rose rapidly, but with such a low level inversion as that represented on the tephigram the depth of convection was not appreciably increased. Even by 1200 GMT the upper limit was only 1,800 ft. above Lasham—as

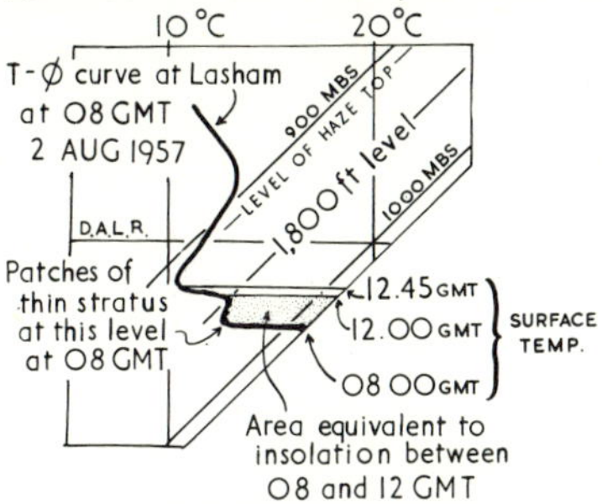

Fig. 12.7. The lower inversion was "broken down" soon after 12 GMT.

pilots who made brief local flights may well testify. Soon after this time, however, even a small rise in the surface temperature was sufficient to push the upper limit of convection appreciably higher—or, more colloquially again, the low level inversion was "broken down," and between 1245 and 1345 GMT competing pilots were able to set off on the day's task of racing to Nymphsfield.

One of the features to note in this example is that the breaking down of the inversion may have been detected at ground level by using a thermometer or thermograph to note the sudden decrease in the rate of rise of temperature. The deduction that convection currents would become deeper immediately after this change of rate would be based on the reasoning that the deeper the layer of air being effectively heated the slower would be the rise of temperature, and the use of or familiarity with the tephigram helps to keep such reasoning in accord with the thermodynamical rules of meteorology.

INSOLATION ON THE TEPHIGRAM

(The following notes and tables are included in this chapter for readers who wish to study more details of the method of forecasting the effect of insolation on the T–Φ curve. It is not essential, however, to study these details before passing on to the next chapter.)

The effective heat energy received from the sun during any interval of time in the morning and early afternoon can be directly related to the area on the tephigram between the T–Φ curves at the beginning and end of the interval. One method of applying this relationship to clear sky conditions over low level terrain in the British Isles is based on the "insolation" table below.

THICKNESS OF LAYER (IN MBS.) WHICH IS CHANGED FROM AN ISOTHERMAL TO AN ADIABATIC STATE BY INSOLATION

Hours from Sunrise	*1*	*2*	*3*	*4*	*5*	*6*	*7*	*8*	*9*	*M m*
Jan	16	29	41	50 (A)	58 (B)	—	—	—	—	6
Feb	18	33	46	57	65	73	—	—	—	8
Mar	20	37	52	63	73	82	90	—	—	9
Apr	22	40	56	69	80	89	98	106	—	11
May	23	42	59	72	83	93	102	110	118	12
June	(A) 23	42	60	73	84	94	103	112	119	13
July	23	42	59	73	84	94	103	111	118	12
Aug	22	41	57	70	81	91	99	108	115	11
Sept	21	38	54	66	76	85	93	100	—	10
Oct	(A) 19	35	49	60	69	77	85	—	—	8
Nov	17	31	43	53	61	—	—	—	—	6
Dec	15	28	40	49 (A)	— (B)	—	—	—	—	5

Notes

1 Over damp soils the energy corresponding to the values given is not available for heating the lowest layers of the atmosphere during the first few hours of sunshine. In such localities the values to the left of the lines marked (*A*) should be reduced by one-third and the values between the lines (*A*) and (*B*) should be reduced by one-fifth.

2 Modifications appropriate to mountainous districts or sea breeze effects must be judged according to the situation; for example temperature may rise relatively quickly on sun-facing slopes while in coastal districts on-shore winds may delay or check the rise of temperature just inland.

3 The effect of fog or a complete cover of cloud may be assessed using the following factors as a guide:

For thin cloud (about 500 ft. thick) use 60%–95% of the tabulated values

For thick cloud (3,000 ft. or more thick) use 40%–75% of the tabulated values

For shallow fog use 60%–70% of the tabulated values

For deep fog use 40%–60% of the tabulated values

Examples

While it must be realised that adequate routine information and some experience are required to make reliable predictions using the

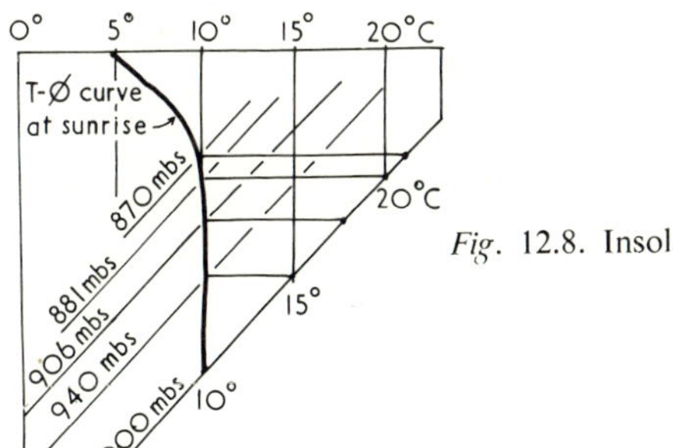

Fig. 12.8. Insolation example (i).

insolation table, familiarity with the method can be a valuable aid to assessing thermal soaring prospects even when detailed temperature observations are not available. The reader is recommended to work through the examples below and then to devise and solve some hypothetical problems as an exercise.

1 T–Φ curve at sunrise on a cloudless June day as shown in Figure 12.8.

Forecast of temperature at 3 hours after sunrise would be 15° C.
Forecast of temperature at 6 hours after sunrise would be $17\frac{1}{2}$° C.
Forecast of temperature at 9 hours after sunrise would be 20° C.

Forecast of maximum temperature (in early afternoon) would be $21\frac{1}{2}°$ C.

2 *T–Φ* curve at sunrise on a cloudless March day as shown in Figure 12.9.

To forecast the maximum temperature at screen level: Draw a line *MN* such that *N* is on the pressure level 97 mbs.

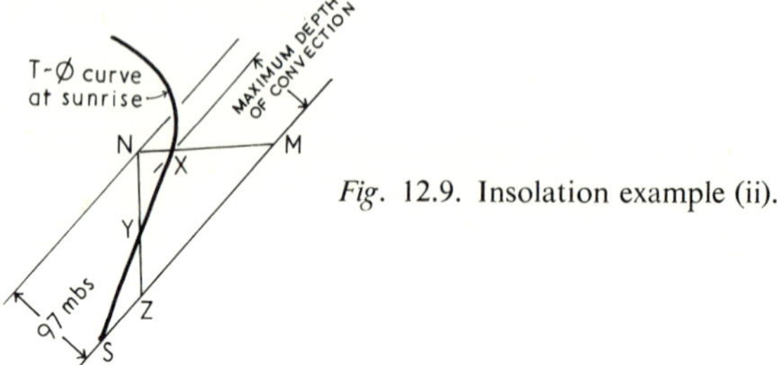

Fig. 12.9. Insolation example (ii).

(the tabulated March "maximum" value) less than that at the ground and area *NXY* equals area *SYZ*. This makes area *SXM* equal to *MNZ* which in turn is the area calculated to correspond to the effect of insolation between sunrise and the time of maximum temperature. Therefore *M* will denote the maximum temperature. Note also that, since *MX* denotes the maximum depth of convection, thermal soaring will not be possible above the level of *X*.

3 The temperature structure at 0845 GMT on a cloudless mid-August morning in central England is denoted by the *T–Φ* curve

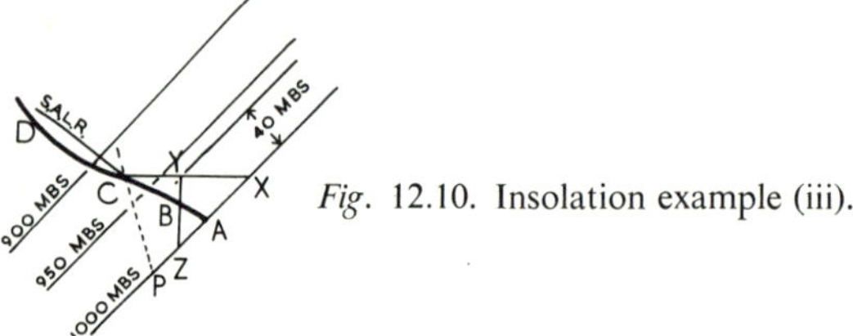

Fig. 12.10. Insolation example (iii).

ABCD shown in Figure 12.10 while the dew point at screen level is indicated by the point *P*. To predict the time at which cumulus will begin to form: Draw a dry adiabatic *CX* as shown in the figure, *X* being the air temperature required for thermals from ground level to rise to their condensation level at *C* and to

LOCAL MEAN TIMES OF SUNRISE AND SUNSET, AND SOLAR ALTITUDE AT MIDDAY AT LATITUDE 52° N. ON THE MIDDLE DAY OF EACH MONTH

	Jan	Feb	Mar	Apr	May	June	July	Aug	Sep	Oct	Nov	Dec
Sunrise	0802	0716	0615	0505	0407	0339	0357	0443	0533	0624	0720	0801
Sunset	1617	1713	1804	1856	1946	2021	2013	1925	1817	1708	1609	1549
Correction (minutes) per deg. of latitude	5·5	2·9	0·4	−2·3	−5·1	−7·4	−6·4	−3·6	−1·2	1·7	4·5	6·5
Solar altitude (degrees)	17	25	36	48	57	61	60	51	41	30	20	15

For each degree of latitude *north* of 52° N.

add / subtract } the correction to get the time of { sunrise / sunset

For each degree of latitude *south* of 52°N.

subtract / add } the correction to get the time of { sunrise / sunset

The solar altitude at midday in latitude L degrees may be obtained by adding the algebraic value of $52 - L$ to the figures given in the last row of the table.

continue rising in the form of cumulus cloud. Draw an isothermal *YZ* (as shown) such that area *CYB* equals area *ABZ*. Then area *XYZ* equals area *YXABC*—which represents the area corresponding to the heat energy required to change the T–Φ curve from *ABCD* to *XYCD*. Thus the heat energy required is equivalent to that which will change a 40 mb. thick layer (*YZ*) from an isothermal to an adiabatic state. Sunrise in mid-August in central England is about 0445 GMT, so by 0845 GMT on this cloudless morning the insolation already received would have been sufficient to change a 70 mb. thick layer from an isothermal to an adiabatic state.

Therefore (remembering that the heat energy is proportional to areas on the tephigram and not simply to the depths of the layers involved) we can calculate the total depth of equivalent isothermal layer to be transformed to an adiabatic state between sunrise and the time of formation of cumulus to be $\sqrt{(70^2 + 40^2)} = 80$ mbs. approximately. Reference to the insolation table shows that this change would be effected by about 5 hours after sunrise. Therefore, cumulus would be predicted to form just before 1000 GMT (1100 BST).

In practice such a prediction may be modified in the light of forecasting experience; it is not uncommon for small isolated cumulus clouds to be produced from particularly active thermal sources before the countryside is warm enough to generate widespread convection.

CHAPTER 13

Convection

It is as well to understand right now that this chapter will not be a simple guide to the sizes, shapes and locations of those upward convection currents we call *thermals*. Convection in the atmosphere can be considered in a general way as buoyant air rising through a relatively cold environment, but the thermals which constitute this convection are much less amenable to easy description.

However, we need not be too alarmed at the complexity of convection phenomena; simple, logical concepts of thermal structure are quite adequate for extensive thermal soaring and these ideas can be gradually elaborated in the light of accumulated experience. Many thermal soaring pundits do not supplement their flying skill and experience with more than elementary views on what thermals are and where to find them. Rather than confuse themselves with rigid or ultra-complicated ideas, these pilots are ready and quick to assess the characteristics of thermal conditions they actually encounter, and an understanding of the meteorology of convection can ensure that such assessment is realistic.

The problem of thermal structure

We are interested not only in the likelihood or the depth of convection at a particular time and place but also on the more detailed structure of the thermals themselves. Thermals in the atmosphere, however, are as varied as, say, trees throughout the world; no two are exactly alike and no particular specimen can be described as typical of all the others; we can talk of their observed characteristics and try to deduce the species likely to be found in various meteorological circumstances. An elementary, though inadequate, concept of a thermal is to regard it as a blob of buoyant air which breaks away from a particularly warm patch of ground and quickly organises itself into a more or less spherical bubble—in much the same manner as a drip of water falls from a wet ceiling. This concept could be augmented by visions of vertically elongated bubbles or "chimneys" of rising air, but, while containing germs of truth, none of these embellishments would make the concept fit the observed features of thermal soaring. Two significant features are:

1 the region of lift in a thermal appears to be between about 200 and 600 yds. at 1,000–2,000 ft. above ground level and wider at higher levels;
2 it is often possible to obtain lift for a number of minutes in what appears to be a single thermal.

To explain these two features it is now necessary to consider the effect of the mixing of thermal air with the environment and the motion of air within a thermal itself. When discussing these and other aspects of thermal structure it is expedient to consider the convective régime as a 3-layer sandwich, the uppermost layer containing the clouds, the bottom layer occupying the lowest 1,000 ft. (approximately) of the atmosphere, and the middle layer which we shall consider first.

"Isolated" thermals in the adiabatic layer

In convective conditions it is usual for the layer of air from about 1,000 ft. above ground level up to within a hundred feet or so of cloud base (or to the top of the convection, whichever is the lower) to have neutral stability, i.e. its lapse rate is the D.A.L.R. and we can refer to it as an adiabatic layer. It is this layer of the atmosphere that offers best opportunities for discerning the characteristics of thermals by soaring experience. Modern experience has underlined the importance of the motion of the air within the thermal itself and laboratory experiments initiated by Dr Scorer have provided a coherent picture of such motion.

Instead of experimenting with warm fluid rising from a heated surface, a "bubble" of relatively heavy liquid was released just below the upper surface of water in a glass tank. With a white precipitate making it visible, this heavy bubble was then filmed as it sank through the water. The conditions of each experiment were such that during its descent the heavy bubble exhibited the same type of motion as that of an isolated bubble of buoyant air ascending in an adiabatic layer of air with no wind shear.

Bubbles of various densities and sizes were released in the water and the feature common to them all was the vortex ring-like pattern of their motion. Assuming that atmospheric convection behaves in a similar fashion we can take the sketch in Figure 13.1 to represent the motion of an isolated thermal at between about 1,000 ft. above ground level and a hundred feet or so below cloud base. With its central core rising faster than its perimeter, the thermal is being turned inside out and, as the outside air becomes entrained in the circulatory motion, the thermal expands as it ascends. At some stage

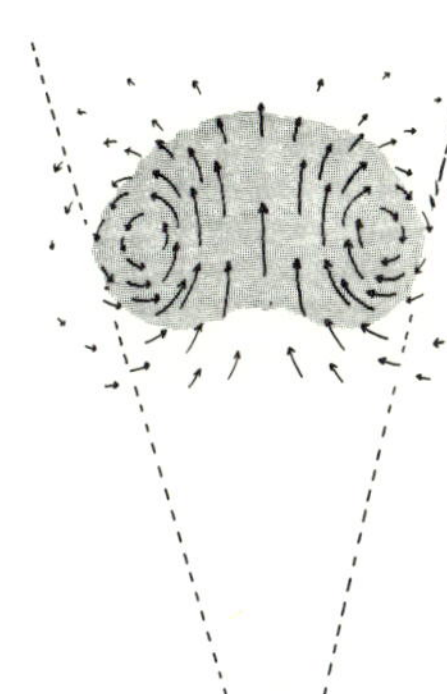

Fig. 13.1. The length of the arrows gives an indication of the speed of air motion in an "isolated" thermal.

it becomes so diluted that it is practically indistinguishable from its environment of non-buoyant air. The laboratory experiments suggest that, whatever their sizes and buoyancies, the motion of all isolated bubbles rising in the conditions already stated will be geometrically similar. As may be expected, the greater the initial buoyancy the greater the rate of ascent and the deeper will be the convective penetration before the thermal is eroded by entrainment, but the pattern of motion associated with a small isolated thermal is likely to be very similar to that exhibited by a large bubble.

The feature of particular relevance to thermal soaring is that the upward velocity of the air in the centre of the thermal is greater than the rate of ascent of the whole bubble. As long as this difference in velocity is greater than about 200 ft./min. a glider in the centre of a thermal will rise through the thermal itself; then, having climbed to somewhere in the top half of the thermal, the glider will rise at the same rate as that of the bubble as a whole until the thermal becomes too dilute and slow moving to sustain soaring flight.

Using the water tank experimental technique, Betsy Woodward has determined the patterns of vertical and horizontal speeds of the motion in and around an isolated thermal. Sketched in Figure 13.2, the vertical speed pattern shows the centre of such a thermal to be rising at more than twice the speed of the thermal as a whole. The effect of the horizontal outflow from the top half of the thermal and inflow towards the base is to reduce slightly the operationally effective

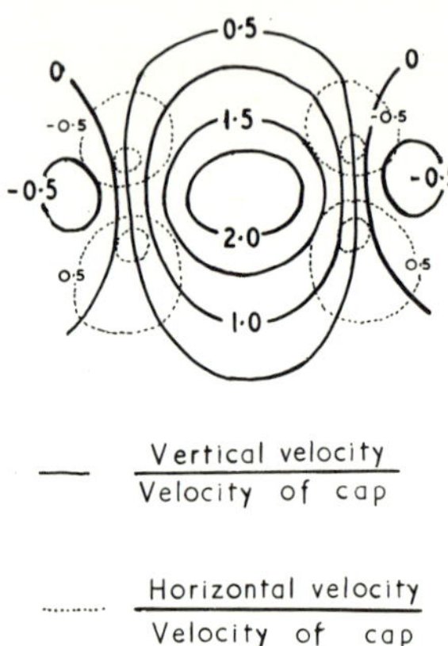

Fig. 13.2. Vertical and radial velocities in an "isolated" thermal in proportion to the upward velocity of the cap.

zone of lift in the upper half of the thermal and to allow slightly more efficient circling flight in the lower section.

Naturally thermals in the atmosphere are seldom isolated and are frequently distorted by wind shear but the concept of the expanding and diffusing vortex ring structure is a useful frame on which to form our ideas.

The superadiabatic layer

During the mornings and early afternoons of most warm and sunny days insolation supplies heat to the ground faster than it can be transported both upwards by turbulence and convection and downwards (but not very far down into the ground) by conduction. Thus the lowest hundred feet or so of the atmosphere becomes a superadiabatic layer whose temperature distribution may be represented by a T–Φ curve typified by the line *ABCDE* in Figure 13.3. The depth and degree of instability of this superadiabatic layer are determined mainly by the intensity of the sunshine, low level turbulence and the nature of the ground. Blazing sunshine with light winds over a desert can produce a superadiabatic layer several thousand feet in depth, but in temperate maritime climates superadiabatic layers are more likely to be several hundred feet deep on warm sunny days, and scarcely discernible if the sun's heating is either distributed upwards too readily by turbulence or used up in evaporating moisture from wet and soggy ground.

If a parcel of air (*X* in Figure 13.3) in a superadiabatic layer is displaced slightly upwards, either because it has become warmer than

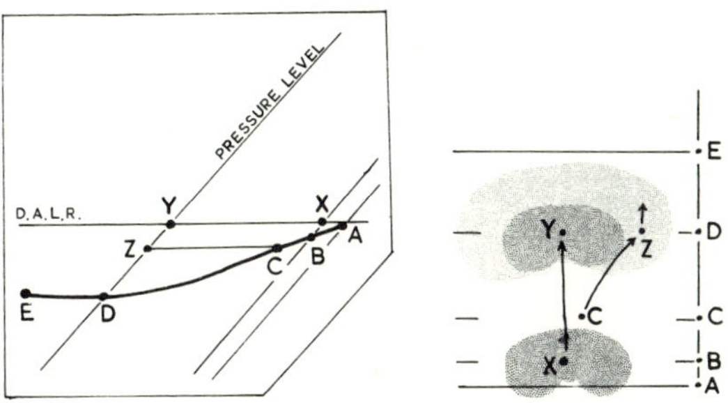

Fig. 13.3. Suppose a bubble of buoyant air rises in a superadiabatic layer from *X* to *Y* and displaces part of its environment from *C* to *Z* then the displaced air will acquire buoyancy and the incipient thermal will grow. Temperatures in and around the incipient thermal (shaded) in the sketch on the right are denoted schematically by corresponding letters in the tephigram on the left.

its immediate surroundings (*B*) or as a result of both buoyancy and turbulence, then its buoyancy in the unstable layer will urge it higher still. This incipient thermal mixes with the air into which it rises and also displaces the air (*C*) in its path slightly upwards. The entrained air and the air just above the thermal will also acquire buoyancy as a result of their upward displacement, so as the thermal ascends through the superadiabatic layer its total buoyancy and size increase rapidly; the volume of buoyant air at, say, 500 ft. above ground level is bigger and more buoyant than its embryo which may have been quite a small bubble at the start of its journey from ground level or thereabouts.

The superadiabatic layer is unstable for both upward and downward displacements of air, hence air which comes down to take the place of the ascending thermals also tends to accelerate during its progress. The nascent shape of these parcels of descending air is a matter for conjecture, but the important point is that, by entraining and displacing its immediate environment, a parcel of descending air can effectively increase in size and downward speed—rather like an upside down thermal.

The maximum strengths of both the thermals and the downdraughts depend mainly on the depth of the superadiabatic layer and its degree of instability. On many a convective day in the British Isles the superadiabatic layer is only just unstable and both thermals and downdraughts at very low levels are of only weak or moderate strength, but it can be taken as axiomatic that whenever superadiabatic layers produce strong thermals they are also liable to harbour disconcertingly strong downdraughts.

The interplay between ascending thermals and downdraughts (let us call them "negative" thermals) in the superadiabatic layer is usually such that neither species has the chance to reign supreme. A large proportion of both types lose their identities in the general convective confusion, but the thermals that do manage to preserve their identities to, say, half-way up through the superadiabatic layer have more than a fifty-fifty chance of developing into a mature thermal; the higher a thermal gets in the superadiabatic layer the bigger it becomes and the lesser are the chances of it being diluted and nullified by negative thermals. Thus the superadiabatic layer acts as a sort of filter from which relatively durable thermals emerge into the adiabatic layer above.

Thermal sources

One of the factors contributing to the characteristics of convection at low levels is the type and distribution of thermal sources. We can talk of *heated thermal sources* as those spots over which the air close to the ground tends to become warmer than that over the immediate surroundings. This excess warming of the air over a thermal source depends on the rate at which the temperature of the ground surface itself rises and on the length of time the air remains close to the surface before being carried away in the general wind flow. For a given intensity of sunshine the rate at which the ground surface temperature rises is controlled by several factors which include:

1 The angle of incidence of the sun's rays; the temperature of sun-facing slopes will rise faster than adjacent horizontal but otherwise similar surfaces, and indeed such slopes often are efficient sources of thermal activity.

2 The dampness of the ground; the wetter the surface the bigger will be the proportion of incoming radiation wasted in evaporating some of the moisture—especially in strong winds.

3 The moisture content of the soil; the wetter the earth the bigger will be the proportion of incoming heat wasted by absorption within the soil itself. The chalky soils of the Chilterns or the North and South Downs, for example, drain more quickly and appear to provide more thermal activity than damper fields in the Vales of Taunton or Yorkshire.

4 The crop of foliage cover. A thick crop or dense trees will intercept much of the incoming insolation before it reaches the ground, and usually a large part of this intercepted heat is used up in transpiration, that is, evaporation from the leaf surfaces of moisture which makes its way up through the plant from the ground. The amount of moisture evaporated in this manner is very considerable—a large tree transpires about three tons of water per day. During periods of drought, however, the water content of the ground may be inadequate for adequate transpiration and some crops become overheated and shrivel up.

5 The wastage of incident solar radiation by reflection from the ground. The power of a surface to reflect heat is difficult if not impossible to estimate but it is instructive to compare some actual measurements relating to a few types of surfaces. Here they are:

Type of surface	*Insolation wasted by reflection*
Various cereal crops	3–15%
Black mould	8–14%
Patches of damp sand	10%
Bare ground	10–20%
Patches of dry sand	18%
Various grass fields	14–37%
Dry ploughed fields	20–25%
Desert	24–28%
Snow or ice	46–86%

The length of time the air remains close to the surface of a particular field or potential thermal source depends on the general wind speed and on the effect of local sheltering. The airflow through, say, the plants of a wheatfield is usually slowed down by the crop foliage, and on a sunny day the temperature within the crop (at about 1 to 2 ft. above ground level) is often about 5° F. higher than that in the faster airflow at about 1 ft. above the top of the crop. Mid-afternoon temperatures within a potato crop are sometimes about 3–10° F. (depending on crop density) higher than the air temperature at the 4-foot level, and it seems probable that, on sunny days with light to moderate winds, locally high temperatures are attained at the foliage level of the trees in woods.

Groups of buildings, towns and steep leeward escarpments in hilly country offer similar though larger scale shelters to the general wind flow and the last type has acquired the name *wind shadow*. A wind shadow, however, is probably active as a thermal source mainly when the lee escarpment is also a sun-facing slope. Buildings and small towns are often efficient thermal sources; they are usually dry, their reflective power is probably low and they usually have some internal heating.

It needs but little imagination to appreciate the difficulties of predicting the efficiency of heated thermal sources. For example, we may argue that since the reflective power of patches of damp sand is low then, in very light winds, the exposed sandy banks of an almost dried up river may be useful thermal sources, but with fresh winds the air close to ground level would not remain over the sand long enough to gain excessive heat; furthermore, evaporation, with its wasteful consumption of insolation, would be greater with fresh winds, and it is practically impossible to predict just how slow the wind must be to allow particular sandy banks to become efficient thermal sources in particular synoptic situations.

To consider another illustration, we can argue that a dry wheatfield is likely to be a more productive thermal source than a neighbouring ploughed field, but if the crop is wet, and if the wind is very light, it is open to conjecture whether or not the air temperature within the wet wheatfield would be higher or lower than that close to the surface of the ploughed field. Of course, we could theorise on the combined effects of sun-facing slopes, wetness of the surface, moisture content of the soil, transpiration, heat reflection and wind shelter (to say nothing of the effects of irrigation) at great length, but since it is practically impossible to know how much of each effect applies to particular places at particular times such theorising is mainly inconclusive. However, this sobering inconclusiveness is no cause for pessimism;

it merely means that we must be wary of forming preconceived notions of where and when to find heated thermal sources. Instead we must be aware of the factors which create such sources and let nature reveal how these are combined on particular occasions, then if we can deduce the reasons for the efficiency or lack of efficiency of one thermal source there may be a better chance of predicting where to find the next.

Another type of thermal source can be provided by a hill ridge in the path of an airstream in which the humidity decreases sharply with height. If the initial tephigram representation of the airstream and the flow over the ridge are like those illustrated in Figure 13.4, then over the crest of the ridge the airstream will be unstable—

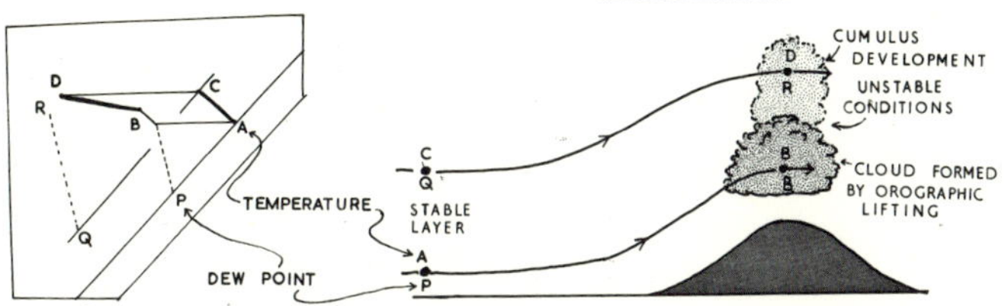

Fig. 13.4. In this illustration the temperature and dewpoint at the bottom of a stable layer is represented on the tephigram by *A* and *P* while *C* and *Q* represent the temperature and dewpoint at a higher level. Because this airstream is moist at low levels orographic lifting can transform the stable T–Φ curve *AC* into unstable curve *BD*.

because the air rising from level *A* to *B* has cooled less than the drier air ascending from *C* to *D*, and this difference in cooling is sufficient to produce instability in the layer *BD*. An airstream which is liable to become unstable when lifted in this fashion is said to be *potentially unstable* and the origin of the thermal activity can be called an *orographic thermal source*. This potential instability need not occur at low levels; a sharp decrease of humidity with height at medium levels may yield convection cloud over the ridge without producing thermals at low levels.

Dust devils

Since both the thermal capacity and conductivity of loose sand are low, insolation is especially effective at raising the temperature of the surface of a desert, and over such regions the superadiabatic layer is particularly unstable and often extends up to a few thousand feet. Thermals and negative thermals in this layer are usually vigorous but, since the desert surface is likely to be of uniform type, the thermal sources will be numerous without being outstanding in relation to their surroundings and the thermals will be abundant but generally small. However, the bubbles that do manage to emerge in one piece from the lower part of this superadiabatic layer will have exceptional chances of developing into strong, mature thermals, probably with characteristics like that of the isolated thermals already described.

One of the by-products of the convergence in any fluid is the

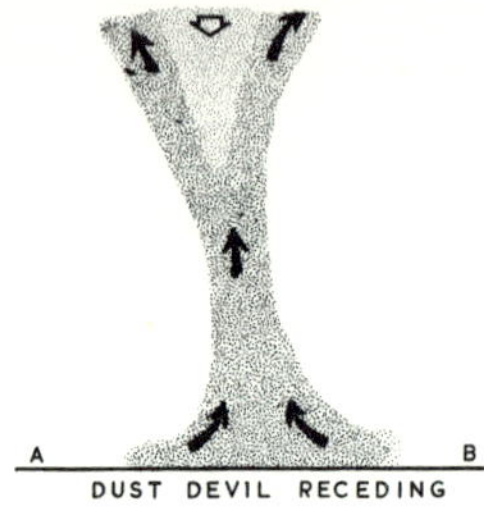

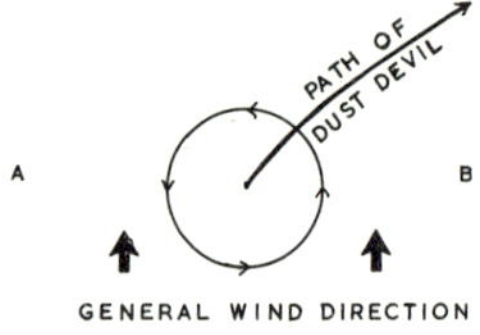

Fig. 13.5. Cross-section and schematic plan of a dust devil.

boosting of whatever rotation happens to be present in the converging elements, and convincing proof of this statement can easily be obtained by watching the motion of bath water as it converges towards the open plughole. The convergence of air in towards the bottom centre of a thermal can also accentuate whatever horizontal rotation happens to be imparted to the air by eddy motion or by the effect of neighbouring thermals. Usually this rotation is insignificant and not readily detectable, but if it does attain a critical value, which is intricately determined by the local state of the atmosphere and topography, then centrifugal force acquires a leading rôle in the subsequent events. This centrifugal force acting on the elements of the rotating thermal delays ready mixing of outside air into the centre of the thermal, so that the buoyant bubble is not diluted and tends to accelerate upwards with a consequential increase in the convergence and rotation of air drawn in towards its base. If this now vigorously rotating thermal picks up enough dust or sand to reveal its whirling motion then it is called a *dust devil.* Over hot deserts these dust devils may reach heights of several thousand feet above ground level. The hydrodynamics of the phenomenon are such that a well developed devil may be in the form of a hollow rotating shell inside which dust-free air descends into the upper part—as depicted in Figure 13.5.

Small dust devils are common sights in convective conditions in most countries, but it is often difficult to guess whether a small swirl of dust from the ground denotes an incipient thermal or an eddy in the wind. Dust devils can spin in either sense of rotation and move in any direction, but most of the large species revolve cyclonically and move very approximately in the direction of the general low level wind flow but with a tendency to swing slightly towards high pressure.

The effect of wind and wind shear

The efficiency of a thermal source is enhanced if the warm pocket of air at ground level has overhead a supply of relatively cool air which effectively boosts the buoyancy of the thermal. Therefore, although thermals might be well formed in hypothetically calm conditions, a light wind favours the production of more frequent, though perhaps distorted, thermals. However, winds across the countryside tend to smooth out the spatial variations in temperature produced by insolation at ground level and strong winds also tend to reduce the rate of rise of surface temperature by distributing heat up through the deep turbulent layer likely to exist in such a flow. On these counts, therefore, winds of moderate strength or more tend to inhibit the creation of thermals from ground level sources. As if to compensate for this suppressive action, the turbulent motion itself displaces parcels of air vertically and if the temperature lapse rate is superadiabatic (even only slightly) then the parcels displaced upwards will become incipient thermals. Hence, there may well be an appreciable number of thermals in moderate or strong winds, but many of them will originate above rather than at ground level and, although some buoyant bubbles may also rise from the land surface, it is usually difficult to relate fixed thermal sources with the thermals actually encountered in the air. The distorting effect of the turbulence also adds to thermal soaring difficulties in such conditions.

The effect of wind shear (i.e. wind change with height) is twofold.

Within a few hundred feet of ground level a wind increase with height in a superadiabatic layer can produce an effect which we could call a "*thermal wedge*," whose action is illustrated in Figure 13.6. Here the incipient thermal sketched in the picture is presumed to have been produced either by a ground level thermal source or by turbulent displacement in the superadiabatic layer; how the thermal was born is not important here, but once the ascent of the thermal starts, air also flows down from the immediate environment to take the place of the rising bubble. With the wind shear illustrated, the air descending on the upwind side of the thermal will be moving faster

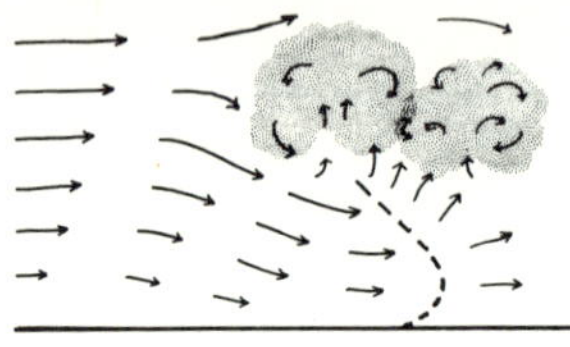

Fig. 13.6. The "thermal wedge."

than the air it begins to follow. So it will act as a cool wedge prising up the air just ahead of it. This vertical displacement of air in the superadiabatic layer will rejuvenate the thermal, whose motion will induce further descent of cold air from its immediate and especially upwind environment. So the process will persist for a while and the thermal soaring effect will be a patch of lift, which drifts with, but somewhat slower than, the wind at the same level, and which may persist at mediocre heights of a few hundred feet or so above ground level without necessarily producing a more active, penetrating thermal.

At higher levels the principal effect of wind shear is to distort a thermal in such a way that the upshear* side tends to be rather more favourable for lift than the downshear region which may include a marked downdraught at the periphery of the thermal. This tendency is worth remembering, but in practice it is not easy to discern the direction of the slight wind shear, and when the shear is very strong then turbulence is likely to destroy practically all semblance between the vertical motion experienced and the simplified patterns so convenient for discussion. A study by J. Findlater of thermals over the British Isles suggests that, on good convection days, soaring in

*Frequently the wind increases with height but changes little in direction, and in such circumstances "upshear" and "downshear" may be interpreted as "upwind" and "downwind."

Date	*District*	*Surface wind*	*Depth of dry convection*	*Wind at top of convection layer*	*Wind shear through convection layer*	*Wind shear in knots per 1,000 ft.*	*Thermal character*
2.4.56	Hants	290/3	3,500 ft.	320/6	350/4	1·1	Moderate and well formed
2.4.58	Middx	090/8	3,500 ft.	070/13	040/6	1·7	Moderate and well formed
3.4.58	Dorset	060/12	3,500 ft.	080/30	090/18	5·1	Plentiful but not well formed
5.5.57	Middx	230/10	3,500 ft.	210/35	210/26	7·4	Very turbulent. Difficult to use
0.7.57	Hants	Calm	4,000 ft.	300/3	300/3	0·8	Strong with narrow cores
3.8.57	Hants	080/14	4,000 ft.	100/12	190/6	1·5	Strong. Easy to use
4.8.57	Hants	090/10	4,000 ft.	140/15	180/12	3·0	Occasionally strong but some distortion
7.4.58	Devon	270/17	4,000 ft.	300/29	330/18	4·5	Strong but difficult to use
7.5.55	Glos	270/13	5,000 ft.	270/12	090/1	0·2	Plentiful. Moderate strength. Easy to use
.0.4.57	Shropshire	248/5	5,000 ft.	220/9	190/7	1·4	Moderate. Easy to use
3.4.58	Cambridge	050/14	5,000 ft.	080/26	100/15	3·0	Moderate. Well formed
3.4.58	Middx	210/9	5,000 ft.	250/17	270/12	2·4	Moderate strength but distorted and difficult to use
5.2.58	Cambridge	240/20	5,000 ft.	260/37	280/19	3·8	Moderate but difficult to use

dry thermals is likely to be possible but difficult due to turbulent distortion when the wind shear is greater than about 2 to 3 knots per 1,000 ft. His study also includes the effect on thermal soaring conditions of the surface wind speed and the depth of penetrative convection and, to perceive the orders of magnitude of these effects, we can note some records of actual conditions on page 161—keeping in mind that these observations by no means tell the full story of thermal structure.

Thermal streams and thermal streets

Occasionally thermals appear to be organised into streets orientated in the direction of the wind. Local streams are likely to develop downwind of quasi-continuous thermal sources such as small towns, factories or orographic sources, the principal condition for such streaming being that the wind direction does not change radically up through the convection layer. The length of streams which stem from particularly active thermal sources is often between two and ten miles. When several parallel streams form, the spacing between them is determined primarily by the distribution of the thermal sources. Certain types of wind and stability conditions, however, are favourable for the organisation of thermals into much longer and more or less regularly spaced streets which do not spring from individual thermal sources. The stability condition is that the convective layer should be capped by a very stable layer. This stabilisation will impose a firm limit on the ultimate sizes of the largest and most significant thermals in the convection layer, and it is virtually the control of these ultimate sizes that allows the regular spacing between the streets to be maintained. The distance between adjacent streets is usually about two to three times the general depth of the convective layer. The wind condition favourable for regular street development is that the wind speed has a maximum in the convection layer, that is, it increases with height up to some unspecified level, then decreases again up towards the top of thermal activity. To illustrate the conditions suitable for local or regular thermal streets some examples are given on page 163.

Truly broad systems of very long, regularly spaced thermal streets are not uncommon features of convection structure over large, flat or uniform regions. Convection in the trade winds over the oceans is very frequently organised into evenly spaced streets. Even

Stability conditions	*Example of wind conditions*	*Probable nature of thermal streets*
Low level convection layer merges into a layer of small stability	Fresh winds. No change of direction with height	Local thermal streams, unevenly spaced
Convection layer capped by inversion at 6,000 ft.	270° 15 knots at 2,000 ft. 270° 18 knots at 4,000 ft. 270° 20 knots at 6,000 ft.	Tendency for small groups of thermal streets to develop
Convection layer capped by inversion at 6,000 ft.	270° 15 knots at 2,000 ft. 270° 20 knots at 4,000 ft. 270° 18 knots at 6,000 ft.	Broad system of long, regularly spaced thermal streets lying West–East likely to form over flat terrain. Spacing between streets 2–3 nautical miles. Streets not linked to particular thermal sources.

over the Arctic pack-ice as far north as 80° N. convection at low levels is characterised by the regular street pattern during the prolonged solar heating of the summer months.

The soaring potential of organised lines of thermals is easily realised in flights directly into wind or downwind, but when flying on cross-wind routes it is wise to anticipate considerable downdraughts likely to be induced between adjacent streams or streets.

Thermals at cloud levels

On being cooled to its dew point the air in a thermal becomes saturated and any subsequent adiabatic cooling will be at the S.A.L.R. Much of the discussion of dry thermal structure can be tentatively applied to thermals in cloud simply by substituting the words saturated adiabatic for dry adiabatic. For example, the buoyancy of an adiabatically ascending thermal will tend to increase, remain constant or decrease according to whether the temperature lapse rate of its environment is greater than, the same as, or less than the S.A.L.R.—Figure 12.3 on page 138 illustrates the reason why.

The structure of the cloud thermal, however, has additional

complications in that it is influenced by both the temperature lapse rate and the moisture content of its environment and by the effects of evaporation.

Suppose a saturated thermal ascends in a layer of air whose temperature lapse rate is greater than the S.A.L.R. and whose water vapour content is very low. The environment air pushed upwards just ahead of the ascending thermal will cool at the dry adiabatic lapse rate and so become denser than its new surroundings (see Figure 13.7) while the difference between the temperature of the saturated

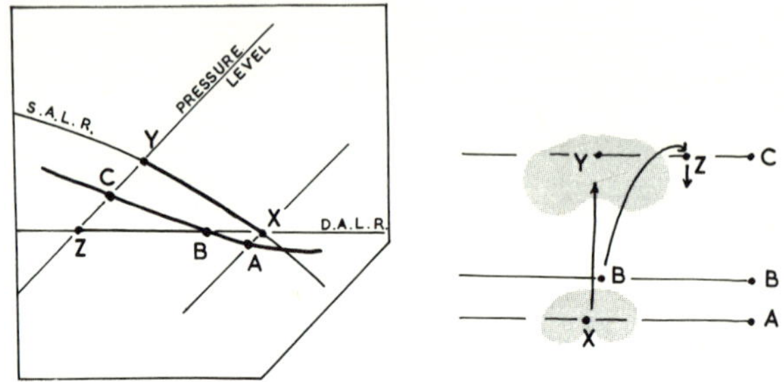

Fig. 13.7. Suppose a cloudy thermal, *X*, rises in an environment represented by *ABC* to *Y* and displaces a parcel of the environment air from *B* to *Z* then the cloudy thermal will remain buoyant while the parcel *Z* will tend to sink because it becomes colder than the environment.

thermal air and that of the surroundings will increase. So while the thermal receives an upward boost, dry air in the newly acquired cap will sink. Descent of air is also likely just within the sides of the saturated thermal itself; this is due to the cooling of the thermal air by evaporation of some of its moisture into the dry surroundings. The net result of these buoyancy changes is that a well developed cloudy thermal exhibits a fairly clear cut outline at its leading surface as it penetrates into a dry and stable environment, although the contrasting vertical velocities at the sides usually produce small scale turbulence. In the initial stages of the process the thermal lift is likely to become stronger and may also be reduced in horizontal extent, but at all stages the entrainment of air will tend to enlarge and eventually destroy the thermal by dilution. We can only conjecture which process will dominate the character of thermals in any specified conditions, but first we must be aware of the processes involved so that we shall have a better chance of guessing how nature

Plate 8 CUMULUS MEDIOCRIS

Besides illustrating one of the cloud types described on page 36, this photograph shows Commander H. N. C. Goodhart's Skylark 3b on the approach to Lezno Airfield, Poland, during the 1958 World Gliding Championships.

combines these processes to form the thermals we actually encounter.

If a succession of saturated thermals ascended adiabatically then the temperature distribution up through the cloud it forms would be represented by a S.A.L.R. on the tephigram. Of course, the concept of adiabatic ascent is only a first approximation to the truth; evaporation and entrainment of the environment air modifies the adiabatic process. For example, if the *T–Φ* curve *ABCDE* in Figure 13.8 represents the environment conditions and *B* denotes the condensation level of rising thermals, then saturated adiabatic ascent from *B* upwards would yield cloud temperatures represented by the S.A.L.R. curve *BP*. But evaporation of the sides of the cloud and entrainment of environment air would probably reduce these temperatures to those represented by, say, *BXRD*—i.e. the temperature of a well-developed cloud would be somewhere between that of the environment and the saturated adiabatic curve through the condensation level. (If the cloud is not well developed then the evaporation may cool the cloud even more.) Suppose now another saturated thermal ascends well within the cloud itself. In this case of a saturated thermal ascending through saturated air evaporation will play no part and the thermal will behave in a very similar way to a dry thermal in a dry environment; in the saturated superadiabatic region of the cloud (between the levels *B* and *C* in Figure 13.8) the size and strength of the thermal will increase rapidly as it ascends; in the saturated adiabatic layer just above the level *C* it will behave as a dry thermal in a dry adiabatic layer and towards the level *D* its demise will be rapid or slow according to whether the temperature

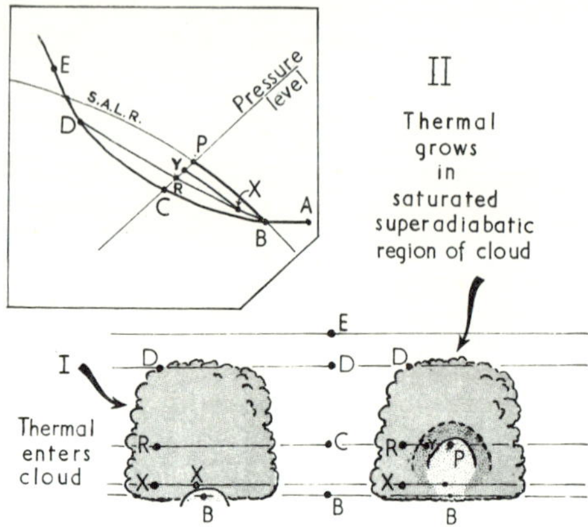

Fig. 13.8. At stage I a thermal is shown just entering cloud. Temperatures of the cloud and its environment at levels *B, C, D, E, X* and *R* are indicated by corresponding letters on the schematic tephigram. At stage II the cloudy thermal, now at level *P*, has become warmer than the cloud around it. Furthermore, it has lifted some of the cloudy air, *X*, just above it at stage I to *Y* in stage II. The tephigram shows that such upward displacements in this region are unstable; therefore the volume of the buoyant air increases. Note that, in this and several other diagrams of this type, sizes of displacements on the tephigram are greatly exaggerated to illustrate the theoretical reasoning.

lapse rate of the cloud is extremely or only just stable with respect to the S.A.L.R.

The subcloud layer

On a sunny day with fair weather convection clouds floating in the sky the total cloud averaged over, say, 10,000 square miles (approx. 40,000 sq. km.) usually covers less than half the sky, and the widespread descent of environment air which usually, but not necessarily, compensates for the ascent of thermals is, on average, very slow. Nevertheless, this descent is important because the environment is adiabatically warmed in the process, thereby

Plate 9 ALTOCUMULUS *R. S. Scorer*

Unlike low level cumulus clouds, these incipient towers of *altocumulus castellanus* are not fed by a supply of thermal up-currents at their bases. Therefore, the individual clouds are being eroded by evaporation into fragmentary towers of the *altocumulus floccus* type shown in this picture. Because the sizes and shapes of these clouds can vary within a wide range, even skilled observers can seldom be confident in their estimate of the height of this type of cloud.

reducing the chances of thermals from low levels reaching their condensation level. This means that thermals have a better chance of rising up past their condensation level into cloud that already exists than into a cloudless region—as may be observed when a large convection cloud virtually damps down convection around it, or when persistent and vigorous convection from the sun-facing slopes of a mountain escarpment inhibits the development of cumulus over the adjoining lowland. The process is often very noticeable when convection occurs over large areas of an ocean or a continent and in such regions the convection clouds may virtually organise themselves into bands, streets or groups between which subsidence of the environment produces a stable layer down to about 200–600 ft. below the general level of the cloud base; such a layer is frequently referred to as the *subcloud layer*.

Persistence and spreading out of cumulus

We have noted that during the initial stages of its ascent in cloud a saturated thermal is likely to receive an upward impetus. This upward surge is often strong enough to draw in more air from below, but all too often this air converges horizontally towards the base of the cloud and unless the cloud is very large with vigorous convective currents, this inflow towards cloud base contributes little to the lift below cloud. Once it is drawn up above its condensation level into cloud, however, this air acquires buoyancy as its water vapour condenses and releases latent heat and so forms a new thermal at or just within cloud base. Thus, a convection cloud, once formed, does not necessarily decay when its supply of thermals from ground level is cut off, and a significant, if perhaps vexing, corollary is that convection clouds in the sky are not necessarily guarantors of abundant thermals far below.

One of the principal factors governing the life history of a convection cloud is the humidity of its environment; in a fairly dry environment evaporation at the periphery of the cloud will considerably reduce the chances of small individual clouds persisting for longer than about ten minutes, but if the environment is very humid then not only will the rate of evaporation be reduced but its effect may be to increase the water vapour content of the immediate environment of the thermal to the saturation value; in effect the cloudiness would spread outwards from the thermal, and if the convection cloud is not too deep and vigorous it will degenerate into a large patch of stratocumulus which will literally cast a shadow over thermal soaring prospects for anything between 15 minutes and a few hours. It may or may not be blown away, or "burnt off," or "dried out" by warming due to subsidence, or evaporated into drier air above; each case must be considered in the light of the prevailing synoptic conditions.

The effect of wind on cloudy thermals

Wind and wind shear exert much the same effects on cloudy and dry thermals; wind shear up through the convection cloud layer causes the cumulus clouds to lean in the downshear direction and excessive shear considerably distorts the thermal structure. When the tops of the cloudy thermals are limited to a fairly definite level

Plate 10 CLOUD STREETS OVER WIMBLEDON *R. S. Scorer*

In the late afternoon of 24 May 1958 cumulus cloud formation over S.E. England became organised into parallel streets along the general wind direction. Wind and stability conditions suitable for this street formation are described in the text.

and the wind direction is practically constant up through the convection régime, cumulus clouds, like dry thermals, are apt to organise themselves into streets along the wind direction. The formation of a broad system of evenly spaced streets is enhanced if the wind speed has a maximum in the convective layer, and the distance between such streets will be two to three times the general height of the cumulus tops above ground level.

The density of water vapour

Because water vapour is a gas whose density is about five-eighths that of dry air, a mixture of dry air and water vapour is less dense than completely dry air at the same temperature and pressure. When discussing buoyancy forces this density difference is sometimes taken into account by converting the temperature of the air into a "*virtual temperature*"—that is the temperature at which completely dry air would have the same density as the damp air being considered. A formula for calculating this virtual temperature is—

$$(T' + 273) = (T + 273)\left(\frac{1{,}000 + \frac{8}{5}x}{1{,}000 + x}\right)$$

where T' = the virtual temperature in degrees centigrade
T = the actual temperature in degrees centigrade
x = water vapour content in grams per kilogram of dry air.

A sample calculation shows that damp air at a temperature of, say, 22° C. (72° F.) with a water vapour content of 10 gm./kg. has a virtual temperature of 23·7° C., i.e. it is as buoyant as dry air 1·7° C. warmer would be in the same environment. Compared to the other factors governing thermal characteristics this distinction between actual and virtual temperature is often (but not always) small enough to be ignored; when its effect does succeed in tipping the scales of thermal behaviour it can be held to account for such phenomena as thermals slightly colder than their surroundings and thermals from moist surfaces or even small lakes.

CHAPTER 14

Showers, Thunder and Lightning

The order of magnitude of the diameter of cloud droplets in cumulus is 20 microns, a micron being one thousandth of a millimetre. A raindrop of, say, 2 mm. diameter contains 4 milligrams of water and is equivalent in size to about a million or so cloud droplets which, as part of the cloud, would be dispersed through a volume of about 1 litre (the size of a small melon). The spacing between the cloud droplets is about fifty times their diameter. The production of rainfall which involves the transformation of billions of cloud droplets into millions of rain drops is not a straightforward process because the physical make up of the tiny cloud droplets gives them little or no chance of growing by direct condensation of water vapour on to their surfaces. Rainfall is the end product of more complicated processes, one of which is described by a theory due to the meteorologists, Bergeron and Findeisen.

This process requires the cloud to extend above the freezing level before showers can be produced, the argument being that the physical structure of an ice crystal does allow it to grow by condensation of the water vapour which evaporates from neighbouring supercooled cloud droplets—and here we should note that the atmosphere contains abundant condensation nuclei on which cloud droplets can form but relatively few nuclei of the type suitable for the formation of ice crystals, so at temperatures just below the freezing point ice crystals in cloud are likely to be surrounded by myriads of supercooled water drops. As the ice crystals grow in size so they tend to fall down through the cloud, growing even more by collision with liquid droplets both above and below the freezing level.

When a tiny water drop gradually freezes in the atmosphere its surface usually freezes first; when the interior subsequently freezes and expands slightly it is liable to shatter the outer shell and eject tiny ice particles which form suitable nuclei on which more supercooled water drops can freeze. Thus once the production of ice crystals (*glaciation*) has started in the freezing region of a cloud it is likely to proceed rapidly. This glaciation also helps to prolong the life of the cloud; ice crystals evaporate much more slowly than water drops so that when a convection cloud becomes glaciated it suffers less shrinkage and cooling at its sides by evaporation into its environment.

The Bergeron theory is sound enough for forecasters in many temperate latitude regions to predict showers or no showers according to whether convection cloud is expected to reach or not to reach up to above the freezing level. In practice this has proved to be a useful working rule, but more recent researches have shown that under certain conditions showers can develop from convection clouds which do not extend up to the freezing level. The mechanism of this type of shower production is the coalescence of cloud droplets on to unusually large droplets which can form on some of the sea salt nuclei in maritime airstreams. These large droplets grow by collision and coalescence with the smaller droplets amongst which they fall and their ultimate size is controlled mainly by the time spent in the cloud; if thermal support is too weak the drops will fall out of the cloud long before reaching raindrop size and soon evaporate at what may become a somewhat diffuse cloud base; if the thermals are strong and the cloud not of great depth then these droplets will be carried to the top or periphery of the cloud and will evaporate into the environment. Calculations by F. H. Ludlam suggest that for thermal updraughts of about 200 ft./min. a convection cloud must be at least 1,500 ft. deep to produce coalescence showers, for 600 ft./min. a 6,000 ft. depth of cloud is required, and for 1,000 ft./min. thermals the cloud must extend to 10,000 ft. above its base. In deep clouds which extend to above the freezing level, both coalescence and glaciation are likely to contribute to shower development.

Like glaciation, the coalescence process is sometimes self-exciting; raindrops in the atmosphere are liable to disintegrate on reaching certain critical sizes; in calm air 7 mm. is about the maximum diameter and in turbulent air about 4 mm. is the maximum diameter to which a drop can grow before disintegrating into several smaller droplets, each of which may grow by the coalescence process.

Plate 11 CUMULONIMBUS FROM ABOVE *R. K. Pilsbury*

Once the top of a cumulus cloud becomes higher than the general level of the surrounding cumulus tops, the cloud tends to grow even more at the expense of the neighbouring convection clouds. In this photograph the large convection cloud is growing rapidly but has not yet reached the glaciation stage of its development.

Hail

When a pellet of ice collides with a water drop the water coats the pellet with either a partly frozen opaque mixture of air bubbles and water or a glassy shell of ice according to whether the temperature of the water drop was initially above or below 0° C. If the water content of the cloud is high and the ice pellet takes some time to fall through the regions of water droplets then the ice pellet will grow to form a hailstone. In vigorous convection clouds growing hailstones encounter and are sometimes carried aloft by several thermals before they eventually fall out of the cloud, and, with the accumulated coatings of opaque or glazed ice, their ultimate size is commonly comparable to that of peas or small marbles. In the powerful updraughts in violent convection clouds some hailstones may not fall out of cloud until they have grown to the size of golf balls or even larger. Hailstones with diameters of two inches have been encountered at ground level in freak showers in the British Isles, while in some warmer climes hailstone diameters of five inches have been recorded. Hailstones of half an inch in diameter fall through the air at about

30 knots and are therefore formidable missiles capable of inflicting expensive damage on parked or airborne gliders. Fortunately, most hailstones are somewhat smaller than this and hail showers themselves are usually short lived; such showers usually become rain showers after the initial short sharp burst of hail. There is no simple criterion for predicting whether or not a shower will precipitate damaging hailstones. Obviously hail will not fall from an isolated convection cloud whose top does not extend up to above the freezing level. Nor is hail likely in a convection cloud which is so cold that it cannot contain an abundance of water drops to coat the falling ice pellets with a number of shells, and a convection cloud which lacks really strong thermals is likely to let raindrops fall out before the incipient hailstones can grow. But at present no simple rules have been evolved from reasoning such as this, and whenever there is some doubt it is wise to seek a forecaster's advice on the hail risk in the particular synoptic situation.

The effect of wind shear on shower development

For the production of moderate sized raindrops both the coalescence and the Bergeron processes require relatively large liquid or frozen drops to fall through smaller droplets, but if a strong wind shear exists in a convection cloud of small horizontal extent then these relatively large drops are likely to fall out of the cloud before they have attained raindrop sizes. They will probably evaporate before they can fall to the ground in the form of a shower. If, on the other hand, these drops fall into a fresh supply of smaller droplets in a newly formed convection cloud (or in a new centre of thermal activity within the cloud) then the shower production mechanism will acquire an increased efficiency which will help to propagate the shower in a downshear direction—but more will be said on downshear propagation in some later sections of this chapter.

Cumulonimbus

Many of the features of thermal structure and shower formation already discussed lead to the deduction that, in shower conditions, once a convection cloud becomes slightly more mature (in the sense of growing and becoming glaciated) than its neighbours its chances of developing even more at the expense of these neighbouring clouds

Plate 12 CUMULONIMBUS DEVELOPMENT *R. K. Pilsbury*

These four photographs were taken at approximately five-minute intervals. The cumulonimbus clouds are moving from left to right in the pictures and the anvil cloud clearly visible in *A* and *B* reveals that the wind speed increases with height. The top of the large cumulonimbus in the foreground rose very quickly and the cloud produced a shower of rain, but by the end of the fifteen-minute period this cloud was beginning to decay while the rapid growth of new convection cloud was apparent both on its upshear side (in this case on the left) and the downshear side. Notice the relatively firm outlines of the cumiliform tops of the new convection clouds compared to the more fibrous top of the older cumulonimbus cloud. Such outlines indicate that the new clouds are still composed mainly of water drops, while the older convection cloud has matured past the glaciation stage. The significance of glaciation in shower production is described in the text.

increase rapidly and, indeed, shower-producing clouds often do tower well above the general level of the neighbouring cloud tops.

When thermals in a glaciated cloud top reach the upper limit of penetrative convection the layer or region into which they spread out is made visible by a plume of ice crystals which are slow to

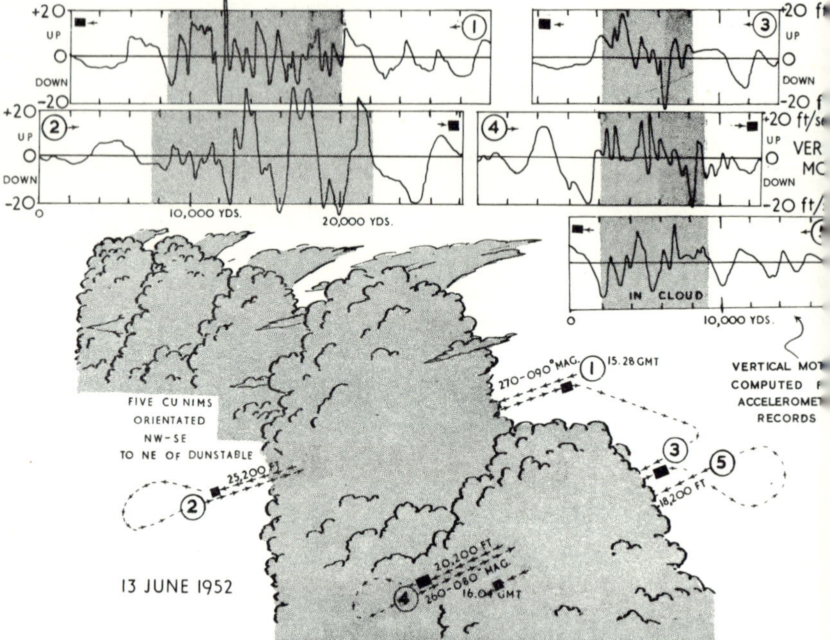

Fig. 14.1. The five vertical motion records corresponding to the five flights through the cumulonimbus clouds revealed a complicated pattern which is difficult to analyse into a simple picture of "ideal" thermals. However, it is easily conceivable that any one of the three large thermals encountered in cloud during run No. 2 could have lifted a glider up through some considerable depth of the cloud. Naturally the complications of the whole vertical motion picture are not apparent to the pilot who can locate and remain in one large thermal for some time.

evaporate. Usually this plume widens laterally as it is drawn out from the bulk of the cloud by whatever wind shear exists up through the convection cloud region, so from some viewpoints the convection cloud appears to support an anvil of white cirrus cloud. Such a convection cloud is called a *cumulonimbus* and, in temperate latitudes, its anvil may be at any level between about 20,000 and 50,000 ft.—the tropopause usually sets the upper limit.

By the time convection clouds grow to cumulonimbus size they embrace complex patterns of updraughts and downdraughts; at any moment the distribution of vertical currents at any one level is typically as complicated as that sketched in Figure 14.1, and may be difficult to link with the vertical motion at any other level or at any other moment of time. Of course, this vertical motion pattern is not revealed to a pilot who is able to stay in one strong thermal as it carries him up through some considerable depth of the cloud; he may well gain the impression of being in a long continuous updraught stretching from cloud base or below up through thousands of feet of cloud. On occasions, it may be apparent that certain regions of the clouds are particularly favourable for updraughts or downdraughts, but in general the vertical motion in a single large cumulonimbus is not organised into a simple pattern.

The strong thermals and downdraughts in a cumulonimbus are usually felt as turbulence when encountered in high speed powered flight through the cloud, but a number of the thermals are so wide (often about 1,000–2,000 yds. in diameter) that their lift seems relatively smooth when used for soaring. However, some small scale turbulence is often encountered in three regions: near the freezing level where the precipitation mechanism is accelerated, towards the top of the cloud where the thermals begin to spread out and where the wind shear is sometimes large, and at the sides of the lower part of the cloud where vertical motion changes quickly across the periphery of the cloud.

Ice accretion

Supercooled water droplets in cloud above the freezing level freeze readily on contact with a solid object and are therefore likely to form ice on a sailplane, especially at the leading edges of the aerofoils, and at exposed joints. Very often this ice accretion is not serious but it is quite feasible for a glider to have its windscreen covered and its control surfaces jammed by ice while still being carried aloft in a thermal and then to enter a strong downdraught in which it descends to a dangerously low level before the ice has melted. To minimise the danger of this it is wise to try to avoid lingering only just above the freezing level too long—this is where the ice accretion is likely to be most rapid; at higher levels where the cloud is composed mainly of ice crystals rather than supercooled water droplets the icing hazard is reduced.

Thunder and lightning

Lightning is the electrical spark discharge which takes place in a strong electrostatic gradient between oppositely charged regions of cloud or between cloud and the ground, and within a range of about 18 miles the noise of this spark may be heard as thunder.

Since the flash and the noise originate simultaneously, the nearness of the discharge may be determined by noting the time interval between the lightning and the thunder and remembering that sound travels about 1 mile in 5 seconds. The lightning flash itself may be a mile or more in length—in fact, inter-cloud discharges of over 50 miles in length have been observed during radar studies of long lines of cumulonimbus clouds. The sound from the whole length of a flash may therefore continue to be heard for several seconds and echoes from hills or buildings add to the reverberations.

A gradient of about three million volts per metre is required to trigger off a lightning discharge and many thousands of volts per metre to extend the length of the spark. Precisely how the atmosphere builds up such gradients is not yet clearly understood. Plausible theories hinge on various experimentally observed facts; when two ice particles of different temperatures cannon off each other the warmer particle acquires a negative electrical charge while the colder piece gains a positive charge; the shattering of ice shells during the freezing process and the breaking up of raindrops also provide mechanisms for separating positive and negative electric charges. The motion within a cumulonimbus is often chaotic enough to break up raindrops and to bring warm and cold ice particles into collision, yet the convective system as a whole is sufficiently organised to build up accumulations of the electrically charged particles in various regions of the cloud.

Rough theoretical reasoning which we will not dwell upon suggests that this differential charging of various regions in the cloud is particularly efficient if the cloud contains an abundant supply of both liquid water and ice particles, and observations confirm that neither clouds which do not extend far above the freezing level nor clouds which are entirely above the freezing level are efficient generators of thunderstorms.

Although the electrical potential associated with lightning is measured in millions of volts, the electric current is very small and the structure of a thoroughly bonded metal glider is adequate to conduct a lightning discharge with no damage. Safety in a basically non-metallic glider, however, often rests on the statistically small chance of it actually being struck by a powerful discharge. A protruding or trailing wireless aerial increases the risk of the aircraft being struck; should this occur it is almost certain that the aerial would be damaged or destroyed and there would be a risk of fire breaking out in the equipment. The most common electrostatic manifestations in soaring in thunderstorms are "St Elmo's fire" (myriads of small spark discharges) associated with instruments and other metal fittings and a hissing or crackling which may build up to a crescendo before a somewhat bigger discharge takes place somewhere in the thunder cloud.

As with ice accretion and small scale turbulence, the region of the freezing level seems to be particularly prone to these electrostatic manifestations. A lightning discharge usually causes electric currents to flow in divers parts of the storm and glider pilots in a non-metallic aircraft receive from the controls electric shocks which range from mere twinges to painful spasms. Bonding the aircraft nose to tail and wing tip to wing tip would increase the chances of its being struck but would considerably enhance the structural safety of the aircraft in the thousand to one chance of it being struck by a really powerful stroke of lightning.

Just over 200 years ago, in an age when electrical experiments were a drawing-room novelty, Benjamin Franklin dabbled with atmospheric electricity by obtaining sparks from a wire stretching up to a kite flying below a thundery cumulonimbus. How lucky he was to survive the experiment! He was virtually prodding the thunderstorm with an efficient lightning conductor. A glider launching wire stretching from a winch or tow car on the ground to a glider at several hundred feet is also an efficient lightning conductor; if a thunderstorm is practically overhead the risk of lightning striking a glider during the launch is quite considerable and the effect of such a strike would probably be to damage the aircraft and, if the winch or tow car were not earthed, to harm the operator or driver.

Fortunately, serious gliding mishaps due to lightning appear to be rare, but it is perhaps sobering to realise that, in the world at large, lightning kills more people than hurricanes, earthquakes and floods

Plate 13 CUMULONIMBUS AT A SEA BREEZE FRONT *P. M. Saunders*

On 18 June 1957 conditions over England were ideal for the formation of deep convection cloud particularly in association with sea breeze frontal effects. This photograph, taken at 1420 GMT from an aircraft east of Brighton on the south coast of England, shows the storm clouds associated with radar echoes illustrated in Plate 16 and in Figure 14.3*b*. The cloud types are *cumulus congestus* and *cumulonimbus incus*, the tops of which extended to above 40,000 ft.

all put together. High up in the casualty lists are golfers, cyclists and picnickers. Golfers are struck at the rate of three per million per year. One-third of lightning deaths occur under trees. Relatively safe places in thunderstorms include the insides of cars, buses and trains. People struck by lightning are not charged with electricity. They can be touched at once and may need artificial respiration if, as is often the case, their breathing mechanism has been temporarily paralysed.

In the world's thunderstorms (which total over 40,000 per day) there are two types of lightning flash—an ultra-rapid flash lasting less than 1/10,000 of a second and a slower, hotter flash of about 1/10 to 1/100 second duration.

The normal zigzag pattern of a lightning stroke with its various branches is appropriately described as "forked" lightning, while "summer" lightning is a popular though most unscientific description of visible lightning which is too far away to be heard, and "sheet" lightning is another colloquial name applied to the illumination of the sky by a distant concealed stroke. The rare "thunderbolts" which are observed appear as slowly moving balls of some glowing

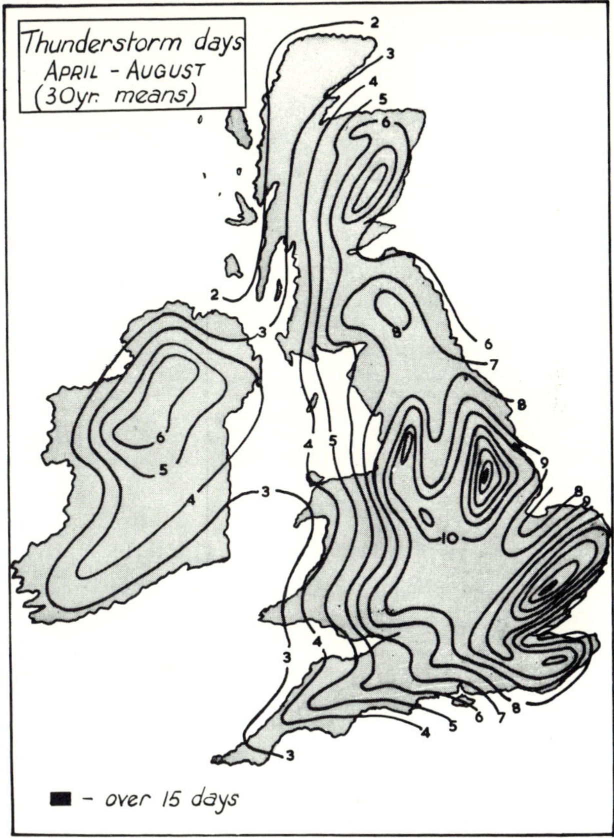

Fig. 14.2. Average number of days with thunderstorms in the period April to August.

form of electrical activity, but both descriptions and scientific understanding of them are very sketchy.

In the British Isles the regions particularly prone to thunderstorms in the five-month period April to August inclusive are found mainly in some of the eastern districts of England and Scotland. Figure 14.2 shows the average number of days with thunder in the period. No doubt sea breeze effects contribute to the development of convective storms in belts approximately parallel to some sections of

Plate 14 ALTOCUMULUS WITH MAMMATUS *R. K. Pilsbury*

Convectively unstable conditions can accelerate downdraughts as well as upward motions. Sometimes the downdraughts within a cloud are denoted by the appearance of globular bulges emerging from the cloud base. Such protuberances, classified as mammatus cloud, are shown in the centre of this picture—emerging from the mass of unstable medium cloud.

the coastline, but at present there is insufficient evidence to judge the measure of this contribution.

Precipitation downdraught

Lift is frequently located in precipitation underneath or inside cumulonimbus clouds, but this precipitation does exert a frictional downward drag on the air and if the lower part of the cloud is a saturated superadiabatic zone then slight downward displacements of the air in this zone will trigger off a negative thermal, and may dramatically reverse the updraughts associated with the precipitation. Below cloud base some of the precipitation evaporates into the initially unsaturated air which is thereby cooled and becomes another source of negative thermals.

If, as is usual in convective conditions, the air at low levels forms an adiabatic or superadiabatic layer the speed of the downdraughts will be maintained or even increased as the descending air approaches ground level where they must then spread out. If no wind shear exists in the convective layer, isolated downdraughts over flat land will spread out more or less radially, but when the wind changes with height the downdraughts arrive at ground level with a horizontal velocity different from that of the surface air and so tend to spread out mainly in the direction of the shear. More often than not the wind shear comprises an increase in speed with height and the downdraughts spread out mainly ahead of an advancing storm. The rain is then preceded by gusts of cold air. A rough prediction of the magnitude of the possible temperature change may be made by noting a simple if crude formula: the temperature (in ° C.) of the downdraught on reaching the ground may be as low but not lower than $1\frac{1}{2}$ times the height of the freezing level in thousands of feet; for example, if the freezing level is at 10,000 ft. then the lowest temperature which a really strong downdraught will have on reaching ground level will be approximately 15° C. (59° F.) and so if the general air temperature well ahead of a storm is, say, 20° C. (68° F.) then a temperature drop of not more than 5° C. (9° F.) may be expected. There appears to be a close relationship between the fall in temperature and the gustiness which marks the advent of the cold air; this relationship can also be expressed approximately by a simple formula, namely, the maximum gust (in knots) likely as a result of a precipitation downdraught is the general wind speed plus about five times the fall of temperature in degrees centigrade, for example, with a general flow of 15 knots, the maximum wind speed in gusts associated with a 5° C. drop in temperature is likely to be about $15 + 5 \times 5 = 40$ knots. Thus a knowledge of the general air temperature and the height of the freezing level is an aid to assessing the possible local gustiness of the wind in the neighbourhood of large precipitating cumulonimbus clouds.

The thunderstorm "high"

The initiation and development of strong downdraughts in a precipitating cumulonimbus is often so sudden that the near balance between the net inflow of air into the cloud base and outflow at high levels is tilted sharply in favour of net accumulation of air with an

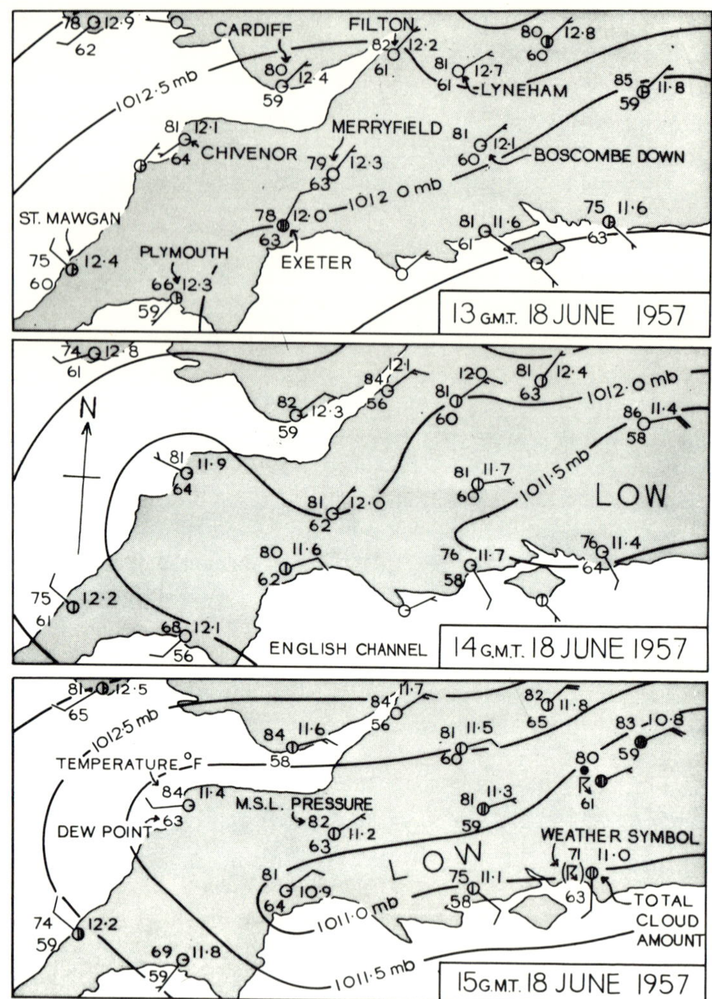

Fig. 14.3*a.* On 18 June 1957 insolation raised inland temperatures to more than 80° F. and created an elongated thermal low over southern England. Isobars are drawn at half millibar intervals to illustrate the sequence of events. Thunderstorms which initially developed in a V-shaped area approximately parallel to and inland of the Thames estuary began to move westwards.

accompanying rise in the M.S.L. pressure immediately under the storm. This dwarf anticyclone is called a *thunderstorm high* and though the majority of such anticyclones are too weak to be obvious,

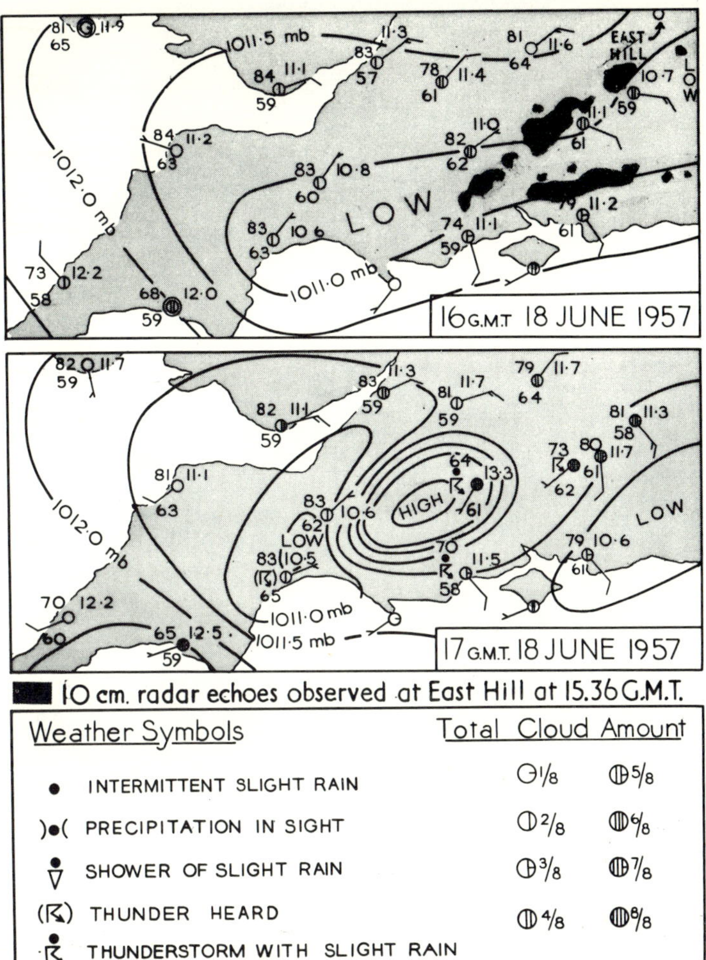

Fig. 14.3*b*. At 16 GMT on 18 June 1957 the principal thunderstorms over southern England appeared to lie between the observing stations. By 17 GMT however, the most intense section of one of these storms had moved westwards across Boscombe Down and the precipitation downdraught had created a thunderstorm high. The sudden development of this new system was evidenced not only by the dramatic change in the pressure pattern between 16 GMT and 17 GMT but also by the changes in wind, temperature and dew points as the cold downdraught spread out over the countryside.

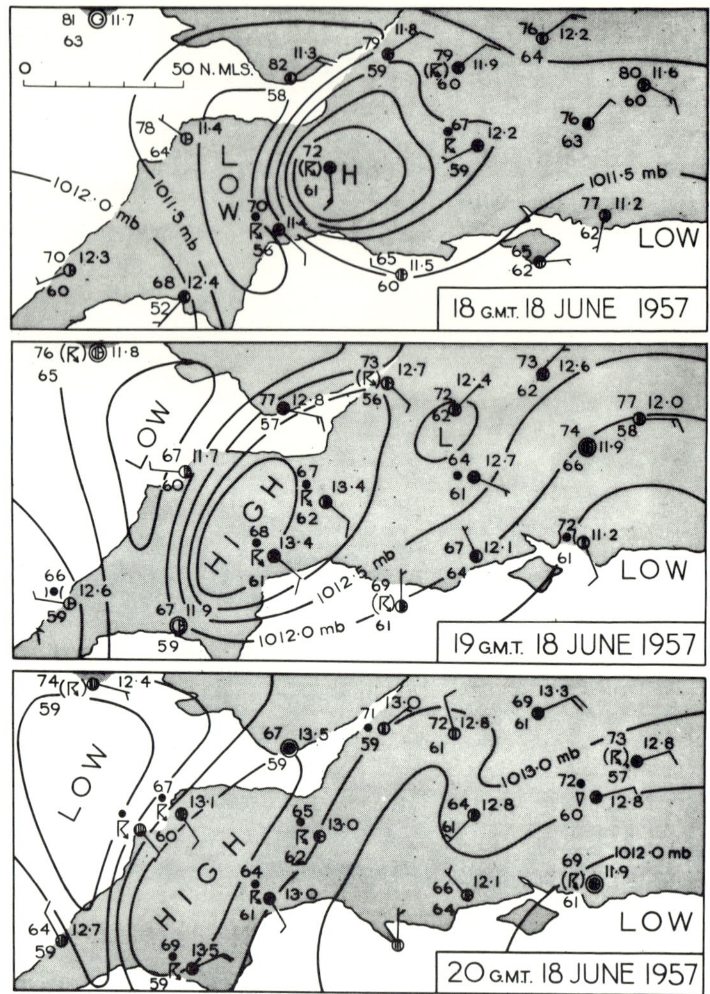

Fig. 14.3*c*. The thunderstorm high which had developed between 16 GMT and 17 GMT moved westwards with the storm area. Barograph records were used to confirm the details of the maps drawn.

it is not unusual for a group or line of vigorous storms to produce pressure surges of a millibar or two and to effect pressure pattern changes like that illustrated in Figure 14.3.

A July night in 1952 happened to provide suitable conditions for an interesting by-product of a thunderstorm high which apparently developed suddenly under a group of severe storms over the English Channel. These storms had intensified while moving north from

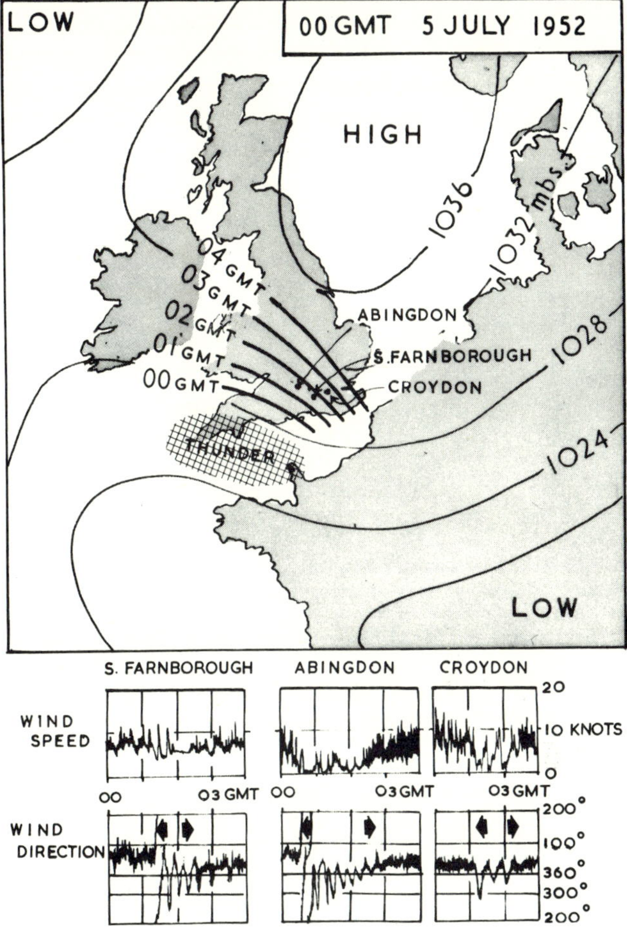

Fig. 14.4. Isochrones of the pressure surge following the sudden development of a thunderstorm high over the English Channel. The surge was accompanied by considerable wind fluctuations of the type shown in the autographic records and the periodic formation and dispersal of stratocumulus in several districts.

France, but at present the only item in their history that concerns us is that the pressure surge following the downdraught developments occurred late at night on 4 July 1952. The airstream (Figure 14.4)

over England happened to include an inversion and a wind shear at an altitude of about 5,000 ft. and, since such conditions provide a means for the channelling and horizontal propagation of wave motion, the pressure surge set oscillations radiating outwards from the storm area—just as a stone dropped into water sets ripples emanating from the initial disturbance. At a speed of about 40 knots these pressure oscillations swept across much of England causing

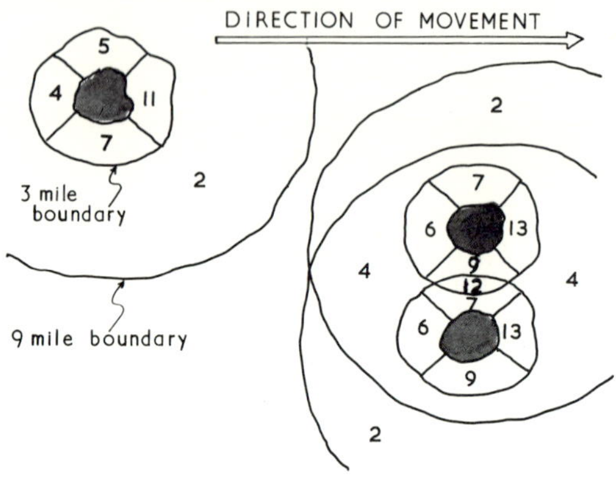

Fig. 14.5. Relative chances of fresh convective development in the vicinity of existing cumulonimbus (shaded).

surface winds to fluctuate (in the manner illustrated in Figure 14.4) for spells of about 90 minutes. Calculations showed the pressure oscillations to be accompanied by travelling waves through which the air near the level of the inversion undulated between 600 ft. above and 600 ft. below its original altitude, and in some localities this vertical motion was evidenced by the periodic formation and dispersal of large patches of stratocumulus.

Line squalls

In spreading out at ground level a thunderstorm downdraught acts as a wedge forcing up the air in its path and if, as a result of wind shear in the convective layer, the spreading out is concentrated mainly in one direction, then this lifting may well be sufficient to trigger off convection on the downshear side of the main storm centre and the production of rain in a convection cloud in this position may be facilitated by precipitation from the older cumulonimbus.

Thus a thunderstorm over flat countryside can virtually propagate itself roughly in a downshear direction without being fed by a supply of thermals from fixed ground level sources.

A study of thunderstorms in the United States showed the statistical chances of fresh convective development taking place in the neighbourhood of an existing cumulonimbus to be like those depicted in Figure 14.5. The details of these arrangements of development probabilities will vary somewhat according to local topography and the prevailing wind shear, but these variations will not detract from the general conclusion that once a few neighbouring storms are arranged into a line across the general wind direction they tend to consolidate and perpetuate the line formation, and if, as is commonly the case, the line is preceded or accompanied by severe gusts of wind, it is called a *line squall*.

In its most pronounced state the passage of a line squall is marked by:

1 a sudden slight pressure rise during the approach of the thunderstorm high (which is often masked by a broader scale troughing of the isobars across a long line squall);
2 a very sharp wind veer;
3 considerable gustiness which reaches a peak at about the same time as
4 a drop in temperature and a rise in humidity, which precedes
5 a burst of heavy precipitation followed by between about 10 and 30 minutes' lighter rainfall.

Line squalls which form either on or parallel to and just ahead of cold fronts are often a few hundred miles in length, but when the organisation of cumulonimbus clouds into a line is the result of local topographical effects (such as preferential heating on the sun-facing slopes of a mountain range) then the line squall is often less than 150 miles in length and may even be too short to be clearly distinguished on routine synoptic charts.

The wedge-like action of the cold air advancing at ground level is often sufficient to produce a belt of lift just in front of the zone of heavy precipitation. Using such lift as this, Hanna Reitsch flew a Zugvogel sailplane at an average speed of 51 knots (102 km./hr.) over a 46 nautical mile (92 km.) course from Orlinghausen to Dortmund, Germany. A schematic cross-section of the cloud structure is sketched in Figure 14.6. Luckily the line squall moved westward across the course with just the right speed to allow a long straight soaring flight in about the position indicated in the sketch. Visibility towards the east was considerably reduced by heavy precipitation, and from time to time the port wing plunged into this precipitation which occasionally included hail and snow. To the west small cumulus clouds illuminated by bright sunshine were still visible but gradually thickening streaks of rain suggested that some development of the cloud and precipitation system was taking place along a line just to the west of the flight path. In order to reduce the

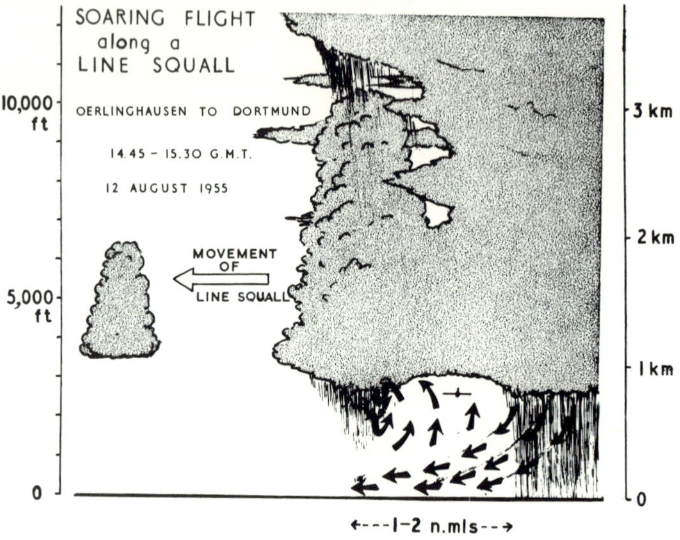

Fig. 14.6. Observations made by Hanna Reitsch suggest that the line squall she encountered was being displaced westwards by both movement and fresh development of convection cloud and rain in advance of the main storm system.

possibility of being cut off from visual flight conditions by this development, an attempt was made to fly the Zugvogel westwards to beyond the newly formed leading edge of the precipitating cloud, but such severe turbulence was encountered in the development zone that a return to the remarkably smooth flight conditions of the rain free channel was preferred. The strength of the continuous lift in this narrow channel may be gauged by the fact that a constant altitude could be maintained at soaring flight speeds of between 60 and 85 knots (120 and 170 km./hr.).

Tornadoes

With a mechanism somewhat similar to that of a dust devil, a tornado is a rotating funnel of cloud pointing downwards from a convection cloud. A tornado, however, has an additional source of energy in the form of the latent heat released during the condensation of water vapour in the ascending and rotating air. Therefore, this phenomenon is usually more vigorous and persistent than a dust devil.

The funnel cloud does not necessarily hang vertically from its parent cloud; it may be tilted or it may swing rather erratically below the main cloud base. It may or may not reach the ground and in some cases (especially at line squalls) several funnels may reach down from the same convection cloud.

The diameter of the tip of a funnel cloud may vary from several yards to a few hundred yards. The winds are very strong within and close to the funnel cloud and in extreme cases their speeds have been estimated* to be over 200 knots (400 km./hr.).

The passage of a tornado is often accompanied by a temporary but very sudden pressure drop whose magnitude is approximately 30 mbs. per 1,000 ft. height of the funnel cloud (10 mbs. per 100 m.). For example, if the tip of a funnel cloud is 1,500 ft. below the base of its parent cloud the pressure at the tip will be about 45 mbs. less than that at the same level outside the tornado. Thus as a tornado passes over a building the outside pressure drops so suddenly that the walls and the roofs are liable to be blown outwards unless doors and windows are left open to allow a freer flow of air.

Most tornadoes persist for only a few minutes but a "twister," as the Americans call it, maintains its identity for an hour or more and leaves a narrow trail of destruction along a path a hundred or even two hundred miles long.

In the British Isles destructive tornadoes appear to occur on an average of about once in two years and funnel clouds not reaching ground level are reported in meteorological literature several times a year. It is practically certain, however, that a number of funnel clouds are not brought to the notice of meteorologists and aviators. The majority of the British Isles tornadoes have occurred in the Midlands and have moved towards the north-north-east in slow

* No anemometer has survived the passage of a violent tornado.

Plate 15 FUNNEL CLOUD *C. S. Lowndes*

After extending from cloud base at 2600 ft. obliquely downwards to about 1300 ft. above ground level, this funnel cloud (tuba) developed close to the Dunstable site of the London Gliding Club on the afternoon of 12 October 1958. During the half an hour before the phenomenon gradually faded away several gliders flew in strong lift and in reasonable comfort close to the rapidly rotating funnel of cloud. J. Costin felt a violent jolt when he flew quickly through the tip of the funnel. Although this rapidly rotating vortex was only a mild species of tornado, winds at ground level were locally strong enough to damage a few farmyard buildings.

moving, unstable air masses on the forward side of a trough of low pressure. Conditions favourable for tornado development also include:

1 the presence of a cold front;

2 moist, unstable air from ground level up to a few thousand feet, capped by

3 a very shallow stable layer under a
4 deep and relatively dry, unstable layer of air.

Convection over the sea can also give rise to funnel clouds which often extend downwards to link up with spray whirled up from the sea surface. The resultant column of spray and cloud is called a *waterspout*.

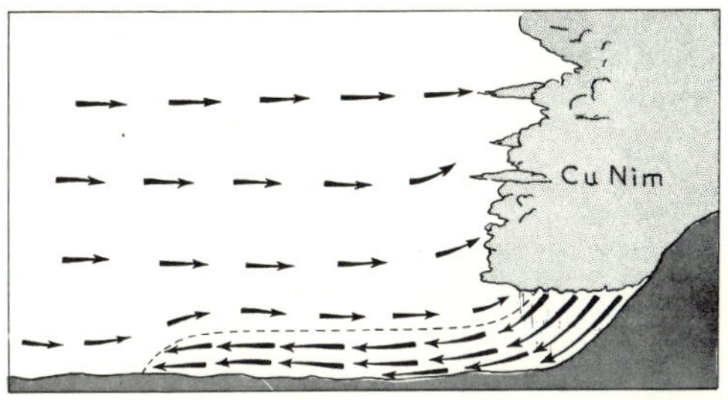

Fig. 14.7. The schematically illustrated spreading out of a downdraught and the associated low level wind shear at Madrid on 11 July 1952 is described in the text.

The spreading out of downdraughts

A low level wind gradient can be particularly dangerous when associated with the spreading out of a precipitation downdraught from a well developed cumulonimbus cloud, and the spreading out of such a downdraught is often extensive when the storm cloud is virtually anchored over a mountainside. Figure 14.7 illustrates the sharp wind shear which can exist between the light winds blowing towards a stationary cumulonimbus situated over a windward escarpment and the precipitation downdraught which flows down the mountainside and spreads out over the adjoining plain. On 11 July 1952, during the World Gliding Championships, the depth of this undercutting cold air was only about 120 ft. (40 m.) at Madrid (about 35 nautical miles from the mountains) and R. Ortner, who signified his completion of the day's task by swooping his Sky sailplane low over the airfield, suddenly found his airspeed rising from 75 to 110 knots (with alarming downward flexure of the Sky's wing tips) as he entered the shallow cold air. Another, and this time tragic, experience was that of a pilot whose two-seater glider stalled

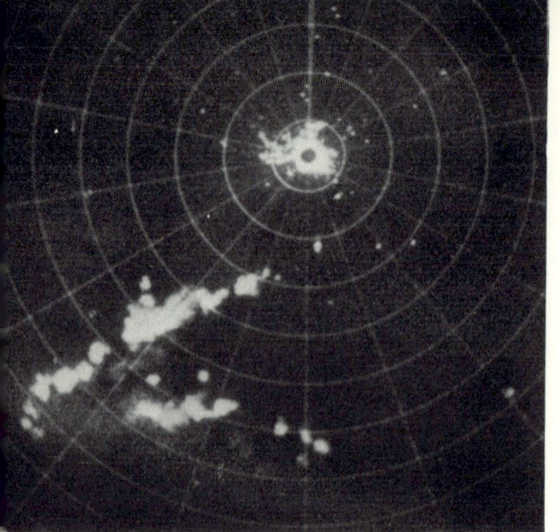

Plate 16

RADAR ECHOES FROM RAIN CLOUDS

Bright patches on the lower half of this radar picture are due to echoes from rain clouds at 1536 GMT on 18 June 1957. The circles, centred on a radar station near Dunstable, Bedfordshire, are range markers at 10-mile intervals. The corresponding map location of the rain echoes are sketched in Figure 14.3*b*, while Plate 13 shows storm clouds associated with the southern band of echoes.

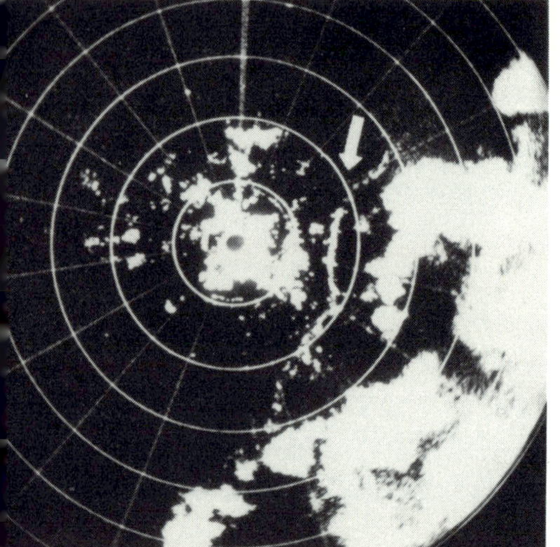

Plate 17

RADAR ECHOES FROM SWIFTS

Bright patches in the centre of this radar picture are due to reflections from buildings and other obstacles in the immediate vicinity of the radar station, but the larger echoes to the east and south-east are caused by heavy showers in a broad band moving from the east. This band was preceded by line squall effects which included the wedge-like advance of cold air at low levels. The thin line of echoes indicated by the arrow was due to the large number of swifts feeding on insects in the narrow belt of lift associated with the line squall effect. The range circles are at 10-mile intervals.

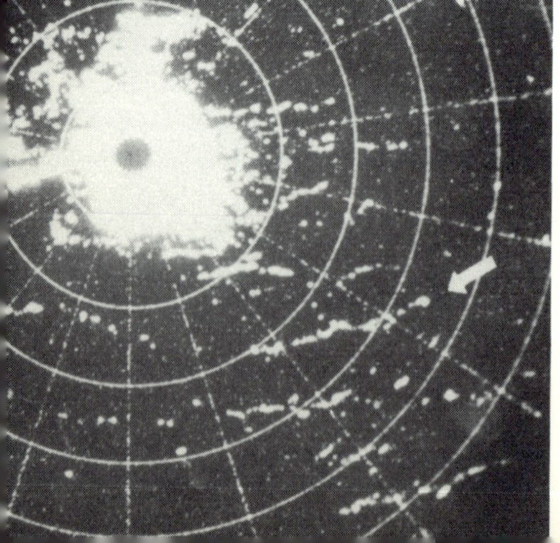

Plate 18

RADAR VIEW OF SWIFTS IN DRY THERMAL STREETS

On 12 July 1956 conditions over England were suitable for the formation of dry thermal streets. Swifts flying on food collection missions in these streets were revealed by the lines of radar echoes shown in the photographs. The range circles are at 10-mile intervals.

(These radar photographs were taken by Mr. W. G. Harper of the Meteorological Office and are reproduced with the kind permission of Her Majesty's Stationery Office.)

and crashed on descending into, and in the same direction as, the undercutting cold flow.

Since the extensive spreading out of such a precipitation down-draught may not be easily detectable from the air it is wise for ground crews or controllers to be alert for signs of the cold air and to try to communicate their observations by radio or signals to pilots flying in the locality.

Radar views of convection phenomena

Precipitation from convection cloud is usually detectable as a bright patch on the radar screen and by watching these echoes the progress of showers can be followed within a range of about 80 nautical miles from the radar apparatus. This radar picture is an extremely valuable aid to predicting the local likelihood of showers up to about two hours in advance but the speed of development and change of pattern of precipitation within the zones of convective activity make longer period forecasting difficult. The radar picture, nevertheless, provides a view of the precipitation pattern in considerably more detail than can normally be gleaned from routine synoptic charts; a short line squall conspicuous as a line of precipitation echoes on the radar screen may be indistinguishable from an isolated shower on the routine synoptic chart and the radar observer will often have a better overall view of the precipitation in a cluster of convection clouds than a pilot flying in or near the actual clouds.

Because the most commonly used "10 cm." radars detect precipitation and not cloud the radar screen does not give a comprehensive view of thermal activity. On some occasions, however, echoes are received from flights of birds who happen to be soaring or searching for insects in convective updraughts. Such echoes may be caused by swallows, martins or gulls but the swift is the most interesting radar indicator of organised thermal updraughts. British breeding swifts arrive on migration in early May and the young adults depart from late July to mid-August. The swifts seen in England in late August and September are thought to be birds moving southwards from Scandinavia. The most intensive aerial activity of swifts is in July when the young are in the nest, and must be fed throughout the daylight hours in good weather. Flying mainly between 20 and 100 ft. but occasionally as high as several thousand feet above ground, the adult swifts collect insects carried aloft by thermals and form these minute tit-bits into food balls in their throats. On a favourable day a single pair of swifts have been observed to make over 40 flights from their nest and collect 20,000 insects—in addition to their own food. Little wonder then that swifts exploit updraughts in sufficient numbers (especially after a few days with no food due to bad weather) to be detectable by radar. Thermal streets have been marked by echoes from swifts; in fact radar echoes in the form of lines or arcs just ahead of line squalls and clusters of thunderstorms puzzled radar operators until a telescope coupled with a radar scanner brought into view hundreds of swifts obviously hunting insects carried up in a very narrow belt of lift just ahead of a storm in a somewhat similar position to that located by Hanna Reitsch on her line squall flight already described. In some parts of Europe the noticeable association between the swift and thunderstorms has earned the bird the name of "thunder swallow." Obviously swifts cannot be relied upon to form a radar target for all occasions but these birds do occasionally provide the only radar indication of organised updraughts; with luck they can help the meteorologist to uncover some otherwise hidden features of convection and with even more luck they may reveal some of these features at opportune moments for gliding operations.

CHAPTER 15

Thermal Soaring Prospects

Before leaving the subject of convection it may be useful to extract from the last three chapters the main points to remember when considering thermal structure and thermal soaring prospects. We can note that:

1 Incipient thermals can be triggered off either by differential heating at ground level, or by the dynamical action of the wind, or possibly by slightly damp sources. Sun-facing slopes are particularly efficient thermal sources.

2 The best breeding conditions for thermals is a superadiabatic layer in which incipient thermals grow rapidly and often accelerate upwards. Pronounced instability produces both strong thermals and strong downdraughts, but even in comparatively tranquil conditions most of the incipient thermals are soon destroyed by turbulence, leaving relatively few to rise as "ideal" thermals into the adiabatic layer above.

3 This "ideal" thermal on which we can shape our ideas of thermal structure grows and becomes diluted by entrainment as it ascends in the adiabatic layer. With an internal motion resembling that of a vortex ring, this thermal virtually turns itself inside out and in doing so enables a glider to be soared in its lift for longer than would be possible if the thermal were simply an internally inert bubble of buoyant air.

4 A steady wind flow with little change of direction with height coupled with a fairly definite lid to the top of convection tends to organise the thermals into streets with downdraughts in between. The likelihood of thermal street development is enhanced if the wind speed has a maximum in the convective layer. A very pronounced wind shear, however, is likely to distort the thermal structure into chaotic forms difficult to use for thermal soaring.

5 On becoming saturated, thermals receive an upward boost especially if they enter an existing cloud. This boost will be even bigger if the cloud has a saturated superadiabatic temperature lapse rate.

6 Some turbulence and descent of air is likely at the sides (and especially the downshear side) of a convection cloud.

7 Cumulus cloud is liable to spread out to form large patches of stratocumulus when the humidity of its environment is high.

8 A decaying cumulus whose supply of thermals is cut off is likely to have a ragged base whereas a steady supply of thermals into a convection cloud will keep the base fairly well marked and probably flat, although there is no reason why a cumulus base should not be slightly concave or convex.

9 Damp air is slightly more buoyant than dry air at the same temperature and pressure. Therefore, thermals are not necessarily warmer than their environment.

10 The nature of the countryside, the state of the ground, wind, wind shear, the distribution of temperature and moisture with height, the intensity of sunshine, and the overall effects of changes in the larger scale weather conditions combine to produce an infinite number of subtle variations on the "ideal" thermal structure.

11 A common, but not always essential, prerequisite for shower development is that the convection cloud should extend to a height above the freezing level.

12 A well-developed convection cloud may persist even after the supply of thermals from ground level is cut off; the cloud can induce, and be maintained by, a horizontal inflow underneath its base.

13 The spreading out of a precipitation downdraught can produce a landing hazard in the form of low level wind changes.

Of course, this summary does not provide a simple unequivocal answer to the question: "Where and when will the next thermal appear?" But nature ensures that such an answer is not possible; if it were then thermal soaring would not be the intriguing sport it is.

Coherent, if somewhat flexible, ideas on convection allow the glider pilot to be more specific in his requests for meteorological advice, and it is appropriate to supplement our summary with notes on thermal soaring forecasts.

Forecasts for thermal soaring

To facilitate discussion we can classify forecasts for thermal soaring into three types, namely:

1 Casual forecasts—usually in the form of impromptu replies by a forecaster to telephone enquiries from glider pilots.
2 Routine gliding forecasts—issued by a meteorological office to a nearby gliding centre according to a mutually convenient schedule.
3 Special gliding forecasts—usually prepared at a meteorological office temporarily established for events such as gliding championships.

When making a casual enquiry the glider pilot should announce that he wishes to have a thermal soaring forecast for a specific place or region for a specified period of the day. Such vague questions as "Is it unstable today?" or "When will the cold front arrive?" are worse than useless as opening queries; the forecaster and the glider pilot are likely to differ unwittingly in their interpretations of the significance of such questions and their answers. The response to a specific question on thermal soaring prospects will vary according to circumstances; the forecaster may or may not be extremely busy fulfilling his routine forecasting commitments and, since the majority of these commitments do not entail more than elementary ideas of convection, he may not have studied the details relevant to the enquiry. He may know little or nothing about thermal soaring. (In his jargon, the word "thermal" relates to thermal wind charts rather than to convection currents.) However, the forecaster's initial reply usually reveals how prepared he is to give a comprehensive thermal soaring forecast, and it is for the pilot to judge what supplementary questions are necessary. Bearing in mind that forecasters usually have only limited time to deal with each casual enquiry, the pilot should try to obtain, either directly or by inference, the answers to the most appropriate, if not all, of the following questions:

1 *Will convection from ground level occur?*
2 *Will convection cloud form?*
3 *What will be the height* (above M.S.L. or ground level, whichever

is specified) *of the convection cloud base at various times of the day?* (There is a general tendency for both meteorological observers and forecasters to err on the low side when estimating or predicting the height of cumulus cloud base. The forecasting error usually arises from an underestimation of the effect of the mixing of the environment air with thermals between ground level and cloud base; when this part of the environment is dry compared to the ascending thermals mixing reduces the humidity of the thermals and thereby raises the condensation level. The observational error arises because the observer usually bases his estimations of convection cloud height on the appearance and movement of the clouds and for many years his main—and sometimes only—facility for checking these estimations have been cloud heights computed by the oversimplified forecasting method just mentioned. These errors are associated mainly with convection cloud inland at heights of 3,000 ft. and more above ground level, but in coastal districts the convection cloud base may occasionally be underestimated in damp unstable air-streams.)

4 *How much convection cloud will there be?* (The forecaster may not be aware that small amounts of cumulus cloud usually provide better cross-country thermal soaring conditions than abundant convection cloud which is likely to reduce the chances of bright sunshine.)

5 *Will the convection cloud spread out to form large patches of stratocumulus?* (If the humidity of the environment of the cumulus is high then occasional spreading out is likely.)

6 *How much medium or high cloud will there be to reduce the chances of bright sunshine?* (Weak, diffuse sunshine can be sufficiently intense to produce thermals active enough to form convection cloud but not strong enough to allow thermal soaring.)

7 *How high will the tops of the convection cloud reach?*

8 *What will be the height of the freezing level?*

9 *Are showers expected? If so, how frequently, and will they be of rain, hail, sleet or snow? Is thunder likely?* (Note that the forecast of the type of precipitation will normally refer to that likely at or near ground levels. A forecaster may not specify the risk of hail at higher levels unless asked to do so, and even then he may not be justified in giving a confident assessment of the risk.)

10 *Will the cloud base lower in showers?*

11 *Will there be dry thermals even if the convection cloud does not form? If so to what height will the dry thermals reach?* (In other words, to what height will insolation create a D.A.L.R.?)

12 *What will be the wind velocities at several levels in the convection layer?* (This information being required for navigation and to assess the likelihood of turbulent distortion of thermals.)

13 *Are thermal streams or streets likely to develop?*

14 *At about what time will active convection at low levels die out?* (Little forecasting experience has so far been built up around this question and, unless the synoptic situation reveals specific evidence to the contrary, the answer will usually suggest about 2–3 hours before sunset.)

15 *Are any regional convective phenomena such as line squalls or sea breeze fronts expected?*

16 *What will the visibility be?* (For navigation.)

17 *How will the large scale synoptic features such as approaching fronts or anticyclonic subsidence affect thermal soaring prospects for the place or region specified?*

Some gliding clubs arrange to collect (usually by telephone) gliding forecasts from a nearby meteorological office according to a mutually convenient schedule. Such an arrangement has several obvious advantages; prior to its inception the forecasters usually acquaint themselves with the nature of the particular forecasting problem, they can allot sufficient routine time to prepare the forecasts, they usually assess and try to improve their service and, with the forecasts available at the gliding club, there are fewer non-routine gliding enquiries to deal with.

At meteorological offices temporarily established for events such as gliding championships forecasts are usually derived from a careful watch on the local weather, temperature measurements on local flights, a detailed study of hourly observations within the area of operational interest and the broader scale analyses and forecasts issued by a central forecast office. Thus the forecaster on the spot is reasonably well equipped to give moderately detailed forecasts for thermal soaring for the day and he can present these forecasts at individual or mass briefings of the assembled glider pilots and the organisers of the daily events. In this country forecasters with experience in forecasting for gliding usually try to highlight the salient features of their thermal soaring forecasts without making unjustifiably precise predictions. Usually it is more justifiable (and useful to the glider pilot) to try to convey some idea of the overall "soarability" of the thermals than to make superficial predictions of the speed of thermal lift. This "soarability" is assessed as a tentative by-product of the forecast intensity of sunshine, depth of convection, wind shear, the observed state of the ground, the nature of the countryside and the current accounts of thermal soaring experiences.

CHAPTER 16

Lee Waves

Have you ever watched the ripples in a shallow brook as the water flows over a submerged rock? The water rises over the rock, dips sharply on the downstream side and, if the rock is in the form of a ridge placed across the stream, the water surface will rise and fall a second, third or several more times downstream. The crests of the ripples form a series of bars parallel to the rock and, with water flowing through them, these bars remain in almost stationary positions in the stream.

Substitute an airstream for the brook, a mountain for the rock and we begin to visualise the form of lee waves in the atmosphere. But before trying to visualise too much let us get a few basic features of wave flow fixed in our minds. These features are illustrated in Figure 16.1 by the airflow across a very long isolated mountain ridge lying at right angles to the airstream. Of course, mountain ridges do not always happen to be at right angles to the wind direction; they are often short rather than very long; they are seldom isolated from other mountains, and they rarely have the smooth symmetrical profile shown in this illustration. But we can consider more complicated shapes later. First the basic features and the terminology used to describe them.

The flow pattern may be dissected into three zones. The first zone contains the undisturbed flow—too far upstream to be diverted far from its steady horizontal course. Then comes the mountain sector wherein the streamlines at low levels tend to follow the high ground profile, and finally we have the lee wave flow with its regular undulating stream bearing little apparent relationship to the flat terrain below.

It is this lee wave flow that merits detailed discussion and the two dimensions most appropriate to such discussion are wavelength and amplitude.

The lee wavelength is a measure of the distance from one wave crest to the next—or from trough to trough. Usually between 2 and 20 nautical miles, this lee wavelength is determined almost entirely by

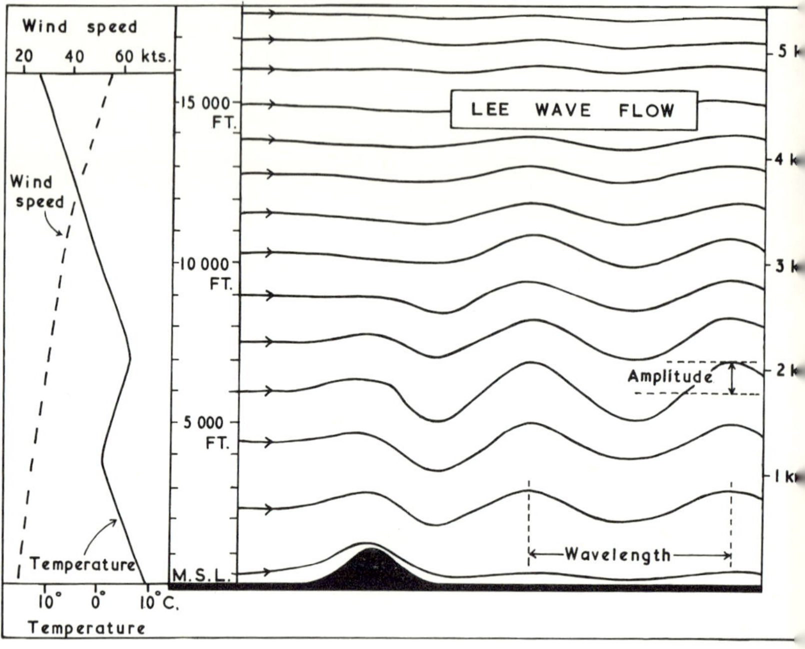

Fig. 16.1. In lee wave flow the air usually dips sharply down in lee of a hill ridge before undulating up and down for some considerable distance downstream. The wavelength of the lee waves is determined entirely by wind and temperature conditions in the upstream flow while the lee wave amplitude depends on both airstream conditions and the size, shape and surface nature of the ridge.
Lee waves are often associated with a stable layer sandwiched between air of lesser stability together with an increase with height of wind components across the ridge.

winds and temperatures at various levels in the undisturbed flow. It is not normally the same as the distance between the summit of the ridge and the first lee wave crest.

The lee wave amplitude is half the vertical distance from wave trough to crest. Notice that the amplitude varies with height. Negligible close to the ground and at very high levels, it attains a maximum at about 6,000 ft. in the illustration of Figure 16.1. The streamline at this level in the undisturbed, upstream flow is displaced from 1,000 ft. below to 1,000 ft. above this level in the lee wave part of the stream, i.e. the lee wave amplitude is 1,000 ft. at the 6,000 ft. level.

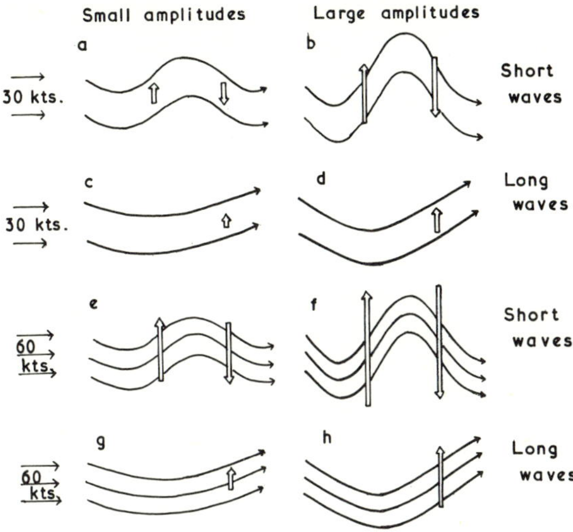

Fig. 16.2. Vertical currents (represented by the broad arrows) in wave flow depend upon the wavelength, the wave amplitude and the wind speed through the waves. Strong up- and downdraughts are favoured by large amplitudes, short wavelengths and strong winds.

Either one or both of these dimensions are bound up with almost every feature of wave flow to be discussed.

Vertical currents in the wave flow depend on the amplitude, the wavelength and the wind speed. As shown in Figure 16.2, strong up- and downdraughts are favoured by:

1 large amplitudes—the larger the amplitude the farther the air moves up and down;
2 short wavelengths—the shorter the wavelength the steeper the ascents and descents in the undulating airflow;
3 strong winds—the stronger the wind the faster the air moves through the wave pattern.

The distribution of vertical speed throughout a wave flow is illustrated in Figure 16.3.

The lee wave flow illustrated was evidenced by variations in the rate of ascent of a radio-sonde balloon released from Leuchars on 21 December 1953, and the detailed structure of this flow was calculated approximately on an experimental but justifiable theoretical basis. In this particular flow it is apparent that a glider

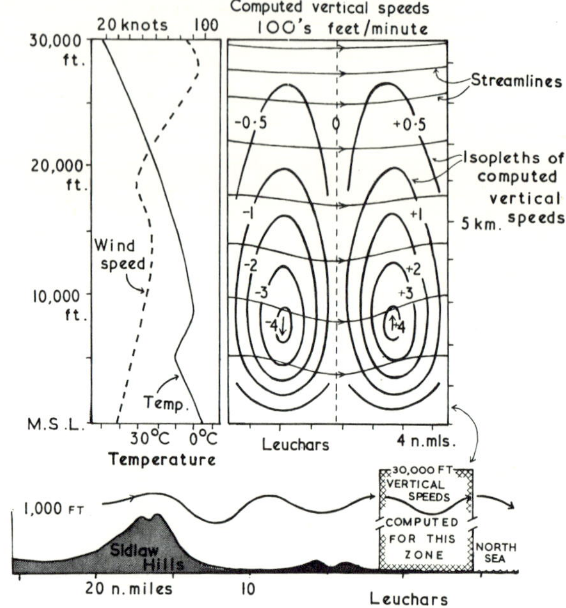

Fig. 16.3. On 21 December 1953 waves were evident in lee of the Sidlaw Hills, Scotland. Vertical speeds in the neighbourhood of Leuchars were calculated approximately on an experimental but justifiable theoretical basis. Wind direction was approximately 290 degrees at all heights.

with a minimum sinking speed of, say, 180 ft./min. (about 60 m./min.) could have maintained or gained height in the updraught of the wave between 3,000 and 17,000 ft. Above and below this height interval the vertical wave currents were too small for soaring.

The egg-like structure representing vertical speeds is characteristic of many a lee wave flow. Of course, details vary from one wave situation to another but it is useful to have the basic pattern in mind.

Wave cloud is another phenomenon linked closely to lee wave amplitude. Air rising in the updraught of a wave cools adiabatically, and if this cooling is sufficient to cause condensation then cloud will form. Subsequent warming in the downdraught causes the

Plate 19 LEE WAVE CLOUDS *P. Lane*

The view towards the west-south-west from R.A.F. Leeming, Yorks, showed a series of wave clouds in lee of the Pennines in the late afternoon of 19 April 1958. The wind at 2,000 ft. was 250 deg. 25–30 knots. The smooth bars of wave cloud lying across the wind were between 8,000 and 12,000 ft. while the relatively ragged patches of wave cloud between 3,000 and 5,000 ft. indicated the tendency for rotor flow to develop at low levels.
(*Reproduced by courtesy of H.M.S.O.*)

condensed water to evaporate and so by a continuous process of condensation at its leading edge and evaporation at the trailing edge the cloud as a whole appears to be stationary in the sky. As illustrated in Figure 16.4, wave cloud owes its existence to two principal factors: the wave amplitude and the humidity of the air before it enters the wave flow. Because condensation of water vapour in the atmosphere is a very rapid process the formation of wave cloud does not depend upon the speed of the vertical currents. Therefore the only certain fact implied by the presence of a wave cloud is that near the level of the cloud the wave amplitude is big enough to lift the air to its condensation level. This in turn indicates anything from small amplitude undulations in humid air to large amplitude waves with low humidity, and remembering that the vertical currents are dependent not only on the amplitude but also on the wavelength and wind speed it becomes apparent that a wave cloud is not an absolutely

Plate 20 WAVE CLOUD IN SICILY *R. K. Pilsbury*

This wave cloud in the vicinity of Taormina, Sicily, shows a small scale globular form of cloud at its trailing edge. A westerly wind was blowing (from right to left in this photograph) at the time.

sure sign of strong updraughts. Nor does it indicate the level at which the waves are most pronounced. An airstream with, say, strong waves but low humidity at 6,000 ft. and weak waves in moist air at 10,000 ft. may have wave cloud at the upper level but no visible signs of the stronger waves below.

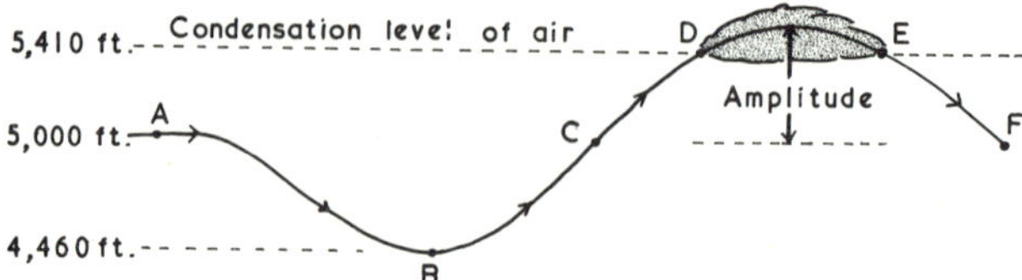

Fig. 16.4. By a continuous process of condensation at its leading edge and evaporation at the trailing edge, the wave cloud as a whole appears to be almost stationary in the sky. In this particular illustration the state of the air at several points along the streamline are as follows:

Position	*A, C and F*	*B*	*D and E*
Pressure	850 mbs.	867 mbs.	837 mbs.
Temperature	5° C.	6·6° C.	3·8° C.
Dewpoint	4° C.	4·2° C.	3·8° C.
Water vapour content	6 gm./kg.	6 gm./kg.	6 gm./kg.
Relative humidity	94%	85%	100%

Humidity can and often does vary considerably with height; some of the more detailed variations can occasionally be deduced from the shapes of isolated wave clouds. In Figure 16.5*b*, for example,

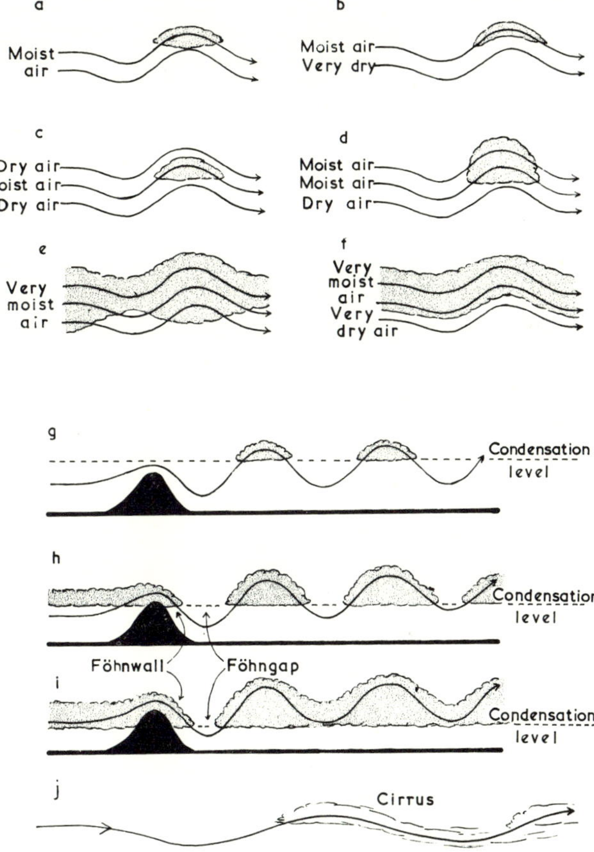

Fig. 16.5. The shape of the wave cloud depends not only upon the streamlines but also on the vertical variation of humidity.
Quite often the streamlines reach their lowest levels in the Foehngap, so that when the cloud base is low this stationary gap in the clouds may be a better indicator of wave flow than the shape of the wave cloud itself, which, as in *i*, may have a deceptively flat base.
Because ice crystals form quickly but evaporate slowly, wave cloud at high levels tends to stretch out some way downstream, as illustrated in *j*.

the concave base of the lenticular cloud denotes an abrupt increase of humidity with height, while a convex base betrays a more gradual vertical variation of humidity. Figures 16.5*c* and *d* show that the streamlines are as steep as the cloud face only when the humidity decreases sharply just above the wave cloud level.

The lenticular (lens shaped) form of wave cloud is most commonly observed at medium levels—between 6,000 ft. (2,000 m.) and 20,000 ft. (6,000 m.) in temperate regions. At lower levels the wave cloud is often torn into ragged patches by low level turbulence. The patches as a whole remain more or less stationary but their detailed outline changes quickly and erratically.

At high levels cloud is usually composed of ice crystals and because these crystals form quickly but evaporate slowly high level wave cloud forms readily in the updraught of a wave but does not always disappear on the descent; it tends to stretch out some way downstream.

Wave conditions

Another way of dissecting the airflow across a ridge is to regard it as a lee wave pattern, typified by the streamline in Figure 16.6*a*, superimposed on the more common type of flow depicted in Figure 16.6*b*. The main problem in planning to soar in waves is that of deciding whether or not the lee wave part of the flow can exist in

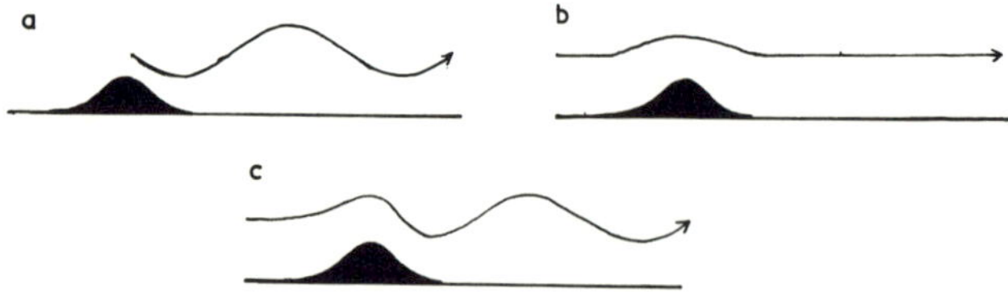

Fig. 16.6. Wave flow may be considered as a flow typified by the streamline in *a* superimposed on the more common flow depicted in *b*. The result is illustrated by *c*.

the prevailing or predicted atmospheric conditions. Experience suggests that the conditions favourable for waves with appreciable vertical currents comprise:

1 a layer of low stability (high lapse rate) at low levels,

2 a stable layer (e.g. isothermal layer or inversion) above the lower layer, and

3 an upper layer of low stability in the troposphere.

Supplementary conditions are that the geostrophic wind, or wind at about 1,500 ft. (500 m.), should be at least 15 knots across whatever mountain ridge is being considered and that the wind

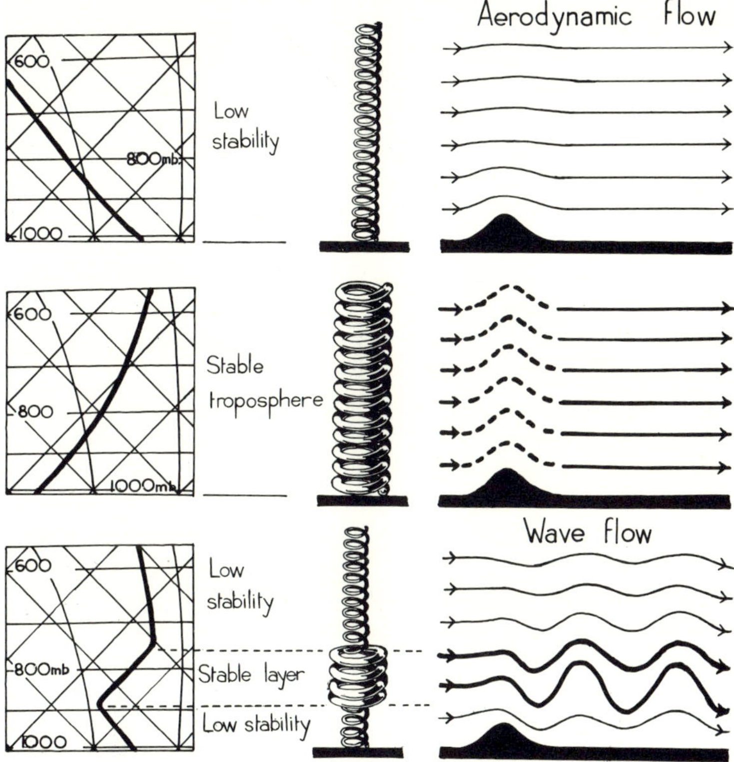

Fig. 16.7. The atmosphere may be likened to a vertical coiled spring. An unstable airstream can be compared with a weak, flimsy spring because it offers little resistance to vertical motion within it, and a stable atmosphere can be likened to a tough, heavy spring which tends to suppress internal vertical motion. The best structure for persistent oscillation is a sandwich of a few strong coils between two weaker springs.

direction should be almost constant with height up to the top of the stable layer. These conditions are illustrated in the left-hand sides of Figures 16.1 and 16.3.

To understand why stable air sandwiched between two layers of lesser stability favours the formation of significant lee waves it may be helpful to resort to an analogy. The atmosphere may be likened to a vertical, coiled spring. An unstable airstream can be compared with a weak, flimsy spring because it offers little resistance to vertical motion within it, and a stable atmosphere can be likened to a tough, heavy spring which tends to suppress internal vertical motion. With the aid of Figure 16.7 it is not difficult to imagine that although the lower coils of the flimsy spring would move easily up and over a mountain ridge the jolt received at ground level would not be transmitted far upwards. Nor would it stretch the imagination too far to suppose that if the heavy spring were forced over a ridge it would be too tough for oscillations to be set up.

But consider now a few strong coils sandwiched between two weaker springs—as depicted in the lowest section of Figure 16.7. With this arrangement it is conceivable that the tough coils will continue to bounce up and down for some time after the structure has crossed a mountain ridge.

The atmosphere works in a somewhat similar fashion. Neither a completely unstable nor a uniformly stable airstream can produce appreciable lee waves but a stream containing stable air between layers of lesser stability is both flexible enough to be set in vertical motion and resilient enough to maintain this motion as a series of vertical oscillations.

The spring analogy has many flaws and we must be cautious in drawing conclusions from it. Nevertheless it does illustrate several features of lee wave flow. Considering Figure 16.7, for example, it seems reasonable to suppose that the heavy coils dominate the leeward oscillations, and indeed lee waves in the atmosphere usually do have their maximum amplitude in the stable layer which contributes so much to their existence. (See Figures 16.1 and 16.3.)

The amplitude and the frequency with which the coils bounce up and down is related in some close but complicated way to the precise depth and resilience of each part of the spring and the lee wavelength is determined by the speed with which these vertical oscillations are propelled downstream. It should be no surprise, therefore, to learn that lee wavelength and amplitude in the atmosphere are determined by the winds and temperatures at various levels in the undisturbed flow. Out of the intricate relationships between winds, temperatures, lee wavelength and amplitude, two deductions which emerge as useful though not infallible supplements to the wave flow conditions already listed are that:

1 the stable layer associated with the wave flow produces larger amplitudes when it comprises a shallow layer of great stability than when only moderate stability extends over some considerable depth;

2 long waves are associated more with strong upper winds than with light winds aloft.

Diurnal variation of lee waves

In the neighbourhood of Cross Fell in the Pennines the local folk assert that "the bar never crosses the Eden," and if you appeared no wiser for this odd piece of information they would explain that the bar refers to a cigar shaped cloud (the Helm bar) sometimes observed downwind of and parallel to the steep escarpment of Cross Fell, and that the Eden is the river in the leeward valley. During the mornings the bar usually moves slowly downwind, towards the south-west, but later in the day, just as the cloud seems about to cross the river, it apparently changes its mind and retreats back towards the escarpment. Thus "the bar never crosses the Eden," or translating the story into meteorological English: there is a tendency for lee wavelengths to increase during the morning and decrease during the late afternoon. An explanation of this diurnal effect starts with insolation, or heat from the sun, which warms the ground, which warms the air at low levels. Any low level inversion present is reduced in depth, or even eaten away, by the convection set up, and it is one of the intricate relationships between temperature and wavelength that links such a reduction with an increase in wavelength. In a complementary manner the subsequent decrease in wavelength stems from the low level cooling which occurs in the late afternoons and evenings of fairly clear days.

Lee wave amplitude is also affected by diurnal heating and cooling. Its variation is such that, in the British Isles,* the wave history of many a day can be classified into three periods:

Early morning in which a sudden and quite early onset of wave flow is often followed by good wave soaring conditions at their best between about one and three hours after sunrise.

The middle of the day is the least likely period for soarable waves. Waves are suppressed or even obliterated by convection.

* The variation being described does not apply to regions where diurnal heating is more intense; in the Owens Valley, California, heating tends to increase the lee wave amplitude in the mid-afternoon.

Late afternoon and evening. Increasing amplitude and a shortening of lee wavelength combine to produce appreciable vertical currents which are often at their strongest from about one to three hours before sunset. If a 15-knot gradient wind is maintained the wave flow may persist until well after dark, but there is a tendency for the wave amplitude to decrease again and when it does so the collapse is often sudden.

Although these diurnal effects are important they play only a subsidiary rôle in the creation of lee wave conditions. It is the synoptic situation that can provide the upper wind and temperature conditions suitable for wave flow. The diurnal heating and cooling, which is itself under partial control of the synoptic situation, superimposes significant but not necessarily dominant variations on these conditions.

Synoptic situations

A synoptic situation favourable for lee waves is simply one in which the airstream conditions required for wave flow are satisfied in the locality being considered. These conditions can be fulfilled in a variety of ways.

Warm sectors over the British Isles often include fresh west to south-west winds whose variation with height shows an increase in speed but little or no change in direction. The well stirred air at low levels usually has little stability from ground level up to between 2,000 and 6,000 ft., and above this layer the stability increases sharply before falling off with height. So warm sectors are likely to promote many a wave flow in lee of mountain ridges whose axes lie across the flow. But it is unlikely that these waves are fully exploited; warm sectors often bring a complete cover of low cloud which not only conceals its own wave top from the observers below cloud but may also mask the hill tops with drizzle and fog.

Anticyclones with their subsidence aloft usually have a temperature structure made to measure for lee waves; a shallow, extremely stable layer centred somewhere between 4,000 and 10,000 ft. is a common feature of high pressure systems in temperate regions. But the centre of an anticyclone also features light and variable winds, so that to locate the wave flow conditions we must search towards the outer fringes—far enough from the centre to pick up winds of 15 knots or more, but not so far that the stabilizing effect of subsidence is lost.

Warm fronts are often preceded by wind and temperature conditions which, for limited spells during the pre-frontal changes, are suitable for wave flow. The nature of this wave flow ahead of a

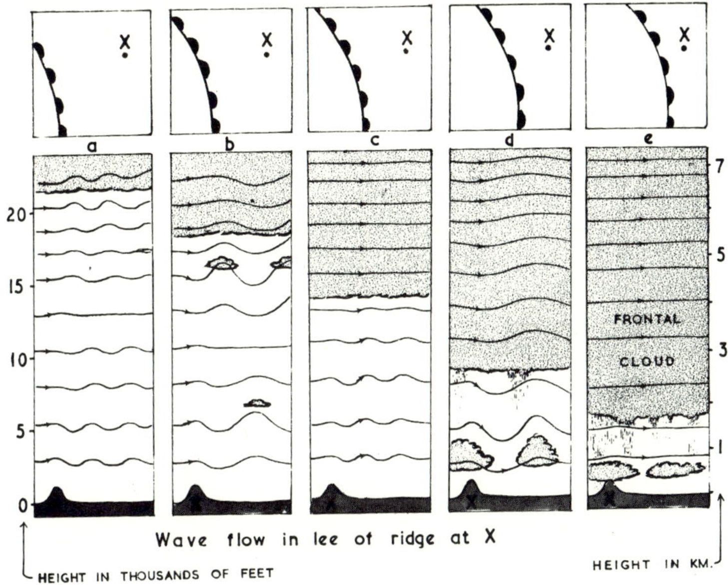

Fig. 16.8. During the approach of a warm front there occur one, two or possibly three spells during which the steadily changing winds and temperatures aloft favour the formation of soarable waves. In this illustration there are two soarable spells, depicted in *b* and *d*.

well marked warm front is illustrated by the sequence of events depicted in Figure 16.8.

The approach of the warm front is accompanied by increasing and lowering cloud and also by changes in the upper winds and temperatures. In practice it is impossible to reason out precisely where or when the airstream conditions will be suitable for wave flow. However, experience and lengthy calculations suggest that some distance ahead of the front (16.8*a*) there are likely to be rather short waves of only mediocre amplitudes, and in noting the effective heights of these waves we meet a new phenomenon—a wave which has amplitude maxima at two distinct levels. Between these levels lies a *nodal surface*, that is a level surface which appears to divide the wave flow above and below it into two separate parts.

Although waves at this distance ahead of the warm front would probably be too weak for soaring they may well show themselves in the form of wave cloud at high or medium cloud levels. And such signs as this may portend better waves to come, for as the front approaches both the wavelength and amplitude of the waves increase and their most effective level descends, so that from about 12 to 18 hours before the front is due the waves may be strong enough for soaring. The end of this spell comes suddenly and is followed by a period of short, scarcely detectable waves (16.8*c*). But once again the wavelength and amplitude gradually increase and between about 100 and 300 miles ahead of the front waves are soarable again (16.8*d*) before a second sudden collapse.

Of course, no two warm fronts are exactly alike and it is not feasible to formulate simple, practical rules relating wavelengths and amplitudes to such factors as the height of the frontal cloud or its speed of movement. All we can do in practice is to be aware that during the approach of a warm front there occur one, two or perhaps three spells during which the steadily changing winds and temperatures favour the formation of significant waves. We cannot predict with any precision when the waves will occur, how long they will last, or just how soarable they will be. But even a knowledge of only the nature of the changes likely can help us to seize more of whatever opportunities arise for wave soaring ahead of warm fronts.

Hill shape and size

Two requirements are needed for waves to form: the wind and temperature conditions of the airstream must be suitable for wave flow and there must be a hill to trigger off the actual waves.* The amplitude of the waves depends partly on the airstream conditions and partly on the size and shape of the hill. If an airstream suitable for waves crossed the three ridges depicted in Figure 16.9*a*, *b* and *c* we should find that although the ridges are of equal height they do not set off waves of equal amplitude. In this particular illustration the width of the ridge producing the best waves happens to be approximately equal to two-thirds of the wavelength of the lee waves.

* Horizontal temperature gradients may also set off waves but observations to date suggest that vertical currents in such waves are usually too weak for soaring.

The jolt received by the airstream in passing over the narrow ridge is not nearly so effective in setting off waves. Nor does the gentle ascent and descent of air over the wider ridge lead to large amplitudes. There is in fact a sort of resonance effect between lee wavelength and hill width. It is not an effect which can be easily formulated and all we can do is to appreciate that short waves are set off best by narrow ridges and long waves are at their best over broader mountains. A corollary from this is that large mountains are not necessarily better than small hills for setting off waves. In the illustration of Figures 16.9*d* and *e*, for example, the larger ridge produces only

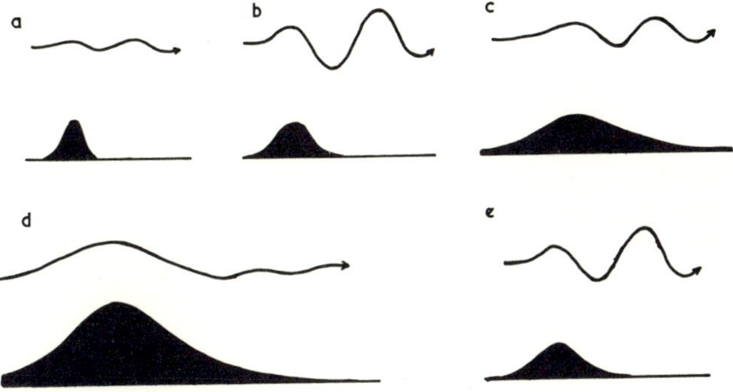

Fig. 16.9. Of the three hill profiles sketched in *a*, *b* and *c* the middle ridge has the best width for setting off lee waves of the particular wavelength illustrated. A big mountain, *d*, whose width is large compared with the lee wavelength does not necessarily trigger off bigger waves than a smaller ridge, *e*.

feeble waves because its width is much too great for resonance with the lee wavelength.

A symmetrically shaped ridge, such as those so far described, has its best wave lift about one-half of a wavelength downwind of the summit of the ridge, but for asymmetrical ridges with relatively gentle upwind slopes such as that sketched in Figure 16.10*b* the best lift is closer to the lee slope of the mountainside. This type of ridge, with its relatively steep lee escarpment, appears to be particularly favourable for setting off soarable lee waves.

When an airstream suitable for lee waves flows past two ridges in succession the eventual amplitude of the waves depends on whether or not the ridges are in or out of phase with each other for the prevailing lee wavelength. If the distance between the ridges is equal to, say, one, two or three wavelengths then the lee waves from the first ridge will be reinforced by those of the second ridge. As shown in Figure 16.11*a*, the net result will be lee waves of larger amplitude than that due to each ridge by itself. If, on the other hand, the ridges

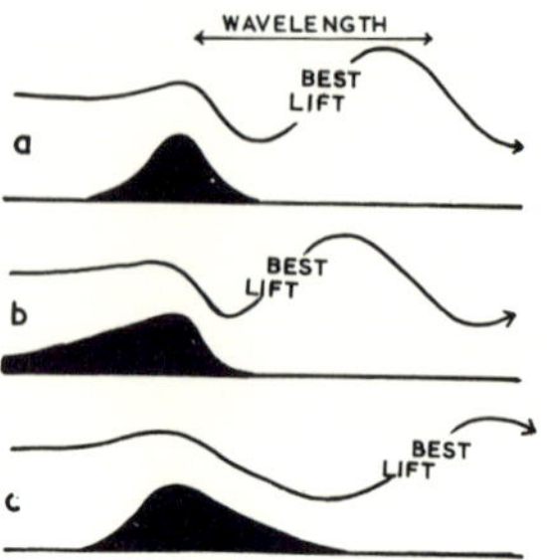

Fig. 16.10. A symmetrically shaped ridge, *a*, has its best wave lift about one-half of a wavelength downwind of the summit of the ridge, but for an asymmetrical ridge, *b*, with a gentle windward slope leading to a steep lee escarpment the best lift is closer to the lee slope of the mountainside.

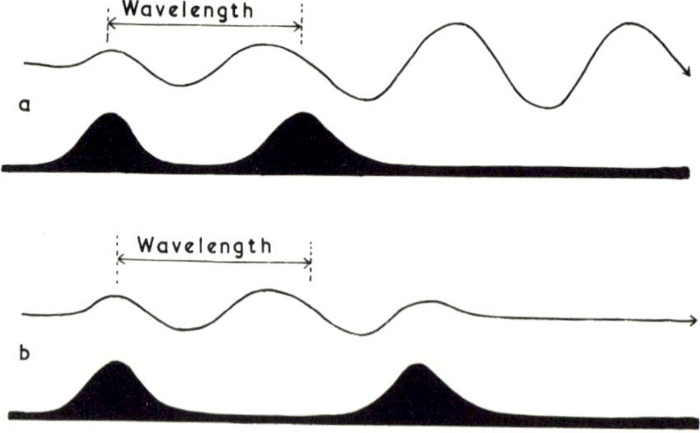

Fig. 16.11. When two ridges are in phase for the lee wavelength in force the second ridge in the flow augments the lee waves due to the upstream hill, as in *a*. If, on the other hand, the ridges are out of phase, as in *b*, the second ridge will tend to cancel out the lee waves set off by the upstream hill.

are out of phase, say one and a half wavelengths apart, as in Figure 16.11*b*, then the second ridge will tend to cancel out the lee waves set off by the upstream hill. In such a situation as this the lee wave flow may well augment the hill lift in front of the second ridge but there would be no soarable train of lee waves farther downstream. An example of this effect occurred in one of the lee wave investigations made in the neighbourhood of the Sierra Nevada, a Rocky Mountain range in California, U.S.A. On 1 April 1955 a westerly airstream blowing across this 14,000 ft. mountain range produced lee waves over the Owens Valley. (See Figure 16.12.) An aircraft used in the investigations was flown through the wave system at 20,000 ft. and from temperature measurements made during flight it was possible

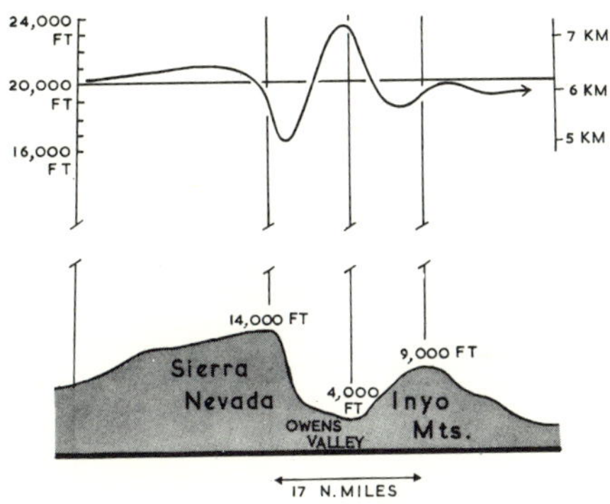

Fig. 16.12. On 1 April 1955 the lee wave flow over the Owens Valley, California, started with a descent immediately to the lee of the Sierra Nevada then passed through one and a half wavelengths before being practically cancelled out by the out-of-phase effect of the Inyo Mountains. The streamline drawn was deduced from temperature measurements made during a flight through the waves.

to deduce the approximate form of the streamlines at about this 20,000 ft. level. This is illustrated in Figure 16.12. Notice how the wave starts with a descent immediately to the lee of the Sierra Nevada and goes through one and a half wavelengths before reaching the Inyo Mountains where it is practically cancelled out by the lee wave effect of this second range of mountains.

Another example of a phase difference between a lee wave flow and a ridge was noted by R. D. Roper on 8 June 1950 at Camphill, the site of the Derby and Lancs Gliding Club. His observations, illustrated in Figure 16.13, showed a retrogression upwind of the wave flow after 1830 GMT. By 1930 GMT the distribution of lift and haze revealed the updraught of the wave flow due to upwind hills to be well away from Bradwell Edge (the steep escarpment which forms the western boundary of the flying field). Thus although wave soaring was possible for gliders already in the waves there was no hill lift close to the escarpment itself.

Because the lee wave effects of successive ridges are additive even

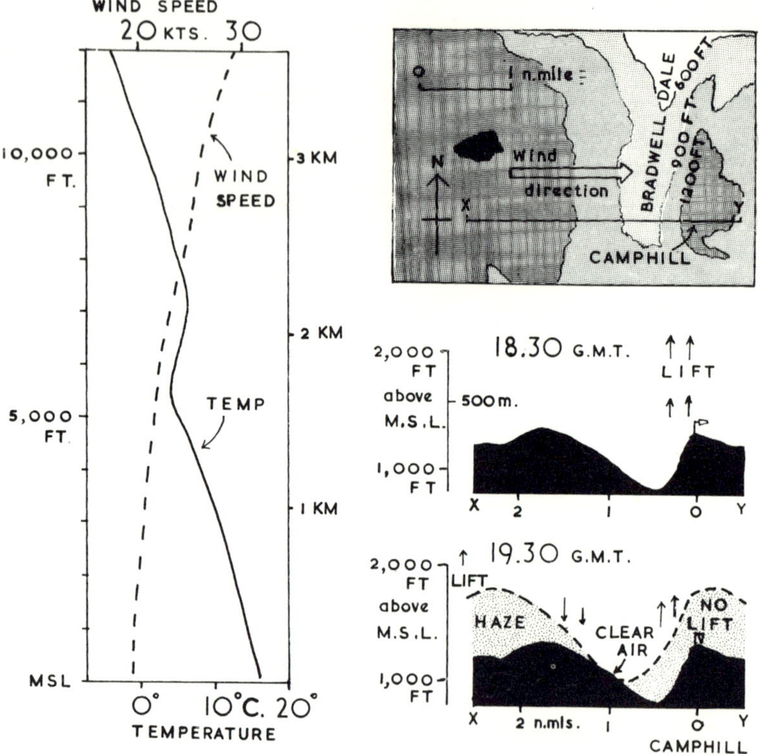

Fig. 16.13. A slowly changing lee wavelength on the evening of 8 June 1950 shifted the wave flow westwards. By 1930 GMT the flow appeared to dip down, to clear the haze from a strip of the windward slope of Bradwell Dale, then rise again west of Bradwell Edge, leaving the wind sock at Camphill limp and lifeless. Although soaring was possible for gliders already in the waves there was no hill lift close to Bradwell Edge itself at 1930 GMT. The wind speed and temperature structure of the airstream is shown on the left.

slow changes of lee wavelength can lead to rapid fluctuations in the resultant flow as the lee waves from various ridges are brought in or out of phase with one another. Figure 16.14 shows some of the variety of forms a lee wave flow can take over rugged terrain. In

Figure 16.14*a*, depicting a flow without lee waves, the most noticeable characteristic is that the orographic cloud is confined to caps right over the mountain peaks themselves. The three other illustrations are schematic sketches of the flow for the indicated wavelengths.

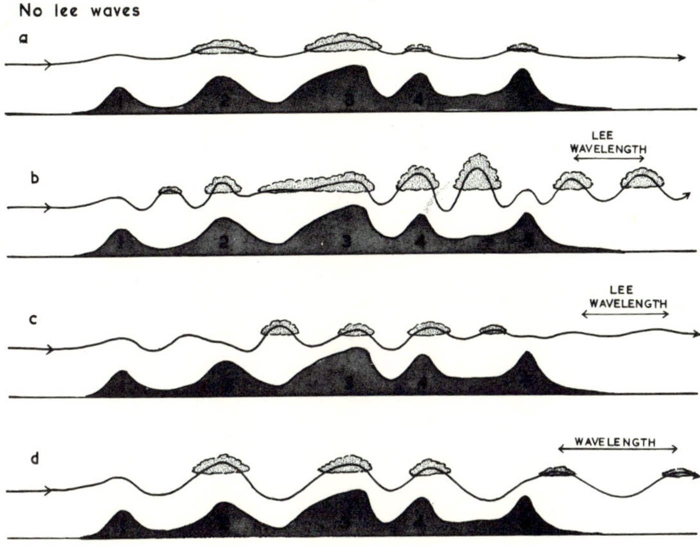

Fig. 16.14. Schematic sketches of the flow over rugged terrain for no lee waves and for the indicated wavelengths. In a flow without lee waves the orographic cloud is confined to caps right over the mountain peaks themselves. The combined resonance and phase effects of the five principal ridges complicate the flow over the mountains themselves; the simple sinusoidal lee wave flow is not apparent until the flow reaches the flat ground.

To the windward of hill 1 the stream is not affected by the lee flow, while immediately downstream of this hill the lee wave flow is not complicated by phase effects so wave lift here is not subject to such fluctuations as must be expected farther downstream among the hills. The waves from hill 2 are out of phase with those from the first hill in 16.14*b* so that although hill 2 is capped by cloud there are no waves over its leeward valley. Hill 3 is the dominant feature of this terrain. It has a steep leeward slope which means that the wave flow turns upwards into the region of best lift not far downstream—before the flow is further distorted by hill 4. And, being broad, hill 3 is particularly suitable for long wavelengths; it may even set off long waves of sufficient amplitude to swamp the out-of-phase effect of hill 4 (Figure 16.14*d*).

The regular sinusoidal form of the lee wave flow is not apparent until the airstream reaches level ground in the lee of the mountainous terrain and in this set of illustrations we see that the short wavelength produces a well marked train of waves; the medium wavelength is not quite suitable for the particular series of ridges illustrated, but a wave train appears again for the long lee wavelength.

Three-dimensional hills

When describing the principal features of lee wave flow it is usually convenient to refer to the flow past two-dimensional ridges; that is, ridges which can be considered as extremely long prisms placed across the airflow. But what about the airflow past real hills and mountains of motley shapes? That's an awkward question. It is practically impossible to observe, calculate or guess the precise effect on an airflow of each spur, peak, knoll or butte of a mountain range. Investigations have, however, revealed that whereas a long straight ridge can set off a train of lee waves extending some considerable distance downstream, a short ridge produces waves whose amplitude decreases rather quickly downwind. The longer the ridge the more lee wave clouds there are (provided, of course, that the lee waves are not cancelled out by some out-of-phase downstream ridge). There is no golden rule relating the length of the ridge to the downwind extent of the lee wave train. Even a ridge of only a few miles in length can set off a long train of waves; but it is often difficult to decide whether or not a ridge can be described as long.

A straight ridge lying obliquely across the airflow produces lee waves parallel to itself—and not at right angles to wind direction. But such waves are usually of small amplitude and seldom extend far downstream.

Compared to long ridges conical hills are poor generators of lee waves, but single stationary clouds, sometimes saucer shaped, sometimes in the form of a crescent, have been observed in the lee of very large conical mountains, such as Mount Fuji in Japan.

Turbulence and eddies

Flight conditions in lee waves are often remarkably smooth; a conspicuous absence of turbulent or eddying motion in the airstream is sometimes the first indication to a pilot that he has flown into a wave flow. But lee wave conditions can also produce some of the most violent turbulence likely to be encountered in the troposphere.

Turbulence in wave flow is usually the combined effect of wind

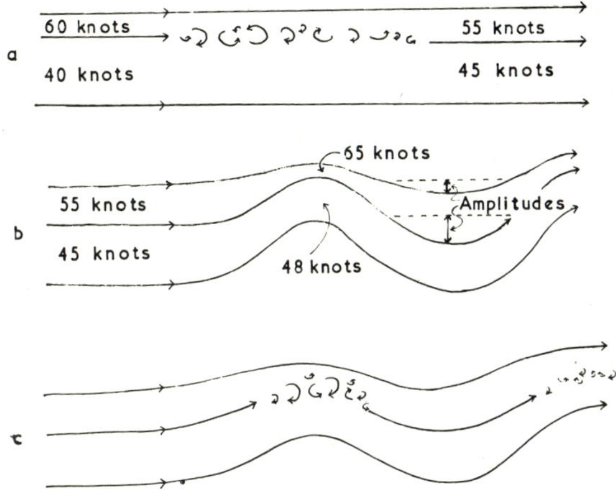

Fig. 16.15. Turbulence due to wind shear reduces the wind shear itself unless there is some mechanism to maintain the shear *a*. One such mechanism involves the variation with height of wave amplitude and wind speed. A situation of the type *b* is likely to produce turbulence in the wave crests, as in *c*.

shear and vertical variation in lee wave amplitude. Suppose that a wind shear takes the form of an increase in wind speed with height, as depicted in Figure 16.15*a* by the 40 and 60 knot winds blowing in two adjacent layers. Between these two layers there will be a sort of friction which will tend to introduce turbulence and eddies into the basic horizontal flow. This tendency for turbulence will be opposed by the stability of the airstream—high stability, as in an inversion for instance, suppresses small scale turbulent motion. But even if the initial frictional effect is large enough to overcome the stability then the ensuing turbulent motion will reduce the wind shear by transferring momentum from one layer to another until the frictional effect is just not large enough to produce more turbulence. The final state will be a smooth airflow with reduced wind shear. So for wind shear turbulence to persist in the atmosphere there must be some process in operation which maintains the wind shear despite the effect of the turbulence itself. One such process involves the variation with height of wave amplitude. Suppose that

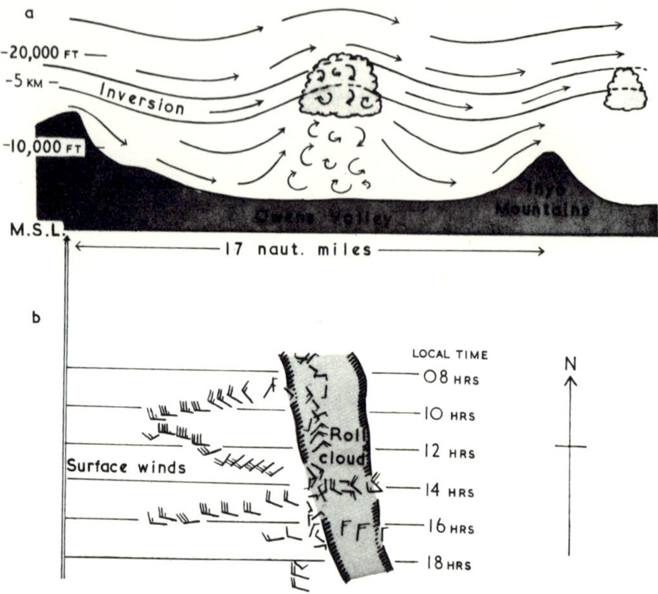

Fig. 16.16. The *rotor flow* in lee of the Sierra Nevada on 18 March 1955 included a turbulent *roll cloud.*
Surface winds were recorded throughout the day at several stations in an approximately east–west line across the Owens Valley, and by a mobile observing unit travelling almost along this line. These wind observations are plotted against time in the lower half (*b*) of the figure. Each full feather of the wind arrows represents a speed of 10 knots.

the wave amplitude decreases with height in the same region that the wind speed increases upwards, as in the illustration of Figure 16.15*b*. Noting that these streamlines are drawn so that the wind speed is inversely proportional to their distance apart, we see that the wind shear is increased in the wave crests. This increase in wind shear may well be just enough to produce turbulence in the wave crests as indicated in Figure 16.15*c*. Furthermore such turbulence as this can persist because the necessary wind shear will be maintained by the prevailing wind and wave conditions.

It is not difficult to reason out other combinations of wind shear and wave amplitudes suitable for turbulence. Such turbulence is often slight; it may amount to no more than shallow patches of ruffled air sandwiched between layers of smooth wave flow. But in the strong wind shears associated with jet streams even weak waves can trigger off high level turbulence rough enough to surprise and shake the unwary pilot, and at lower levels, where the wave amplitude often varies considerably with height, turbulence due to wind shear and waves can sometimes be really violent.

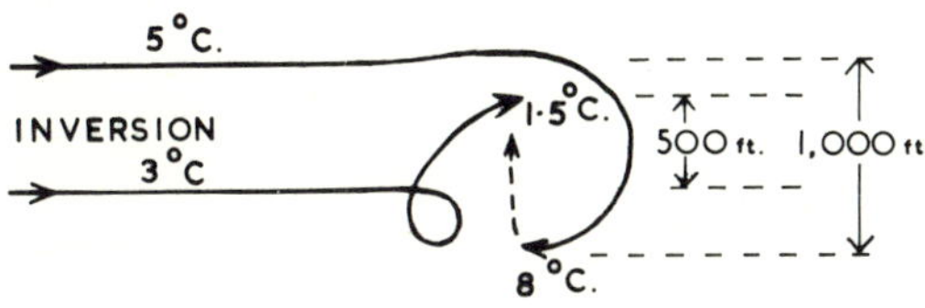

Fig. 16.17. Hypothetical and probably exaggerated example of a stable layer being overturned by turbulence. Adiabatic warming of the descending air and cooling of the rising air would produce tremendous instability.

The flow in lee of the Sierra Nevada on 18 March 1955 included this type of turbulence. Figure 16.16 illustrates the nature of the flow. In the vicinity of the lee wave cloud the wave-like flow had broken down into a region of chaotic motion. The wave cloud as a whole remained more or less stationary, but it was ragged and tattered—quite unlike the well formed lenticulars so characteristic of smoother flow. From a distance this ragged wave cloud looked like a patch of innocuous stratocumulus, but on closer inspection it was possible to observe fragments of the cloud being torn from the trailing edge and to see that the top of the cloud was moving much faster than the base. It was easy to imagine the cloud as a huge stationary roller, and cloud of this type is in fact called *roll cloud*. The type of motion is known as *rotor flow*.

Turbulence in roll cloud is often worsened by a particularly vigorous form of local convection. As we have already noted, wave effects are likely to be most pronounced in or near inversions. Inversions are normally stable, but if turbulence does succeed in overturning air in such a stable layer then local instability will occur very quickly indeed. Figure 16.17 illustrates how such overturning can suddenly transform the affected parts of the stable layer into a highly unstable structure, wherein warm air has suddenly been forced under colder and denser air. The vigorous convection set up in an attempt to restore the equilibrium helps to make the roll cloud a particularly turbulent hazard to both gliders and powered aircraft. On 25 April 1955 a glider used to explore a Sierra wave was broken up by turbulence in such a cloud. Read an extract from the report by the pilot, L. Edgar:

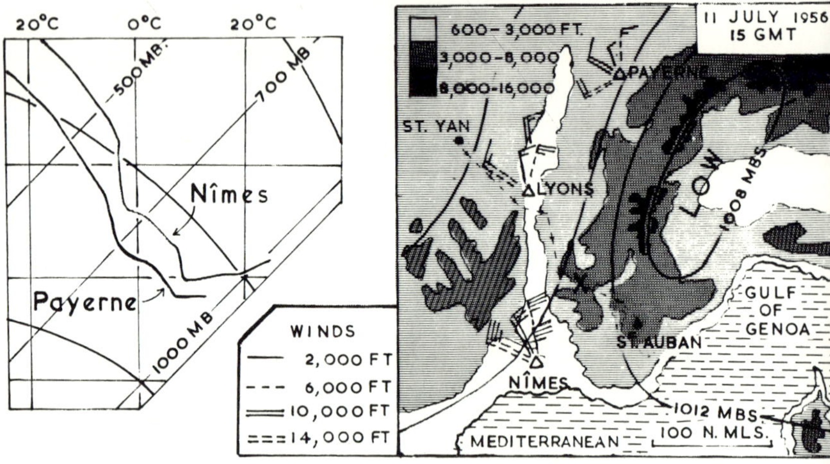

Fig. 16.18. During the flight made by Philip Wills from St Yan to St Auban on 11 July 1956 severe turbulence in rotor flow was encountered over the Drôme Valley (X). Low pressure to the south-east of the Alps, a fresh low level flow down the Rhône Valley with backing winds aloft and tephigrams of the type shown for this occasion are all typical of waves and turbulence amongst the French Alps.

"The flight path went into the very top of the little cloud puff. It seemed to swell up before the nose in the last moment. I looked at the needle and ball. Suddenly and instantaneously the needle went off-centre. I followed with a correction but it swung violently the other way. I was forced sideways in my seat, first to the left then to the right. A fantastic positive G load shoved me down in my seat. Just as I was blacking out it felt like a violent roll to the left with a loud explosion followed by a violent negative G load. I felt my head hit the canopy. I was too stunned to make any attempt to bail out. Just as suddenly as all this violence started it became quiet except for the sound of the wind whistling by. I felt I was falling free of all wreckage except for something* holding both feet."

Turbulence in rotor flow is usually at its worst in the roll cloud itself but it can also be quite formidable in clear air regions of rotor flow. Describing a part of his flight from St Yan to St Auban (see Figure 16.18) on 11 July 1956, Philip Wills said, " . . . we broke cloud, over the Drôme valley, safely south of the mountain I had just left. Suddenly there was a jar and a shock, and my starboard

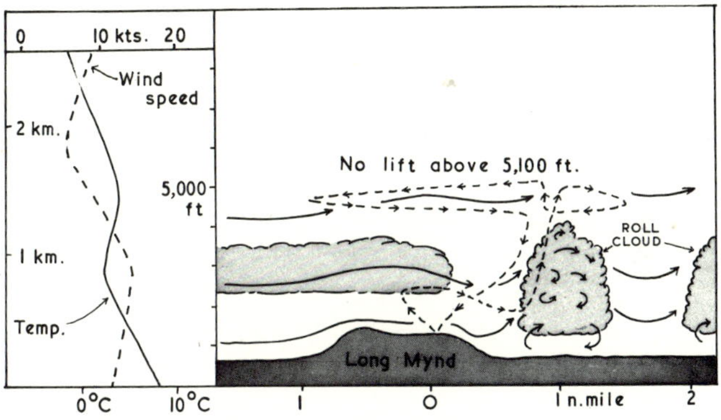

Fig. 16.19. A dotted line marks the wave flight made by S. A. Jones from a winch launch on 19 April 1953. The airstream conditions are shown on the left. As in several other diagrams in this chapter the nature of the flow is depicted schematically by streamlines based on the observed effects.

wing fell into nothing. With full opposite aileron we hung and slid into space for what seemed an age. The next ten minutes were unforgettable. Seven pilots eventually completed this flight, and all of them confessed they had never experienced such wild turbulence before."

Of course not all rotor flow is as rough as this. Flying in the wave flow depicted in Figure 16.19, S. A. Jones found conditions safe enough even though "very rough air was encountered over the top of the roll cloud and full aileron and rudder control was required to keep the Olympia on an even keel. This turbulence was not of the small scale type which sometimes gives a pilot the feeling of riding over cobblestones; it was more like the type experienced on rough hill soaring days."

* The remnants of the rudder bar.

Although rotor flow can often be flown through with safety it should always be treated with caution. The transition between the smooth wave flow and the turbulent zone is usually sharp. The time to tighten safety straps and to secure such movable objects as a camera or a computor is on the ground or in the deceptively smooth air *before* testing the turbulence for strength.

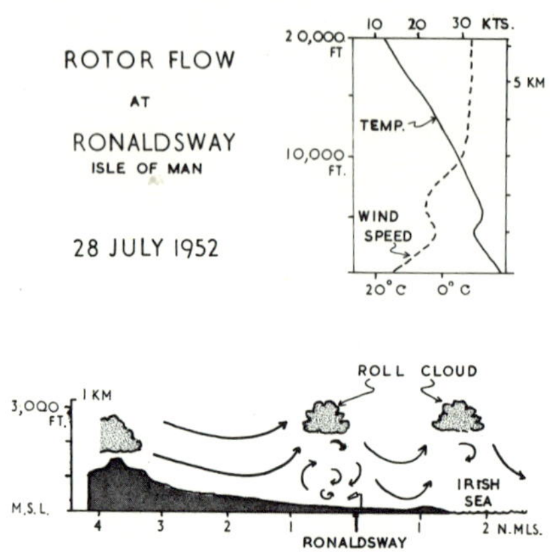

Fig. 16.20. Rotor flow, as evidenced by the roll cloud and variable surface winds at Ronaldsway on 28 July 1952, is often associated with a decrease of wind speed up through a stable layer. The airstream conditions for this occasion are illustrated above.

It is wise to look for signs of rotor flow before taking off in wave conditions. One of the danger signals is a decrease of wind speed or a sharp change of wind direction through the stable layer likely to be associated with the wave flow. Figures 16.18, 16.19 and 16.20 all show the type of airstream conditions likely to promote rotor flow. It must not be deduced that no other types of airstream can produce turbulence in wave flow, but a decrease of wind speed or a sharp change of wind direction up through the stable layer should be regarded as a warning to explore the waves with special caution.

Rotor flow is sometimes betrayed by a relatively low base of the roll cloud compared with that over the ridge. In Figure 16.19 the air flowing up into the base of the roll cloud could not have come from over the hills in a simple smooth wavy flow—if it had then the hills themselves would have been immersed in orographic cloud. The roll cloud base must have been maintained at a low level by air rising from the valley floor, as might be expected in a rotor type of flow, and it seems that the air at low levels over the valley was rather humid on this occasion.

Often the effect of the turbulence extends to low levels, and another sign of rotor flow is the presence of sudden and erratic wind changes on the ground beneath the rotors. Figure 16.20 illustrates the airstream conditions and the nature of the rotor flow at Ronaldsway Airport, Isle of Man, on 28 July 1952 and below is an extract from the wind observations recorded there.

Another example of variable winds in a rotor flow is illustrated by Figure 16.16 showing wind directions and speeds measured at various times and places during a day of rotor flow in lee of the Sierra Nevada. Throughout most of the day a fresh westerly wind

WIND OBSERVATIONS AT RONALDSWAY, ISLE OF MAN, 28 JULY 1952

Time GMT	*Wind at Control Tower*		*Wind at wind sock 800 yds. east of Control Tower*	
	Direction	*Speed*	*Direction*	*Speed*
07·00	S	15 knots	—	—
07·16	Calm	—	—	—
07·28	360° Cycle	8 knots	—	—
07·31	SE	14 knots	N	14 knots
07·36	N	10 knots	SW	9 knots
07·41	SW	6 knots	N	14 knots
07·48	ENE	14 knots	N	5 knots
07·52	Calm	—	N	14 knots
07·54	W	10 knots	N	9 knots
08·02	SW	10 knots	N	14 knots
08·08	E	6 knots	NW	9 knots
08·24	Calm	—	NW	9 knots

blew down the lee mountain slope but with the turbulent motion in the rotor extending down to the ground the winds under the roll cloud were extremely variable in both direction and speed.

The upwind jump

Wave patterns and wave clouds are not always stationary. The way in which the composite effect of a succession of ridges coupled with a slowly changing wavelength can produce fast and erratic changes in the flow pattern has already been mentioned. But there are movements which cannot be accounted for in this way. Perhaps the presence of eddies on the hill slopes and in the valleys changes the effective shape of the high ground; perhaps these eddies form periodically; perhaps they break away from lee slopes and drift downstream at, say, 2 to 20 minute intervals. Such conjectures as these are based on observations, but at present they are little more than vague though plausible ideas. Research into this aspect of wave flow is still at the stage of delving deeper into the theory of airflow over mountains and of accumulating sufficiently detailed observations to highlight the features requiring explanation. Observations so far collected have, however, revealed one feature of special interest. Occasionally a wave cloud has been seen to move slowly downwind, travelling between $\frac{1}{4}$ and 1 mile in 5 to 10 minutes before suddenly, in a matter of seconds, jumping (i.e. re-forming) upstream back to its original position. This process of a slow downstream drift followed by an upwind jump is then repeated over and over again. The reason for such a periodic movement is not yet clear. The phenomenon is most impressive when studied through the medium of time-lapse photography, but it usually requires more than casual observation to be detected from the ground.

To pilots in the air the upstream jump is often all too obvious; at one instant they may be flying just upwind of the wave cloud, at the next they are in cloud which has suddenly developed around them.

Long waves aloft

Most waves used for soaring are of the type whose amplitude simply increases from the ground up to a maximum in or near the stable layer likely to be present, and then fades away at higher levels. But some airstreams can undulate on more than one wavelength, and it is not abnormal to find two different wavelengths in operation at once. The shorter wave is usually most pronounced at some low level while the amplitude of the longer wave is at its maximum at a greater height. Furthermore, the long wave pattern includes a nodal surface, usually in the lower half of the troposphere. Because the wave pattern is reversed on passing up through the nodal surface the most effective part of the longer wave lee flow starts with an ascent

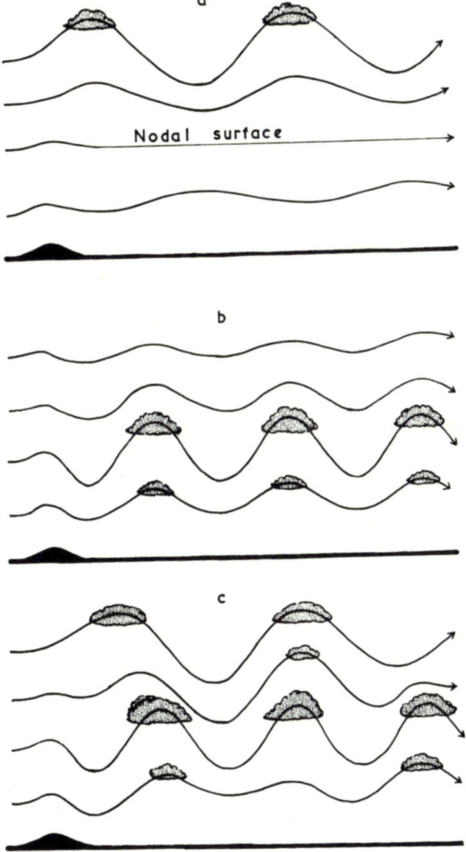

Fig. 16.21. A double wave system comprises:
a a long wave pattern which includes a nodal surface and which is most pronounced at high levels, and
b a short wave pattern most pronounced at a lower level.
The combined effect of these two sets of waves (*c*) can tilt a stack of wave clouds away from the vertical structure characteristic of the simpler type of lee wave flow.

immediately to the lee of the hill crest. Figure 16.21 shows how the combination of the two sets of waves can appear to tilt a stack of wave clouds away from the vertical structure characteristic of the simpler type of lee wave flow. Although these double wave systems complicate the flow pattern they can at least provide occasional opportunities for soaring up through a considerable depth of the atmosphere. The shorter, lower level waves might well form a stairway to the longer waves aloft, and the really ambitious glider pilot may even dream of confirming meteorologists' suspicions that more sets of waves can exist well up into the high stratosphere.

CHAPTER 17

Wave Soaring

There is, and no doubt always will be, a lot of luck in finding soarable waves, but modern knowledge of wave flow can at least help the glider pilot to judge where is the right place and when is the right time to be in the air.

The place

If a pilot is planning a wave soaring expedition he should try to choose a district where the topography includes some long, well marked ridges or lee escarpments across the prevailing wind direction. If the ridges are not high, say less than 1,500 ft. (500 m.) above the valley floor, they should be reasonably smooth—bare rock, moorland, grassland, or covered with thick snow. Well wooded or jagged terrain tends to break up the smooth low level flow, but if the ridges are high the precise nature of their surface will not be quite so important. The district should also be one which has an appreciable quota of airstreams favourable for lee wave flow.

The British Isles often has such airstreams—with such a variety of wind directions that most of its mountain ridges set off lee waves at some time or other. The Sidlaw Hills and many other Scottish ranges are ideal triggers for waves in north-westerlies. The backbone of the Isle of Man is a frequent spur to lee waves in winds between west and north. Waves in westerlies are favoured by many of the Pennine ridges, although the Cross Fell wave occurs with a suitable north-easterly flow. North-easterlies or easterlies also seem to favour waves in lee of such terrain as the Shropshire Hills, Dartmoor and the Black Mountains of Wales. And we must not forget the Cotswolds and the Chilterns; they, too, can set off waves in both north-westerly and south-easterly airstreams whenever the wind and stability conditions are particularly favourable to lee wave flow. Many more hills and mountains could be mentioned as likely sponsors of lee waves. Several of the more common wave locations are well known at various gliding clubs but there is plenty of scope for further exploration. Such exploration can take a variety of forms but in general it is advisable to consult a meteorologist during the planning stage and to arrange a procedure whereby a team of investigators can swing into action at short notice; waves are too unpredictable to justify rigid, inflexible plans being made weeks in advance.

For expeditions to the Continent the site at St Auban in France is conveniently situated amongst mountain ridges running across the northerly flow associated with depressions to the east.

The time

In the British Isles spring and autumn are slightly better suppliers of wave conditions than winter, while summer, with its convection and lighter winds, offers least hope of soarable waves.

The diurnal tendency for lee wave amplitude to increase in the evenings is often well marked, and several hill site clubs can boast of their "evening waves."

Early morning waves may well be just as soarable and no doubt provide many unrealised opportunities for brisk wave flights before breakfast.

Noticeable though they are these seasonable and diurnal tendencies are often swamped by the broad scale airstream changes; lee waves can, and do, occur in any season at any time of the day or night, and usually it is impossible to obtain more than short notice that waves are likely in any particular spot.

Lee wave forecasts

Lee wave amplitude is determined by the precise details of airstream and high ground structures in such an intricate manner that it is usually unrealistic to attempt or to expect consistently accurate lee wave forecasts to be made. After studying the upper winds and temperatures, the meteorologist can often predict the general likelihood of waves over a region for a period of several hours, but he will seldom be able to predict the precise soarability of the waves at any particular spot or any particular time. He seldom has the means of predicting the speeds of the vertical lee wave currents, but in some situations he can forecast the height at which these vertical currents will be strongest and thereby give some indications of the chance of contacting the waves (i.e. reaching the soarable zone) from below. Lee wavelengths are not normally predicted but occasionally the situation allows the forecaster to specify some range within which the wavelength will lie.

When seeking the forecaster's advice on the chances of wave soaring the relevant questions are:

1 Will the airstream temperature and wind conditions be suitable for lee wave flow for whatever period and region are being considered?
2 What will be the wind direction at low levels?
3 Will the airstream change appreciably as a result of
  (*a*) synoptic changes?
  (*b*) diurnal heating or cooling?
4 At about what height will the wave amplitude be at its maximum?
5 Are the wave crests likely to be marked by wave cloud? If so, at what levels?
6 Is turbulence likely at low levels?
7 What will be the lee wavelength? (If it is at all predictable.)
8 Between what levels and of what intensity is icing likely?

Of course, the forecaster may not be able to answer several of these questions. He, too, is feeling his way towards a better understanding of mountain airflow and at present his lee wave forecasting techniques are at the early prototype stage. In normal routine work the forecaster is more often concerned with waves of a different variety; in fact in his conversational circle waves usually refer to broad scale horizontal undulations discernible on the synoptic chart, so when making lee wave enquiries it is wise to ensure that the discussion relates to wave flow which goes up and down vertically, not horizontally.

Local signs

Wave clouds are usually branded with the characteristic lenticular shape and stationary nature, but remember that, when viewed from a distance, many a patch of non-wave cloud has a lenticular outline

Plate 21 WAVE CLOUD NEAR MT COOK *P. A. Wills*

Taken from about 30,000 ft. in the vicinity of Mt Cook, New Zealand, this photograph shows a large bank of cloud over the main mountain ranges. With the wind blowing from right to left in the picture, it is easy to visualise the air flowing downwards at the edge of the main cloud sheet, then up again towards the patches of cloud in the first lee wave crest.

and appears to be almost stationary, while at very close quarters, low level wave cloud may be recognisable as wave cloud only by observing that it is more or less stationary.

It is not uncommon to see thin wafers of lenticular cloud adorning the tops of cumulus clouds, and convection clouds can indeed be considered as mountains in the sky, but transient mountains whose lenticular crowns (pileus clouds) seldom last for long.

Other clues to the detection of lee waves aloft may be gleaned from surface winds which tend to be stronger under wave troughs than

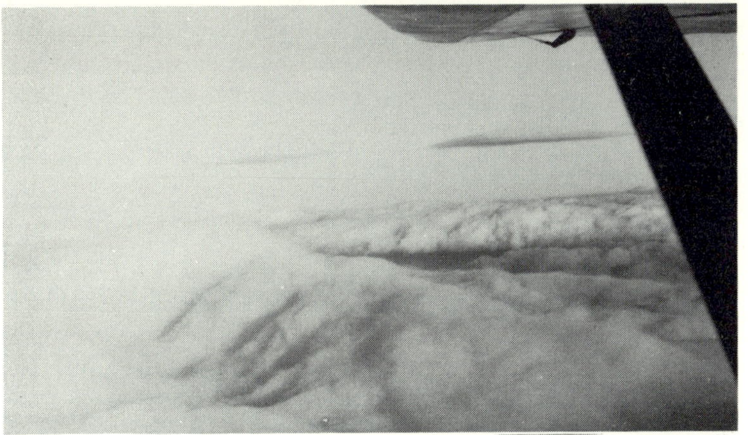

Plate 22 WAVE CLOUD FROM ABOVE *O. W. Neumark*

This photograph was taken from just over the top of low level wave cloud in the neighbourhood of Camphill, Derbyshire. Because the underlying terrain is generally rugged with few predominant mountain ridges, the irregularly spaced zones of wave lift are not always easy to find. However, with the wind blowing from left to right in the picture, it is easy to visualise the airstream flowing approximately up and over the top of the wave cloud in the foreground.

those under the crests, and if rotor flow is present the surface winds will probably be quite erratic under the wave crests.

Waves in flight

During flight a lee wave flow can often be detected either by the rotor flow turbulence which may be associated with the waves or by the uncanny smoothness of flight conditions. On first locating the lift in a wave flow it is usually wise to turn into wind in an attempt to start a climb up through the wave system directly over the spot at which the wave lift was detected. Keeping the egg-shaped pattern of lift depicted in Figure 16.3 in mind it is understandable that circling flight or premature horizontal exploration of the wave at low levels may easily lead to the glider "dropping out" of the soarable zone. But having cautiously climbed well up into the wave system a pilot can then explore the wave in an attempt to find the dimensions of the zone of wave lift. If the wave flow is over rugged terrain it may be impossible and unnecessary to determine the lee wavelength; wave lift over such terrain is likely to be scattered in variegated bands. Over relatively flat terrain, however, wave flow from an upwind mountain range will be free to undulate regularly up and down and the lee wavelength may be easy to determine and to use for planning the next stage of the flight.

The dangers

In the smooth luxury of lee wave lift a pilot can soar high, far and into trouble. Many of the potential hazards are dangerous not because they are difficult to understand but because they tend to be overlooked in planning or training to fly in waves. So here is a check list for the wave soaring pilot to consider.

1 The downdraught down a lee escarpment may be particularly strong.

2 Remember that small gaps between low wave clouds can soon fill up, especially if rain begins to fall from cloud above.

3 With a changing synoptic situation the humps of wave clouds may not keep their positions relative to the mountains below them.

4 Due to cooling by ascent the freezing level will be lower in wave crests than in wave troughs.

5 An airstream with a shallow freezing layer below thick relatively warm cloud can provide the stability conditions for lee waves and conditions for freezing rain, that is rain falling from the cloud and freezing in the freezing layer. Ice accretion in such conditions can be thick and sudden. This type of danger is rare, but when a cold winter spell is about to be broken by the approach of an active warm front ask the local meteorologists whether freezing rain is likely.

6 When landing remember that ground level winds may be very variable beneath the wave crests, especially if rotor flow is present.

7 The transition from smooth wave flow to turbulent rotor flow is often very sharp.

8 When visiting strange clubs believe the local stories of hair-raising turbulence in rotor flow, no matter how innocuous such flow appears to be at your home site.

9 Waves extending to high levels are often associated with a considerable increase of wind speed with height. Do not rely too much on dead reckoning navigation in such conditions.

10 Strong winds aloft are sometimes associated with double wave systems, a long wavelength at high levels and short waves below. Such a combination of wind and wavelength changes can also upset navigation.

11 A pilot has been carried up beyond the safety limit of his oxygen equipment. The quickest way to get out of the updraught of a wave is to fly downwind into the descending air.

12 When flying close to the windward side of a wave cloud be prepared for a possible upwind jump of the cloud.

CHAPTER 18

The Altimeter

The fact that pressure decreases with height could be demonstrated by carrying a sealed can up and down a mountainside and noting the changes in its volume; during ascent the decrease in atmospheric pressure would allow the can to expand and during descent the can would be compressed. To measure the amount of the expansion and contraction one side of the can could be fixed to a frame and the other side to a pointer pivoted at the focus of a scale graduated in

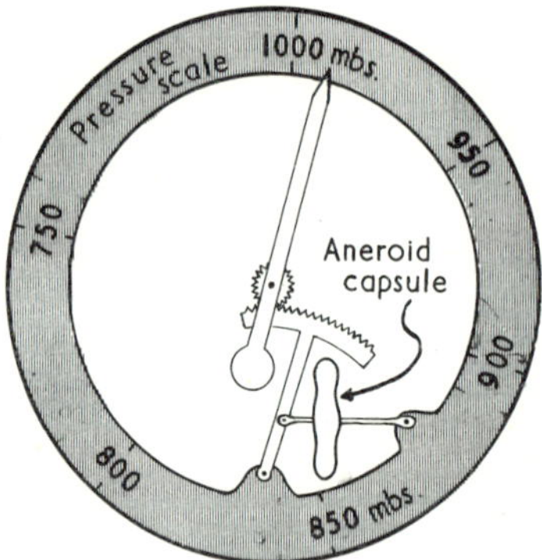

Fig. 18.1. Atmospheric pressure can be measured by noting how much it compresses a sealed can (known as an aneroid capsule).

millibars (Figure 18.1). But the rough and ready pressure/altitude relationship we have already used in general discussion is not accurate enough for a precise conversion of millibars to altitude. Pressure surfaces are seldom truly horizontal; they dip down over depressions and bulge upwards over highs—as illustrated in Figure 18.2. Changes in temperature can also distort the pattern; heating at low levels pushes the isobaric surfaces upwards and low level cooling brings them down a little. Thus the pressure surfaces move almost incessantly—not by very much and not very fast, but enough to make the pressure/altitude relationship an awkward and international problem.

The approach to this problem has been to devise a reasonably simple formula which describes the approximately average state of the atmosphere. Known as the ICAO* Standard Atmosphere, the agreed formula is based on the following specifications:

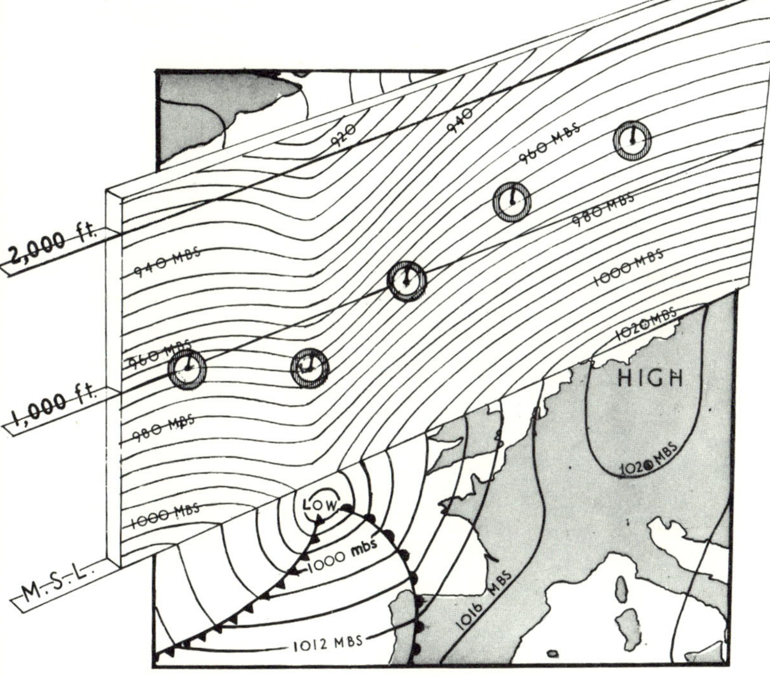

Fig. 18.2. Pressure surfaces dip down over depressions and bulge upwards over highs. Any instrument designed to measure pressure will indicate a constant value as it moves along a pressure surface. The five instruments sketched would all measure a pressure of 968 mbs. in the situation illustrated.

1 A pressure of 1013·25 mbs. at M.S.L.

2 A temperature of 15° C. (59° F.) at M.S.L.

3 A temperature lapse rate of 6·5° C. per kilometre (2° C. per 1,000 ft.) up to a height of 11 km. (just over 36,000 ft.) above M.S.L.

4 An isothermal stratosphere (at − 56·5° C.) from an altitude of 11 km. upwards.

* International Civil Aviation Organisation.

The pressure/altitude relationship derived from these specifications is tabulated at the end of this chapter and partly illustrated in Figure 18.3. It provides an internationally agreed scale for graduating an *aneroid altimeter*, that is a pressure-measuring instrument which uses the sealed can principle and which is calibrated in units of height instead of pressure.

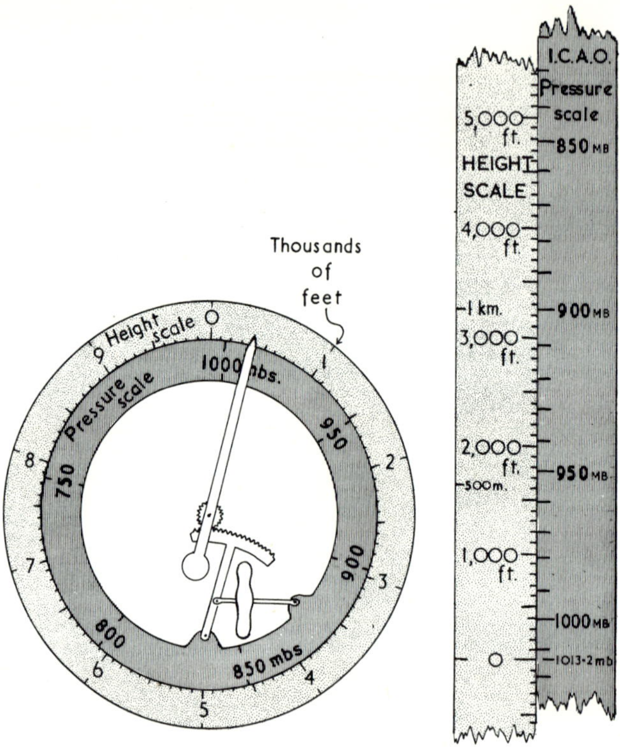

Fig. 18.3. The ICAO Standard Atmosphere provided an arbitrary but internationally agreed scale for converting pressure readings to altitudes.

Of course, a conventionally calibrated altimeter does not always indicate true height above M.S.L. or above ground level. The schematically drawn altimeter in Figure 18.4 is certainly not at 2,000 ft. above ground level. This altimeter could be made to indicate height above the airfield by moving the zero of the ICAO height scale to correspond to a pressure of 980 mbs.—which is equivalent to recalibrating the altimeter by rotating the mechanism in such a way that a pressure of 980 mbs. corresponds to zero on the height scale. This action is known as setting the *pressure subscale*. With this subscale setting left as it is during flight the altimeter will now indicate height above this particular airfield, the corrections for non-standard temperature usually being negligible (about 3·3 ft. per 1,000 ft. per ° C. difference between actual and standard temperatures). However, if the pressure at the airfield level rises the altimeter

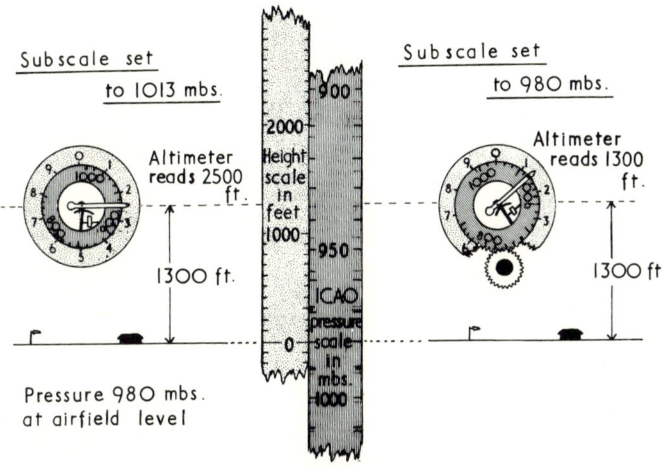

Fig. 18.4. It is often convenient to adjust the ICAO Standard height scale so that the zero coincides with the pressure at airfield level. In the aneroid altimeter this adjustment is achieved by setting the pressure subscale.

will begin to err on the low side and if the airfield pressure falls then a pilot relying on the instrument will be lower than he thinks he is. Desultory errors will also arise from the altimeter mechanism whose tendency to stick a little is often revealed by watching the indicator needle jerk to a new reading when the instrument is tapped. When using the altimeter for flying in the immediate vicinity of an airfield in low, flat countryside, the altimeter should therefore be set to read zero height at the launching point before take off and used in flight as a rough indicator of height above take off level. It is most important to remember that the instrument will not indicate height above all points of a sloping airfield, that the mechanism is liable to move in jerks and that, even if the instrument were mechanically perfect, it would be bad practice to rely on the altimeter on the approach to a landing.

At high level airfields, the pressure at airfield level may be below the range incorporated in the subscale setting mechanism and at such sites it is often expedient to set the altimeter to read the runway elevation (height above M.S.L.) before take off and then to use this as a reference level.

During thermal soaring the jerkiness in an altimeter mechanism occasionally provides a facility for noting the net change of height over a short period; such an instrument usually responds to a gentle tap by jumping across a small but easily noted height interval.

During cross-country flying it is usually more useful to set the altimeter to indicate height above M.S.L. rather than height above any particular piece of ground and this requires a knowledge of the expected changes of M.S.L. pressure over the route and with time. On most thermal soaring cross-country flights the M.S.L. pressure changes en route will not amount to very much, but in wave soaring and especially in line squall soaring neglect of the probable M.S.L. pressure changes en route could easily contribute to disaster. In contrast to thermal soaring conditions, both wave situations and line squalls can provide the means for soaring considerable distances across the M.S.L. isobars in conditions in which a pilot can, intentionally or otherwise, lose sight of the ground for long periods. If the flight is towards a low pressure region and the pressure subscale is left unchanged then every millibar change in M.S.L. pressure en route brings the pilot another 30 ft. or so lower than his altimeter reading and the possible consequences do not need elaborating.

Altimeter setting in air-lanes

Besides worrying about his own height above ground a glider pilot who is likely to venture close to or into civil air-lanes must also be aware of the systems of vertical separation of aircraft with these lanes. Every "C" licensed pilot is obliged to know the rules governing heights at which he may be allowed to cross or fly in air-lanes.

But the rules would be useless without standard subscale settings for the aircraft altimeter. There has been some international controversy over this particular point; on the one hand a universal standard setting of 1013 mbs. seems simple, but the counter argument is that it is more practical to use forecast pressures which would yield a closer indication to true altitude yet at the same time ensure the desired standardisation over conveniently sized flight regions. At present the standard setting of 1013 mbs. is in force for the vertical separation of aircraft in air-lanes. The pros and cons of the system as applied to airline operations are not for discussion here but the important rule to remember is that (at the time of writing) flight levels in air-lanes must be maintained with the altimeter pressure subscale set to 1013 mbs. and failure to make allowance for this may easily cause a glider pilot to fly across an air-lane at the wrong level and to provoke a dispute if nothing worse.

To lessen the chances of ambiguity in messages used in international aviation procedures some words relating to altitude are used with limited meanings:

height is used to denote the vertical distance of an object above the ground immediately below
altitude is used to denote height of an aircraft above M.S.L.
elevation is used to denote the height of ground (an airfield or runway) above M.S.L.

The Q code

International procedures also include a system called the Q code which facilitates the exchange of common questions and answers. The code groups relevant to altimeter settings are:

	As a question	*For information*
QFE	What is the ground level pressure at ..?	The ground level pressure at............is ....mbs.
QFF	What is the M.S.L. pressure at ......?	The pressure at M.S.L. at.......... is...... mbs.
QNH............	What must my pressure subscale be set to so that my altimeter reads the correct elevation on landing at ....?	If the pressure subscale is set to........mbs. then the altimeter will read the correct elevation on landing at ....

These three Q signals are used so frequently in aviation and meteorological procedures that it is common practice to use them colloquially. "What is the QFE?" is a common question asked by enquirers at an airfield who wish to know the barometric pressure at the level of the runway in use.

THE ICAO STANDARD ATMOSPHERE (DRY AIR)

Pressure	*Temperature*		*Density*	*Altitude*	
mb.	°C.	°F.	gm./cu.metre	m.	ft.
1013·2	15·0	59·0	1225	0	0
1000	14·3	57·7	1212	111	364
950	11·5	52·7	1163	540	1773
900	8·6	47·4	1113	988	3243
850	5·5	41·9	1063	1457	4781
800	2·3	36·2	1012	1949	6394
750	−1·0	30·1	960	2466	8091
700	−4·6	23·8	908	3012	9882
650	−8·3	17·0	855	3591	11,780
600	−12·3	9·8	802	4206	13,801
550	−16·6	2·1	747	4865	15,962
500	−21·2	−6·2	692	5574	18,289
450	−26·2	−15·2	635	6344	20,812
400	−31·7	−25·1	577	7185	23,574
350	−37·7	−36·0	518	8117	26,631
300	−44·5	−48·2	457	9164	30,065
250	−52·3	−62·2	395	10,363	33,999
200	−56·5	−69·7	322	11,784	38,662
150	−56·5	−69·7	241	13,608	44,647
100	−56·5	−69·7	161	16,180	53,083
90	−56·5	−69·7	145	16,848	55,275
80	−56·5	−69·7	128	17,595	57,726
70	−56·5	−69·7	112	18,442	60,504
60	−56·5	−69·7	96	19,419	63,711
50	−56·5	−69·7	80	20,575	67,503

CHAPTER 19

More about Fronts

In Chapter 5 fronts were introduced as some sort of sloping surfaces between warm and cold air, but this concept should be regarded as an oversimplified aid to visualising fronts in three dimensions. As such, it is an extremely valuable concept, but fronts are not simple

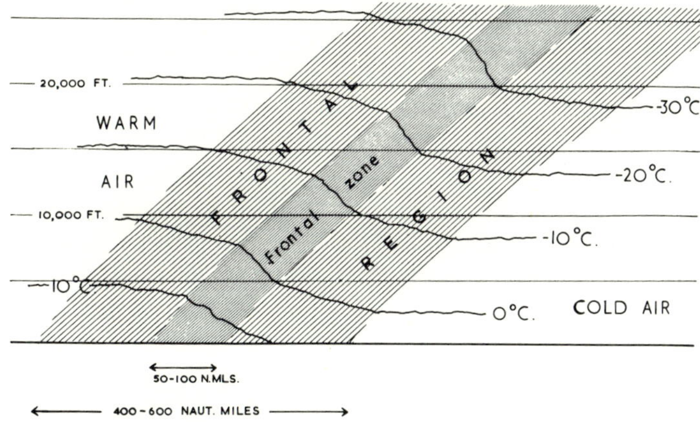

Fig. 19.1. Temperature changes across a warm front are often gradual across a wide *frontal region* and somewhat sharper within a relatively narrow *frontal zone*. Frequently the outer boundaries of the frontal zone are blurred by random non-frontal temperature variations in the atmosphere.

phenomena and if we keep our ideas at too elementary a level we shall merely be perplexed by some of the frontal weather we actually encounter.

Recent research by J. S. Sawyer of the Meteorological Office shows that temperature changes across warm fronts over the British Isles are usually of the form typified by the cross-section illustrated in Figure 19.1. Based on meteorological research flight data, this cross-section shows a gradual temperature increase from the cold air towards the warm side of the front across a belt whose boundaries are often ill-defined but usually about 400–600 miles apart. Within this broad belt, which has come to be known as the *frontal region*, there is a 50–150 mile wide zone (now called the *frontal zone*) across which the temperature change is more pronounced.

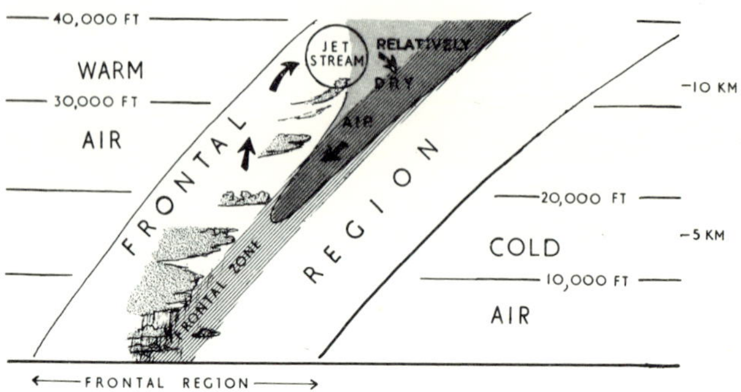

Fig. 19.2. Relatively dry air is usually located at high levels in the warm frontal zone.

In our earlier oversimplification the tacit assumption that the transition between the warm and the cold air was sharp enough to be depicted as a single line on the chart was tantamount to ignoring the existence of the broad frontal region and referring to the frontal zone as the frontal surface. It is still useful to associate a front with a single line on a chart but we must now realise that such a line is a conveniently detectable marker usually within or at one of the edges of the frontal zone. Sometimes the synoptic changes at both the leading and trailing edges of the frontal zone are noticeable enough to track from chart to chart, in which case a pair of parallel red lines may be used by some forecasters to represent the warm front.

The same research flights also revealed the frequent existence of a tongue of rather dry air dipping downwards into and behind the frontal zone—often in the position shown in Figure 19.2. Investigation prompted by these flight observations suggests subsidence as a cause of the dryness of the air in this tongue, and this downward motion obviously calls for a modification to the idea of warm air sliding up the frontal surface (or frontal zone). The warm air does ascend, but as part of an incipient vertical circulation like that depicted in Figure 19.2, and a consequence is that the slope of the frontal zone is slightly less than that formed by the leading edges of the pre-frontal clouds. Frequently the pre-frontal cloud is in layers, whose leading edges do not form a well defined slope, and occasionally the development of the tongue of dry air aloft produces a hiatus in the pre-frontal cloud sequence.

Rainfall ahead of warm fronts

It is very convenient to talk of a "belt" of rain preceding a warm front and for many practical purposes it is apt to view the rain area

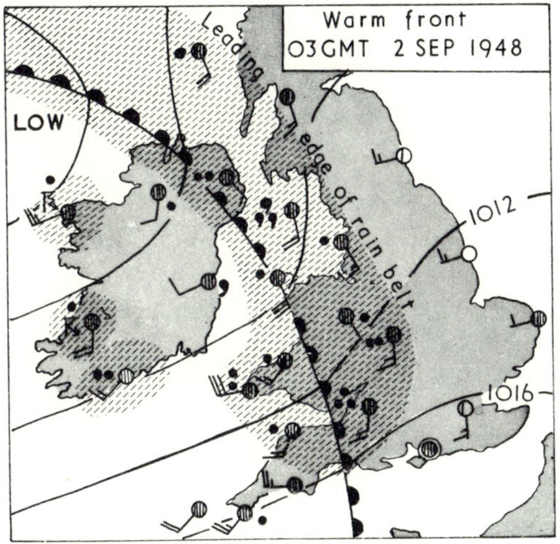

Fig. 19.3. Extracts from the synoptic chart for 03 GMT 2 September 1948.

as a belt with a discernible leading edge approximately parallel to the front. Such a leading edge is marked on the chart reproduced in Figure 19.3, but, after mapping the more detailed rainfall records kept at a number of stations, the hourly distribution (Figure 19.4) revealed several cells or tongues of rainfall moving in such a way that the description "belt" of rainfall was justifiable only when considering periods of at least a few hours at a time.

We shall not pause to explain this particular distribution except to say that the warm front rainfall mechanism (i.e. ascent of air leading to condensation and precipitation) is frequently augmented by

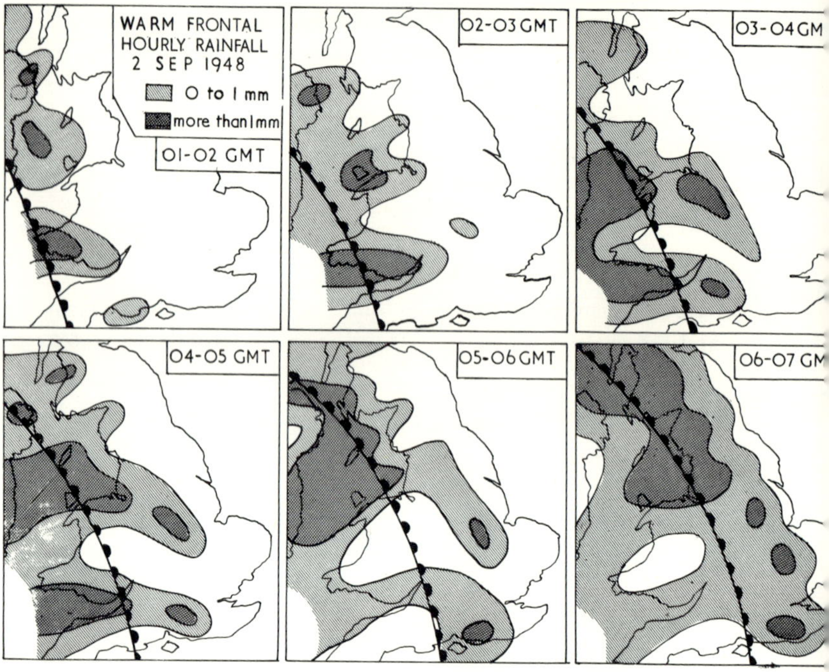

Fig. 19.4. Details of the hourly rainfall pattern on 2 September 1948.

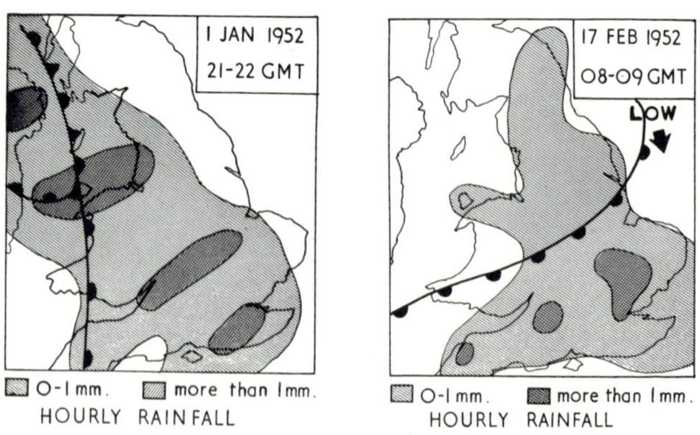

Fig. 19.5. Cellular distribution of rainfall.

orographic effects, and by wave motions and instability blended into processes which are as yet mostly unexplored. Occasionally the power of these supplementary frontal features is revealed by distinctive patterns of rainfall; the patterns illustrated in Figure 19.5 suggest that ascent of the frontal rainfall mechanism is given a boost in several cells about 150 miles apart. At present it is suspected that this type of frontal rainfall distribution is produced by some sort of atmospheric wave motion (whose characteristics differ considerably from those of mountain lee waves) on wavelengths of about 150–250 miles coupled with *hydrodynamic instability* (a form of instability which triggers off compound vertical and lateral displacements in the airflow).

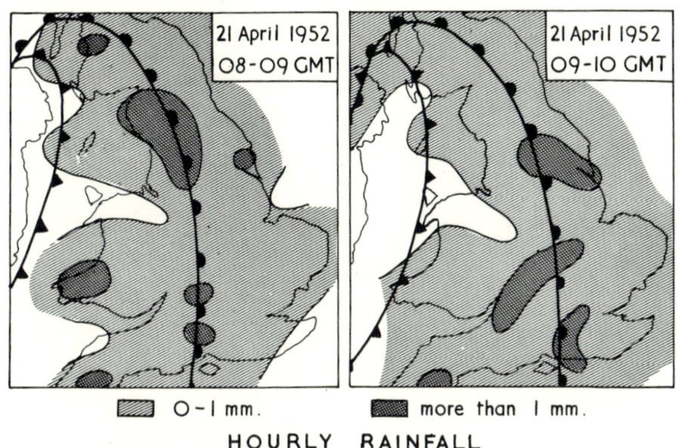

Fig. 19.6. In many frontal situations details of the rainfall pattern change radically from hour to hour.

Unfortunately a large number of warm frontal rainfall patterns (like those in Figure 19.6) are not easily analysed into coherent systems which can be traced hour by hour, and it is difficult to predict or even diagnose just how much orographic effects, wave motions and instability will contribute to the production of frontal rain.

Katacold fronts

As with warm fronts, cold frontal temperature changes usually show a slow change across a frontal region and a sharper change across a frontal zone. The widths of this zone and the frontal region are, on average, about 50 and 250 miles respectively but they vary considerably from one cold front to another. Within the frontal zone there may be a wind veer, a cloud clearance, a fall of temperature and a decrease in dew point—and occasionally these synoptic manifestations happen to be particularly well marked and concentrated into a single line.

The complexity of cold fronts arises not so much from the width of the transition zone as from the shape of the cold frontal structure aloft. Subsidence often follows a cold front and not infrequently the slowly descending air moves forward faster than the M.S.L. position of the front and the front develops a forward bulge—as sketched in

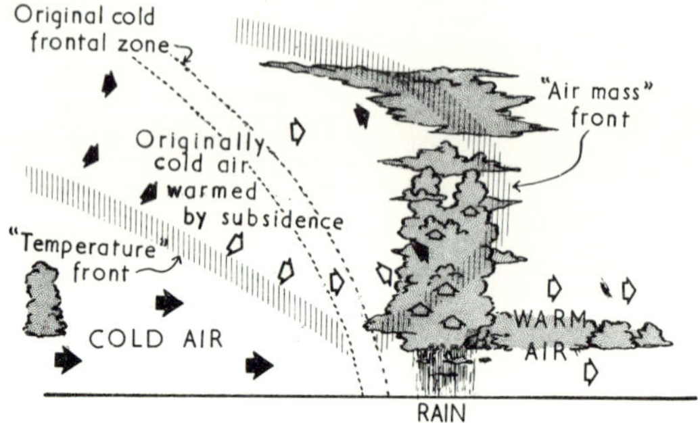

Fig. 19.7. Cross-section of a katacold front. The original frontal zone is ultimately replaced by an "air mass" front separating the originally cold and warm airstreams, and a "temperature" front between the subsided air aloft and the cold air below.

Figure 19.7. As an indicator of the descending air, the prefix *kata* is sometimes applied to this type of cold front, but it is not uncommon for this descent to be checked in a belt about 50–150 miles

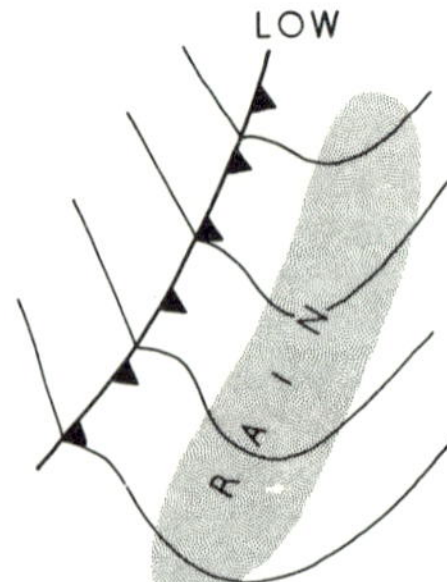

Fig. 19.8. Trough development ahead of a katacold front.

ahead of the M.S.L. frontal position. Ascent of both warm and the originally cold air in this belt occasionally releases the potential instability, and convection cloud, precipitation and possibly thunderstorms may precede the surface front. These developments (frequently at medium levels and not conducive to soaring) are often accompanied by a troughing of the isobars (Figure 19.8) ahead of the surface cold front which, at some later stage, may become scarcely detectable while the new trough acquires more of the characteristics of a rudimentary cold front.

As well as posing problems for more investigation, this katacold frontal type of phenomenon aggravates the practical snags of frontal terminology. Referring to Figure 19.7, notice that the originally cold air subsides, overtakes the ground level position of the front and produces the forward bulge in the transition zone between the originally cold air mass and the warmer air ahead; meanwhile the warming due to the subsidence aloft creates a new temperature contrast in a gently sloping zone behind the original cold front. Thus the "air mass front" and "temperature front" do not coincide in the katacold frontal system, and we have yet another illustration of the inadequacy of the simple word "front" to describe the complex frontal processes of the atmosphere.

Of course, these ramifications may well appear confusing. But it is no use pretending that they do not exist. However, we need not despair of nature's variations on the frontal theme; even the elementary concept of fronts as simple sloping surfaces is very useful—provided we do not let it acquire the status of an unquestionable doctrine to which the weather ought to conform.

CHAPTER 20

Weatherwise

The care taken in planning and carrying out a soaring flight naturally depends on the object of the flight and on the wishes and ability of the pilot. Providing the essential elements of safety are not ignored, an unpremeditated aerial ramble with a surprise ending may be as enjoyable to the happy wanderer as a masterly operation is to the meticulous planner. But for the purposes of this chapter let us assume that the pilot wishes to make substantial use of the meteorological services available and of the weather signs around him.

Medium range forecasts

For most types of club operations serious thoughts on a day's gliding begin about 12–24 hours ahead; many a pilot casts an anxious eye towards the clouds on an afternoon or evening in contemplation of a flight the next day, and indeed this is about the right time ahead to become acquainted with the current weather situation. For background information there are:

1 *The daily press.* Several newspapers publish weather maps which, though sketchy, may be used to view the general pressure pattern and the frontal situation. Weather maps for the morning papers, however, are normally prepared on the previous evening (in time to go to press) and it is advisable to amplify them with more up-to-date information contained in:

2 *Forecast bulletins broadcast by the B.B.C.* These bulletins comprise arrangements of:

(*a*) A "general forecast" giving a broad picture of the weather over the British Isles, usually followed by "district" or "regional" forecasts (for areas mapped in Figure 20.1) in which special attention is paid to such factors as rain, sunshine and temperature.

(*b*) A sentence or two describing the further "outlook."

(*c*) "Shipping forecasts" giving details of the expected weather, wind and visibility in sea areas (Figure 20.2) around the British Isles.

(*d*) "Warnings" of gales, frosts, snow or thaw.

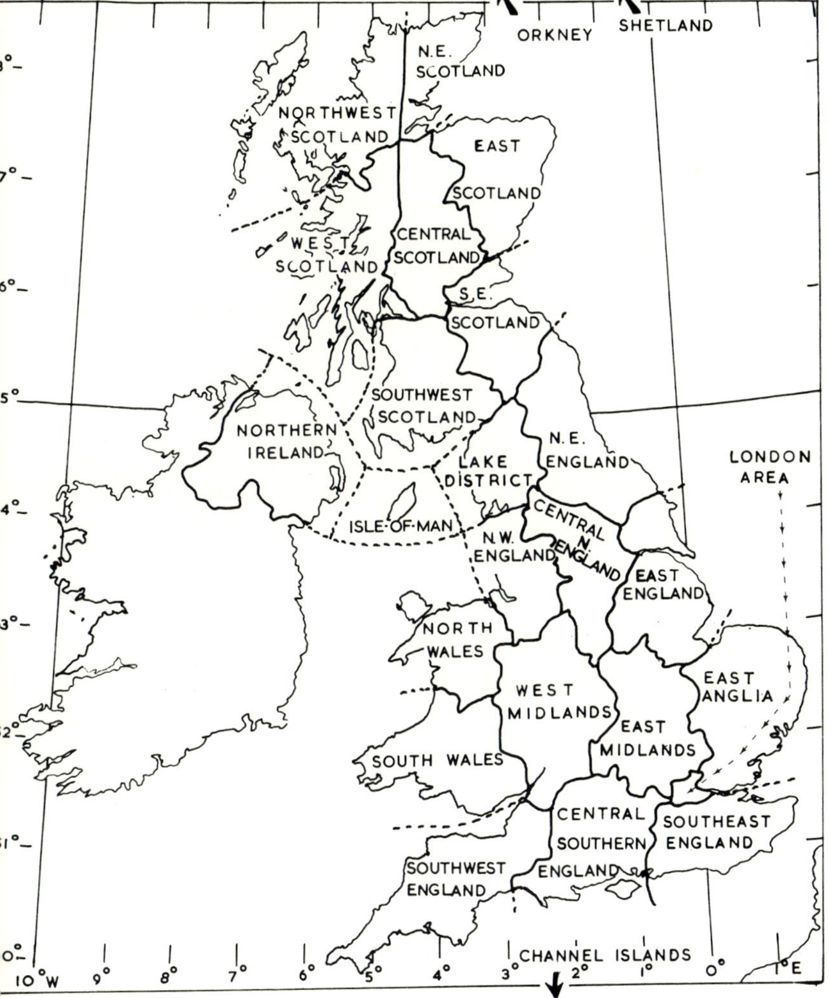

Fig. 20.1. Land areas used in forecast bulletins.

(*e*) A "weather commentary" towards the end of the day.

(*f*) A "general synopsis" describing the principal features of the synoptic situation.

Because most of the bulletins are designed for the general public, careful attention is needed to deduce the synoptic features relevant to gliding. For example, a statement that "Brighter but cooler weather will spread from the north-west" may well refer

Fig. 20.2. Sea areas used in forecast bulletins.

to the approach of a cold front. The discerning listener should also note that, although the forecasts are couched in the language of everyday speech rather than technical terms, descriptive words or phrases are used with careful consistency. The forecasters maintain this consistency by using special definitions of selected common words and phrases; for example, "sunny periods" is used to denote variable skies with considerable blue patches and corresponding sunshine, whereas "bright periods" means cloud rather variable in amount but considerable diffused sunlight at times or even occasionally direct sunshine. The distinction between the two terms when applied to gliding weather is obvious; "sunny periods" suggests mainly good thermal soaring while "bright periods" conveys the warning that insolation is likely to be reduced by cirrus or thin medium cloud, perhaps ahead of a warm front. Notes at the end of this chapter include more details of the terminology used in forecasts for the general public.

A somewhat more direct insight into the broad synoptic situation is given by the wind items of the shipping forecasts and gale warnings. A rough pencil or mental sketch of the wind directions usually reveals the shape of the general flow pattern, but this is discussed in detail in Chapter 21.

Of course, a ready-made viewof this flow pattern is presented in:

3 *The B.B.C. television forecasts.* These are usually brief commentaries by forecasters on the present and predicted weather with illustrations on charts showing recent and forecast pressure and frontal systems. Although these forecasts are products of considerable scientific effort, usually only an elementary knowledge of meteorology is required to follow the forecaster's arguments linking the forecast weather to the actual and predicted pressure and frontal patterns. A period of a few minutes, however, is too brief to allow the forecaster to dwell on the local variations of the forecast for the next day. Local forecasts, however, are available in the form of:

4 *Weather information by telephone.* The latest information about the state of the weather in various parts of the British Isles and the Continent, and local forecasts to cover a period of up to 24 hours ahead may be obtained by telephone from the Meteorological Offices listed on pages 273–4. When asking for a forecast it is important to state the purpose of the enquiry clearly enough to elicit the relevant local features rather than unnecessary general-

ities of the forecast. At this stage, however, the forecaster will not normally be able to give more than a rough indication of the soaring prospects for the next day and no useful purpose is served by trying to press him for superficial details which he cannot honestly predict. Any plans made must be tentative ones based on rather elementary interpretation of the forecast pressure and frontal situations.

To add interest and meaning to the weather information obtained via the press, the B.B.C. or by telephone, it is instructive to make:

5 *Local observations.* Some of the salient features of the synoptic situation can often be deduced from simple local observations of such elements as the barometric pressure and its tendency, the wind direction and speed, the cloud structure and movement and the visibility, and the keen weather student may even try to deduce the characteristics of the T–Φ curve appropriate to his locality. To list principles on which such deductions may be attempted would virtually be to repeat much of the text of the previous chapters. The object of this observing exercise is not so much to make firm predictions as to build up a logical and objective picture of the current situation and its broad potentialities for the next day's gliding.

Short range forecasts

It is usually at about, or soon after, breakfast time that the decision is made whether or not to attempt a flight. By this time the official forecasts in the morning press, the B.B.C. bulletins and local observations will normally provide sufficient information to narrow down the range of possible operations. For example, when fresh winds are forecast it is usually impracticable to plan thermal soaring cross-country flights in any direction outside of a narrow downwind sector from the starting point; in localities predicted to have very light winds it is unlikely that wave soaring will be possible; if showers are not forecast then it is unlikely that low level convection clouds will be very deep.

With slightly more specific plans in mind the pilot is now in a position to consider the relevant details of the synoptic situation and seldom are more than a few of these details included in the routine radio, television and press bulletins. However, there are two supplementary sources of information: the Meteorological Office telephone service and local observations. To get the best out of the telephone service it is wise to remember that it is designed for giving general meteorological advice over a wide range of activities rather than a specialist service to any one type of enquirer. The duty forecaster may not be completely familiar with the techniques or the jargon of soaring; he may not have given serious thought to some of the specialised details required: and, if the enquiry is lengthy, his attention may become distracted by the need to serve other enquirers. Therefore, the request for a gliding forecast should be as specific as possible, for example, "I am planning a gliding flight from............towards the region of............ I hope to start at about midday or earlier if conditions are favourable. Can you, please, give me a general forecast for the route and some relevant details of wind and convective conditions?" Or, "Could you please tell me the prospects for soaring in lee waves in the region of...........today?" The forecaster's initial reply will usually indicate how prepared he is for this type of gliding enquiry, and it is for the pilot to judge what supplementary questions are necessary.

Vague opening questions such as "What will the weather be like today?" does not give the forecaster an indication that the enquirer wants anything more specific than a general forecast of the type issued to the public at large. On the other hand it is most unwise to try to help the forecaster by opening with such questions as "Will this high last?" or "When is the front due?" Before answering such questions the forecaster has to ascertain which high or which front is being referred to, and if he does not seek amplification of the question the way is open for considerable misunderstanding between the forecaster and the pilot. Even such an opening question as "Will there be plenty of convection today?" is charged with potential ambiguity unless properly amplified. The pilot may, in fact, want to know whether or not conditions are favourable for cross-country thermal soaring. He may be elated if the forecaster predicts that there will indeed be plenty of convection. But the elation may well turn to despair if the convection is so plentiful that the sky becomes generally cloudy and thermals are only weak at low levels. If, on the other hand, the forecaster predicts only "limited" convection, it must not be assumed that conditions for cross-country soaring are marginal. Does the word "limited" mean that convection will be limited to a very short period of the day or does it imply that only small cumulus clouds will form?

"Is it unstable today?" is another inadequate question liable to be drastically misinterpreted. In much meteorological conversation the word unstable is applied to T–Φ curves which presage or explain the development of convection cloud at low or medium levels (regardless of the amount or depth of the cloud), while upper air conditions not conducive to such development are said to be stable—even if they produce dry thermals. Thus a simple answer to the apparently simple question will be inadequate and possibly misleading when translated into thermal soaring prospects.

More potential sources of ambiguity arise whenever thermals, waves or gradients are mentioned. In general forecasting practice the word "thermals" is used as an abbreviation for thermal winds and "thermal charts" portray the mean temperature (or its equivalent) in some specified layer of the atmosphere; the word "waves" refers more frequently to kinks on fronts than to soarable waves in lee of mountains and when the word "gradient" is associated with airflow it usually refers to the horizontal pressure gradient rather than the "wind gradient." So when such phrases as "thermals are strong," the "gradient is weak" or "waves on the front" are mentioned it is wise to ascertain in which sense the terms are being used.

No doubt everyday conversation would lack variety and life without its quota of words used in a loose colloquial fashion, but, with suitable preparation and forethought, it is not difficult to seek the forecaster's advice in a colloquial manner designed to get answers to specific questions typified by those suggested at the end of the chapters on thermal prospects and wave soaring.

When listening to a forecast it is sometimes tempting to form a premature overall impression of the prospects for a flight tentatively planned. Such impressions can be misleading; they are apt to be based on casual stresses the forecaster may unwittingly put on items of the forecast and on incidental remarks to which the pilot gives undue thought while the telephone briefing is in progress. Before trying to assess the overall prospects it is wise to note impartially all the relevant elementary items of the forecast and to treat each situation on its apparent merits.

On a number of occasions the forecaster may not be completely prepared to predict some of the details required in a forecast for gliding, either because the situation does not justify a scientifically honest prediction of such details or (more likely) because he has had insufficient notice of the question. Therefore, in many situations it is worth while to give the forecaster notice of an hour or more that a gliding forecast will be requested.

Forecasters are even better prepared when local arrangements can be made with a gliding club for the supply of routine daily or week-end forecasts. When such arrangements are in force the forecaster allocates specific time on his schedule to prepare the forecast and club members are able to study the forecast at their airfield. The details of such arrangements may vary according to local circumstances, but usually it is convenient, for communication at least, to itemise the forecast under headings such as the following:

A Area and period of the forecast.
B Brief description of the synoptic situation.
C Surface winds (and strength of hill lift for a local forecast).
D Upper winds.
E Weather.
F Depth of dry thermal activity.
G Character and distribution of dry thermals.
H Amount, base and tops of convection cloud.
I Distribution of layer cloud.
J Visibility.
K Sea breeze effects.
L Lee waves.
M Height of maximum lee wave amplitude.
N Height of 0° C. isotherm.
O Warnings and remarks.
P Pressure at M.S.L.

The heights mentioned in aviation forecasts are usually heights above M.S.L. if the forecast applies to a large area or route, while in forecasts for a particular airfield and its immediate vicinity the upper wind levels, cloud base, cloud tops and other heights mentioned are given as height above the airfield level.

Ultra-short-range forecasts

Last minute modifications to flight plans or attempts to seize unexpected opportunities for soaring are usually based on the changes in aircraft availability and on local forecasts for the next one or two hours. Successful forecasting for such a short time ahead often calls for careful interpretation of local observations in the light of the general synoptic situation as described by the professional meteorological service. But careful interpretation may be wasted if the observations themselves are haphazard, and it is wise to note local conditions as objectively as possible. For example, by knowing in advance how far a selection of landmarks are from the airfield and by noting which of these landmarks are clearly visible, a far more reliable estimate of visibility can be made than by trying to form a vague impression of the haziness. The direction of movement of medium or high cloud can usually be obtained by watching distinctive features of the clouds as they move past a reference point such as the corner of a building or the wingtip of a parked aircraft, but without a fixed point in the foreground the movement of medium or high cloud can seldom be readily discerned.

Casual glances at the sky at odd moments can be misleading. It is very easy to fall into the trap of noticing a sudden change in, say, the cloud amount and type, or the wind direction, and to be filled with optimism or despair according to whether the soaring prospects appear brighter or worse than was expected, but, unless the change marks an unexpected or recognisable event such as the passage of a line squall, it is usually unwise to act on impulsive feelings without waiting at least ten or preferably twenty minutes to see whether the change was significant or merely a transient fluctuation in the broader pattern of events.

Whenever possible, instrumental measurements are preferable to estimations. Estimations of wind speed at ground level are much less consistent than measurements made with even simple forms of anemometers. Measurement of the air temperature requires a properly sited thermometer or thermograph, and either one or both of these instruments are needed when looking for ground-level temperature clues to the possible depth of convection or to the suspected passage of a sea-breeze front, and without a hygrograph it is extremely doubtful whether an observer would detect the humidity rise which so often betrays the passage of an otherwise obscure sea-breeze front. Precision-made meteorological instruments are costly and need careful maintenance, but for day to day gliding requirements simple, robust home-made apparatus would suffice and there is scope for ingenuity in building an instrument trolley which can be parked at the launching point. With advice from a meteorologist and the talent for improvisation so readily available at most gliding clubs it should not be difficult to incorporate devices for tracing on a 24-hour smoked drum time-graphs of wind speed and direction, temperature and humidity.

Wherever aero-towing is practised it is also feasible to equip the tug aircraft with a form of air temperature thermometer so that measurements of the temperature distribution with height can be made during some of the ascents.

Of course, there will be many days on which instrumental observations will contribute little or nothing to the day's operations, but there will also be a number of occasions when, with even a little experience at interpreting such measurements, a pilot may avoid some minor frustration such as taking off before dry thermals have attained a soarable depth, or he may be able to seize some extra soaring opportunity proffered by such phenomena as sea breeze fronts, line squalls, or unexpectedly deep dry thermals—and at the same time he will be acquiring more skill at interpreting the weather signs he sees and the forecasts he receives.

Although the forecaster predicts what he considers to be the most probable of several possible developments in the synoptic situation, it is unwise for, say, the pilot wishing to attempt an out-and-return flight to assume (without some additional evidence) that the actual winds will turn out to be lighter than forecast—if the situation justified such an assumption then the meteorologist would not have made the forecast in question.

Sequences of weather can also trap the inexperienced pilot into neglecting to study each day's situation on its full merits. For example, several consecutive days with excellent visibility, easy thermal soaring conditions and fresh winds may instil into a pilot the feeling that if only the wind would decrease an out-and-return course could be attempted. Then comes a day with lighter winds. The pilot thinks, "At last. . . ."—and very humanly tends to neglect such other items as convection, which may now be weak, or haziness, which may obscure the turning-points.

Long-range forecasting

If a forecaster could predict the details of weather situations months or even weeks ahead he would undoubtedly make his fortune, and the fact that a millionaire forecaster does not exist is perhaps the most convincing proof that such long-range forecasting is not possible at present. Nor is it likely in the foreseeable future. No doubt more statistical methods of predicting the probability of certain climatic features will be developed. Photographs taken from satellites will literally clarify the meteorologist's view of actual synoptic situations. The use of high speed computers may allow forecasts of the broad scale pressure and frontal pattern to be made a little farther ahead than is justifiable at present. But in many synoptic situations only a slight change of detail can make or mar soaring prospects, and it is unlikely that such details can be justifiably predicted for more than a day ahead.

A realisation of the impossibility of detailed long-range forecasting, however, should not be a deterrent to planning gliding expeditions some time ahead. It merely means that such planning has to be as flexible as possible. Furthermore, it is wise to consult a meteorologist about the region to be explored; even though he will not normally be able to provide a long-range forecast he can usually provide climatic data and draw balanced deductions on the probable soaring prospects. Gliding literature naturally highlights successful flights and, without more general climatological data, a reader may inadvertently acquire an unduly optimistic impression of soaring in regions in which he has not had actual flying experience.

Pilots waiting to attempt a specific task may be in a position to use one of the special services offered by the British Meteorological Office. For a small fee an arrangement may be made for the pilot to be notified by reversed-charge telegram or telephone call whenever the actual or forecast synoptic situation includes specified features. For example, he may ask to be notified whenever the forecast conditions over a specified course satisfy the following requirements:

1 convection up to between 5,000 and 7,000 ft. above M.S.L.;
2 no medium or high cloud;
3 wind speeds less than 15 knots at heights below 5,000 ft. above M.S.L.

The details of the specification are a matter for arrangement between the individual pilot (or club) and the Meteorological Office, but it should be clearly understood that, while it is the forecaster's task to spot the specified meteorological conditions, it is for the pilot to judge whether or not he can achieve his object in those conditions.

CHAPTER 21

Your Own Weather Map

Of the various sources of information required to construct an up-to-date pressure map for the British Isles the most accessible is that provided by the Shipping Bulletins broadcast by the B.B.C. in its long-wave (1,500 m.) programme. These bulletins are broadcast at ordinary reading speeds, but, with the aid of a prepared form, a planned system and simple abbreviations, all the relevant information can be taken down, and, sparse though it may appear at first sight, it is enough to construct a fairly accurate pressure map which will be less than two hours old at the time of the broadcast.

A prerequisite for the task is a specially prepared form with a list of the Sea Areas, Coastal Reporting stations, columns for gale warnings and forecasts and a blank plotting map. It is not difficult to draw up such a form and map but ready-made maps and forms can be obtained from the Royal Meteorological Society,* and this particular version, called a Metmap, is used for illustration here.

Taking down the bulletins

The first essential is to switch on the radio and be ready to listen as soon as the bulletin starts, but it is surprisingly easy to be diverted or distracted just before the broadcast begins. Set an alarm clock to ring a minute or two before the scheduled time; then, after switching off the alarm, wait for the broadcast; do not start another job. The broadcasting times are listed in press and radio publications.

Shipping Bulletins are split into several sections. If there are any gales, the GALE WARNING comes first. This is just a brief statement saying where the gales are likely to occur. For example, at 0645 BST on 8 September 1963, the statement was:

* 49 Cromwell Road, South Kensington, London, S.W.7.

"Gale warnings are in operation in Bailey, Rockall, Malin and Hebrides."

An X in the GALES column of the form alongside each area mentioned is enough to record the warning. The X's on part of the Metmap form are shown in Figure 21.1.

Gales	SEA AREA FORECAST	Wind: At first	Wind: Later	Weather	Visibility
	VIKING	In East S 5-6			
	FORTIES	SW 4	6-7	R P	m
	CROMARTY				
	FORTH	W 3-4	SW 5	R moving E | P	m | g
	TYNE				
	DOGGER				
	FISHER	S 5-6	SW 5	R moving E	g | m
	GERMAN BIGHT				
	HUMBER				
	THAMES Smith's Knoll	SW 3-4	5-6		mg
	DOVER				
	WIGHT	SW 4-5 occ 6	W	R moving SE	m | g
	PORTLAND				
	PLYMOUTH	SW 4-5 occ 6 in E	WNW 3-4	R moving SE	m | g
	BISCAY	V 3	W 4-5 in S		mg
	FINISTERRE	NE 4 near Cape			
	SOLE				
	LUNDY				
	IRISH SEA	WNW 4-5	occ 6-7 in N	occ P	mg
	FASTNET				
	SHANNON	NW 4-5			mg
X	ROCKALL				
X	MALIN				
X	HEBRIDES	SW 4-6	7-8 WNW	occ P	m
	MINCHES				
	FAIR ISLE	SW 4	E bec cyc 6	R moving E	m
X	BAILEY	SW 5-6	7-8 WNW	occ P	m
	FAEROES	SW 4	E then		
	SE ICELAND	SE in SE Iceland	cyc 6	R moving E	m

↖ *Mark gale areas* ↖ *Connect areas grouped in forecast*

Fig. 21.1. Part of a Metmap form listing the sea areas in the order used in B.B.C. bulletins. The X's in the GALES column denote areas for which gale warnings were given at 0645 BST on 8 Sep 1963. The sea area forecasts are inserted in an abbreviated form to allow all the essential details to be noted.

Then comes the GENERAL SYNOPSIS giving the pressure and frontal situation in so far as it affects the Sea Areas within the next 24 hours. Although no rigid pattern of words is used, the synopsis usually mentions the recent positions, predicted movement and forecast positions of a few systems such as depressions, anticyclones, ridges, troughs and fronts. For example, the 0645 BST bulletin on 8 September 1963 gave:

"The General Synopsis at midnight last night. A depression of 983 millibars which was positioned some two hundred miles west of area Bailey is expected to move east and to be centred near the Faeroes with central pressure of 988 millibars by midnight tonight. A trough which extended from Orkney through the Irish Sea to North-west Finisterre is expected to move east to clear the North Sea by midnight tonight but farther south little movement is expected."

In this synopsis only two systems were mentioned: a depression and a trough, and their recent positions, movement and future positions were described in a logical sequence. Thus the salient facts could be taken down with only a few words under appropriate column headings. The process can also be speeded up by abbreviations such as:

L for Low pressure or depression
H for High pressure or anticyclone
R for Ridge of high pressure
W for Warm front
C for Cold front
O for Occlusion
T for Trough of low pressure

Figure 21.2 shows an abbreviated version of the synopsis on the General Synopsis section of the form. In the systems column it is

GENERAL SYNOPSIS *at* 00 GMT 8 SEP 1963

System	*Present position*	*Movement*	*Forecast position*	*at:-*
L 983	200 miles W of	E	Faeroes 988	24
	Bailey			
T	Orkney – Irish Sea –	E	clear of N. Sea	24
	NW Finisterre		but slow moving in S	

Fig. 21.2. An abbreviated version of the general synopsis issued at 0645 BST 8 Sep 1966.

useful to insert the central pressure given for depressions or anticyclones, and if this pressure is changing the predicted pressure can be added after the forecast position. The time 00 GMT stands for midnight GMT at the beginning of 8 September and the 24 in the last column means midnight at the end of the day.

The Sea Area Forecast

The Sea Area Forecast at 0645 BST on 8 September 1963 started with:

> "Viking, Forties. Wind in east, at first South, 5 or 6, otherwise South-west, 4 gradually increasing to 6 or 7. Periods of rain or showers. Mainly moderate."

The areas mentioned always start with Viking and follow a fixed sequence in an anticlockwise direction around the British Isles. The sequence is listed in Figure 21.1. Areas are often combined to save words in the forecasts, and as such combinations do not disrupt the sequence it is easy to bracket them together.

Like the General Synopsis, the Sea Area Forecast comprises particular elements linked together by words which need not be taken down. These elements are: the wind at first, the wind later, the weather and visibility. With these as column headings there is no need to take down all the words of the forecast.

A wind such as "South-west 4" is written "SW 4" (the number denotes Beaufort force), and a set of simple abbreviations can be used to note some of the text. Here is the set suggested on the Metmap:

D = Drizzle	M = Mist	F = Fog
R = Rain	Z = Haze	Fp = Fog patches
S = Snow	T = Thunder	H = Hail
P = Showers	TP = Thundery showers	Q = Squall
s = slight	p = poor	i = intermittent
loc = locally	m = moderate	g = good
c = continuous	occ = occasional	h = heavy
pp = perhaps	LV = light and variable	cyc = cyclonic

Time can also be saved by omitting refinements in the forecasts. For example, in the Viking and Forties forecast quoted above, it is not essential for our purposes to record that the wind is "gradually increasing". The simple distinction "At first" and "Later" will suffice. "Periods of rain or showers" can be condensed to "Rain, Showers" which is abbreviated to "RP," and we can ignore the adverb "mainly" in the visibility forecast. The forecast can thus be taken down with the few words and letters shown in the Viking and Forties section in Figure 21.1.

A vertical stroke is useful for indicating the passage of time in the weather and visibility columns. For example, we could write

R|P for Rain at first, followed by showers.
D| for Drizzle at first
|R for Rain later
g|m for Visibility good becoming moderate.

The remainder of the Sea Area Forecast for 0645 BST on 8 September 1963 is reproduced:

Cromarty, Forth, Tyne

West 3 or 4 gradually backing south-west and increasing to 5. Rain moving away east followed by showers. Moderate becoming good except in showers.

Dogger, Fisher, German Bight

South mainly 5 or 6 gradually veering south-west. Rainbelt moving slowly east to become mainly fair. Good becoming moderate in rain.

Humber, Thames, Dover

South-west 3 or 4 temporarily increasing to 5 or 6. Mainly fair. Moderate or good.

Wight, Portland

South-west 4 or 5 perhaps increasing temporarily to 6 and soon veering west. Belt of rain moving south-east to become fair. Moderate becoming good.

Plymouth

South-west 4 or 5 and perhaps temporarily 6 in east at first soon veering west to north-west and decreasing to 3 or 4. Rain moving away south-east to become fair. Moderate becoming good.

Biscay, Finisterre

Near Cape Finisterre north-east 4 otherwise variable 3 later becoming west 4 or 5 in the south. Moderate or good.

Sole, Lundy

Wind north-west mainly 4 or 5. Moderate or good.

Irish Sea

West to northwest 4 or 5 increasing at times in north to 6 or 7. Occasional showers. Moderate or good.

Fastnet, Shannon

Wind north-west mainly 4 or 5. Moderate or good.

Rockall, Malin, Hebrides, Minches

South-west 4 gradually increasing to 7 to gale 8 and veering west to north-west. Occasional showers. Mainly moderate.

Fair Isle

South-west 4 gradually backing to East and later becoming cyclonic 6. Rain spreading east. Mainly moderate.

Bailey

South-west force 5 or 6 gradually increasing to force 7 to gale 8 and veering west to north-west. Occasional showers. Mainly moderate.

Faeroes, SE Iceland

Wind south-east in SE Iceland otherwise south-west 4 gradually backing to east and later becoming cyclonic 6. Rain spreading east. Moderate.

The words and abbreviations necessary to take this forecast down are shown in Figure 21.1. Such details as "gradually backing" or "temporarily increasing" have been omitted. In the Irish Sea forecast the "west to north-west" is adequately written as WNW. There is no need to note the visibility qualification "except in showers" tacked on to "moderate becoming good" in the Cromarty, Forth and Tyne areas. In the Plymouth area the "perhaps temporarily force 6" is adequately abbreviated to "occ 6." Weather described as "fair" or "fine" need not be noted at all.

The coastal reports

At present the Bulletins at 0202, 0645, and 1155 or 1340 hours include reports from eleven coastal stations. The Bulletin at 0645 BST 8 September 1963 included:

Coastal Reports for 04 GMT

Wick. West 4. Rain in the past hour. 24 miles. 1003. Rising slowly.
Bell Rock. West 5. Shower in the past hour. 16 miles. 1004. Steady.
Dowsing. South-west 5. 5 miles. 1012.
Galloper. South-south-west 5. 5 miles. 1017.
Royal Sovereign. South-west 4. 11 miles. 1018.
Portland Bill. South-west by west 5. 22 miles. 1016 mb. Falling.
Scilly. North-west by north 3. Rain in the past hour. 4 miles. 1017 mb. Falling slowly.
Valencia. West by north 4. 16 miles. 1015. Falling slowly.
Ronaldsway. West-north-west 3. 16 miles. 1010. Steady.
Prestwick. West 3. 13 miles. 1008. Steady.
Tiree. West-south-west 4. 22 miles. 1006. Falling slowly.

The items mentioned in turn for each station are wind, weather (if significant), visibility, barometric pressure in millibars and pressure tendency. Taking down these reports with the aid of a prepared form and weather abbreviations is a straightforward matter, but there are three further aids to time saving. First, there is no need to write miles or yards after visibility figures; one or two figure numbers will always be in miles (e.g. 5 = 5 miles; 10 = 10 miles), while three or four figures will always denote yards (e.g. 300 = 300 yards; 2000 = 2000 yards). Only two figures are needed for pressure readings in millibars; the initial 9 or 10 of a reading can be omitted; thus 1003 can be taken down as 03; 995 as 95. In practice there will be no doubt as to whether a 9 or 10 has been omitted. The third aid to speed is a method of noting the pressure tendency; draw a stroke to illustrate the change; a horizontal stroke for "steady", a stroke sloping downwards from left to right for "falling", or upwards for "rising", the inclination being gentle for slow tendencies and steep for rapid changes. Figure 21.3 shows the coastal reports taken down on the Metmap form. Note the vertical stroke to denote "in the past hour".

COASTAL REPORTS at .04. GMT	Wind Dirn.	Wind Force	Weather	Visibility	Pressure	Change
Wick	W	4	R	24	03	
Bell Rock	W	5	P	16	04	
Dowsing	SW	5		5	12	
Galloper	SSW	5		5	17	
Royal Sovereign	SW	4		11	18	
Portland Bill	SW'W	5		22	16	
Scilly	NW'N	3	R	4	17	
Valentia	W'N	4		16	15	
Ronaldsway	WNW	3		16	10	
Prestwick	W	3		13	08	
Tiree	WSW	4		22	06	

Fig. 21.3 Coastal weather reports noted on the Metmap form.

Plotting the Coastal Reports

Having taken down the Shipping Bulletin, the next step is to plot the information on the map itself. First we plot the Coastal Reports. The positions of the eleven reporting stations are shown by "station circles" in Figure 21.4, and the observations plotted in this figure are those broadcast at 0645 BST 8 September 1963. The plotting system is as follows:

Wind direction. Draw a straight line about one-third of an inch long to the station circle from the direction from which the wind is blowing.

Wind force. As illustrated in the figure, draw short lines, or "feathers", on one side of the wind direction lines, each full feather denoting two steps in the Beaufort scale, e.g., force 5 is denoted by $2\frac{1}{2}$ feathers. Always draw the feathers on the left-hand side of the direction line (when looking along it towards the station circle).

Calm is denoted by a ring around the station circle.

Weather. Plot the weather on the left of the station circle, using the symbols shown on page 102, and use a vertical stroke to denote

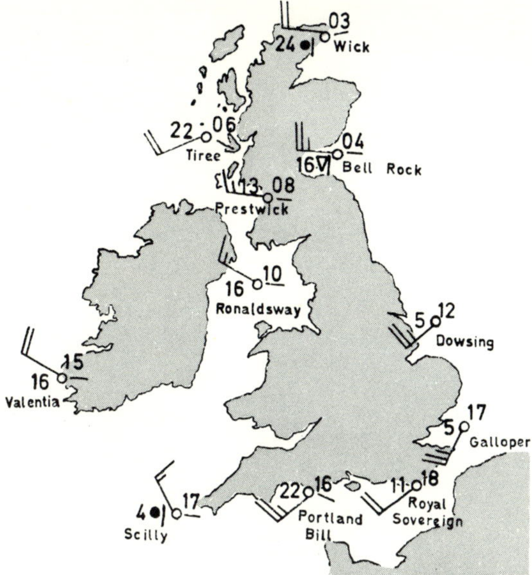

Fig. 21.4. Coastal weather reports plotted in a somewhat similar form to that used on official meteorological maps, but here, for convenience, each full feather on a wind arrow denotes two units on the Beaufort wind scale.

past weather; notice, for example, the dot and vertical stroke at Wick in Figure 21.4 to denote "Rain in the past hour".

Visibility. Write the number denoting visibility at the left of the weather symbol (or at the left of the station circle if there is no weather symbol). One or two figure numbers will always mean visibility in miles, while three or four figure numbers apply to measurements in yards.

Pressure. Write the last two figures of the barometric pressure in millibars just north-east of the station circle. The 03 at Wick in Figure 21.4, for example, stands for 1003 mb.

Pressure change. Just below the pressure, draw a line to indicate the change schematically, i.e., horizontal for "steady", and sloping upwards towards the right for "rising" and downwards for "falling", the inclination being gentle for slow tendencies and steep for rapid changes.

Before plotting the Sea Area information, it is wise to sketch in the positions of the pressure or frontal systems mentioned in the

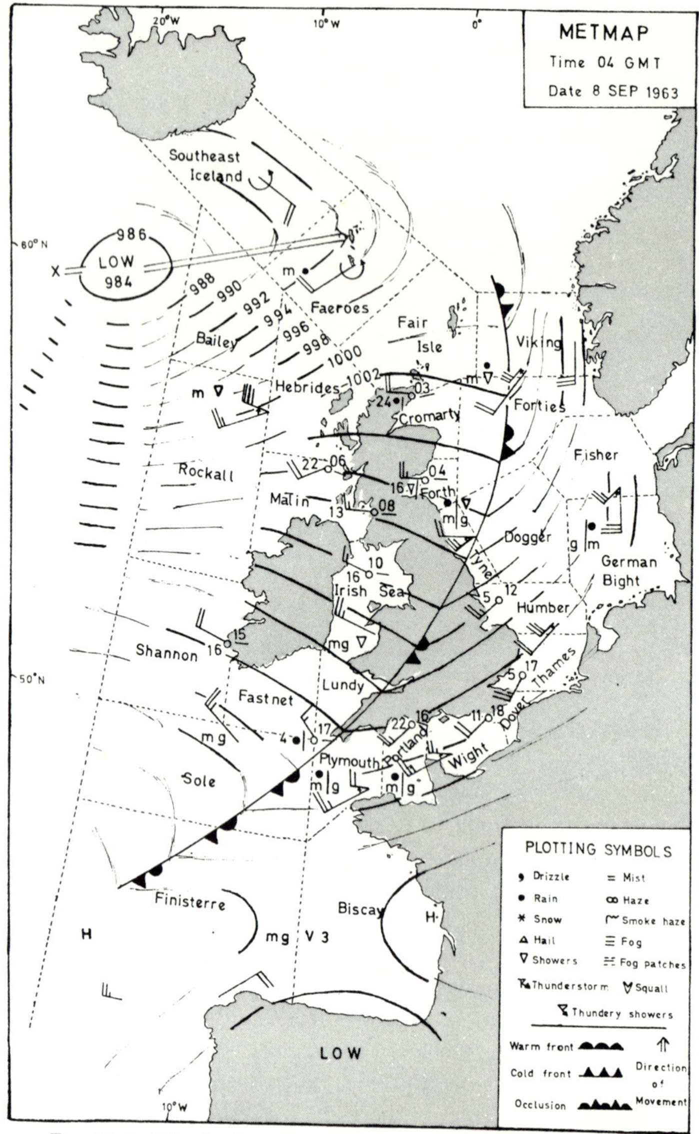

Fig. 21.5. The broken lines mark stated actual and forecast positions of a trough. The interpolated position for 04 GMT is marked as a front—tentatively as a cold occlusion for reasons given later in the text. The isobars are drawn to fit the coastal winds and pressures—not exactly but to yield a pattern without inexplicable irregularities.

General Synopsis. Continuing with the Bulletin for 0645 BST 8 September 1963 as an example, we can mark the initial position of the depression with an "X" 200 miles west of Bailey, and draw an arrow from there to the forecast position at the Faeroes. At the ends of this arrow we also write 983 and 988 to denote the initial and predicted pressure at the centre of low pressure—as shown in Figure 21.5. In this figure broken lines are used to mark in pencil the initial and predicted positions of the trough.

The map we are aiming to construct will be for the time of the Coastal Reports, which was given as 04 GMT. So, on the tentative assumption that the depression and the trough are moving steadily, we interpolate between the initial and forecast positions to find the 04 GMT location of the two systems, i.e., we mark in the depression and trough one-sixth of the way between the initial and forecast positions. To make the trough more distinct, it has been drawn as a line in the 04 GMT position with occlusion symbols; the reasons for suspecting that it is some sort of occlusion will be discussed later. The central pressure of 984 for the "LOW" at 04 GMT is also deduced by simple interpolation.

Plotting the Sea Area Forecast

The recommended system of plotting the Sea Area information is somewhat similar to that used for the Coastal Reports. Winds and weather are plotted with the symbols used for the coastal stations, but the abbreviations used in taking down the forecast are also used to plot visibilities and additional notation is used to denote wind changes. Furthermore, some judgment has to be exercised in selecting items to plot and positions on the map where they are best plotted.

Wind change is best denoted by using large wind arrows for the wind "at first" and smaller arrows for the "wind later". The full range of wind speed given in a forecast can be condensed to a single value, for example, force 5 or 6 can be indicated by $2\frac{3}{4}$ feathers; force 4 or 5 occasionally 6 can be plotted just as force 5 ($2\frac{1}{2}$ feathers). Winds described as "cyclonic" are denoted by circular arrow, large for "at first", small for "later".

The vertical stroke to denote the passage of time plays an important part in plotting the Sea Area Forecast, because we can also use it indirectly to plot the movement of the weather features. The forecast for Dogger, Fisher and German Bight was taken down in our shorthand notation as "Rain moving east, visibility good becoming moderate". In the eastern half of the combined area "Rain moving east" virtually means "Rain later". So we can denote this by the pattern of letters and symbols shown over the German Bight area in Figure 21.5. The "g" stands for good visibility; the vertical stroke means "becoming", the dot signifies rain and the "m" is for moderate visibility.

In addition to the more or less compact groups of wind, weather and visibility plots in Figure 21.5, there are a few wind arrows to denote local variations. For example, there are arrows to denote the "NE force 4" near Cape Finisterre and the "S force 5 or 6" mentioned for the east in the Viking and Forties area forecast.

Drawing the isobars

With the information plotted we can now start to draw the isobars. Drawing them at 2 mb intervals (......... 1002, 1004, 1006........) we use the pressures at the coastal stations to sketch in the pattern over the British Isles. The procedure is just like drawing contour lines to fit heights on a map, but for the pressure map we have the winds as additional guides to the orientation and spacing of the isobars. The winds reported are likely to blow at an angle of between about 5 and 30 degrees to the isobars, the sense of direction being towards the low pressure side of the isobars. Using these directional guides and the reported pressures we can draw the isobaric pattern shown in Figure 21.5—remembering, of course, to include the trough of low pressure whose 04 GMT position has already been tentatively marked.

As in every stage of sketching the pressure and frontal situation, it is unwise to draw the lines in too heavily. Fitting systems to observations is usually a trial and error process entailing much rubbing out and adjustment of tentative lines.

The geostrophic scale

As the winds in temperate and polar latitudes at about 1,500 ft or more above ground or sea level are usually controlled mainly by pressure gradients and the geostrophic force due to the Earth's rotation, the spacing of the isobars can be used as a measure (or,

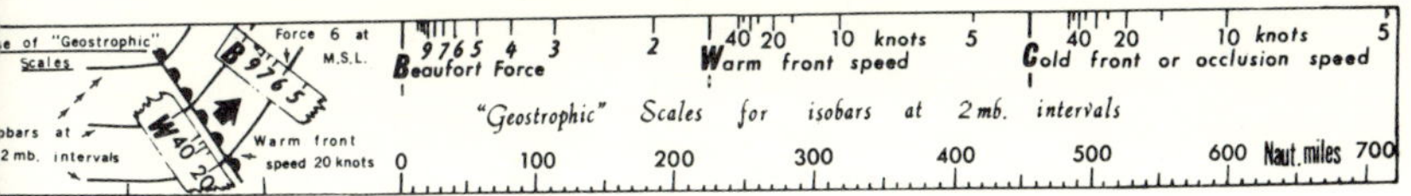

Fig. 21.6. The set of scales includes wind scales calibrated according to approximate relationships between isobar spacing and the surface wind force and frontal speeds. Figs. 21.7 and 21.9 illustrate how the scales are used.

more precisely, an inverse measure) of the wind speed at about 1,500 ft. The surface wind (10 m above ground level) cannot be related quite so easily with the pressure gradient because the effect of low level turbulence brings an additional and complicated force into play. However, as an aid, at least, to constructing the pressure map we can take the surface wind speed to be about two-thirds of the geostrophic wind speed, and use a geostrophic scale with this two-thirds built in. Such a scale is included in a set of scales accompanying the Metmap. Figure 21.6 shows the set. Use of the scale marked Beaufort Force is illustrated in Figure 21.7. If we place the scale across the isobars drawn at 2 mb intervals such that the B mark is on one isobar, then the point on the scale where the next isobar crosses will denote the Beaufort force of the surface wind most likely with such a pressure gradient. This is only a guide, however. When the wind is force 3 or less the speed and direction may differ noticeably from these guides we use. The effects of high

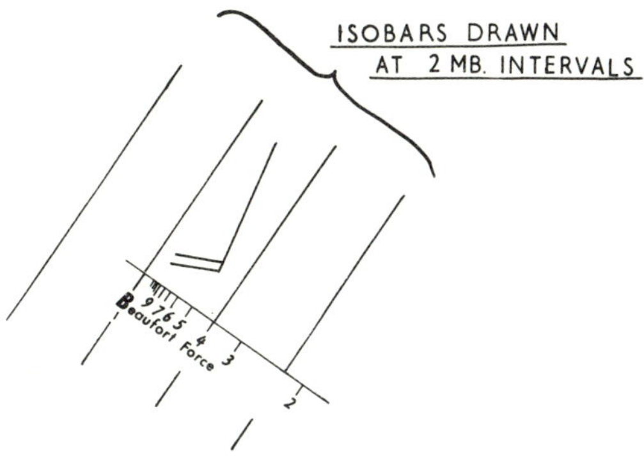

Fig. 21.7. If the wind scale is placed across isobars drawn at 2 mb intervals such that the B mark is on one isobar, then the point on the scale where the next isobar crosses will denote the approximately corresponding Beaufort force of the wind near sea level.

ground can also upset the usual approximate relationships between wind and pressure gradients, and within about 100 miles of a depression centre we must expect the surface wind to be less than the value denoted by the scale.

Nevertheless, with these provisos in mind, we should try to make the pressure gradients fit the winds approximately in accordance with the scale.

Isobars over the sea areas

We can also use the geostrophic scale as an aid to extending the isobars over the Sea Areas.

But first, we can draw a roughly circular isobar around the LOW just west of Bailey, and as the central pressure is taken to be 984 mb we can label this isobar as 986. As we have already drawn the 1002 isobar just north of Scotland, we can insert seven short lines marking roughly equal divisions between the 986 and the 1002 mb isobars, and label them 988, 990, 992........1000. Figure 21.8 shows these short segments of isobars between the LOW and Scotland.

In general, winds over the sea are much closer in direction to the isobars than those over the land, and we shall not be far wrong if we take them as roughly parallel to the isobars.

So the geostrophic scale can be used to sketch in tentative segments of isobars wherever the "At first" wind arrows are plotted over the Sea Areas. For example, in the SE Iceland area where the wind is given as SE force 4 at first, draw two short isobars approximately parallel to the wind direction such that the distance between them is equal to the distance between the B and the force 4 mark on the geostrophic scale.

These segments we draw may not be in quite the right place, but they serve to indicate the direction and spacing of the isobars over this area when we complete the isobaric pattern. Further pairs of lines to denote isobaric directions and gradients are shown near Norway, Denmark, Cape Finisterre, west of Scilly, west of Scotland and near the Faeroes in Figure 21.8. Over Biscay the "Variable 3" is best accommodated by drawing a col in the pressure pattern; we draw curved segments of isobars to suggest low pressure to the south (over Spain) and to the north and high pressure to the east and west.

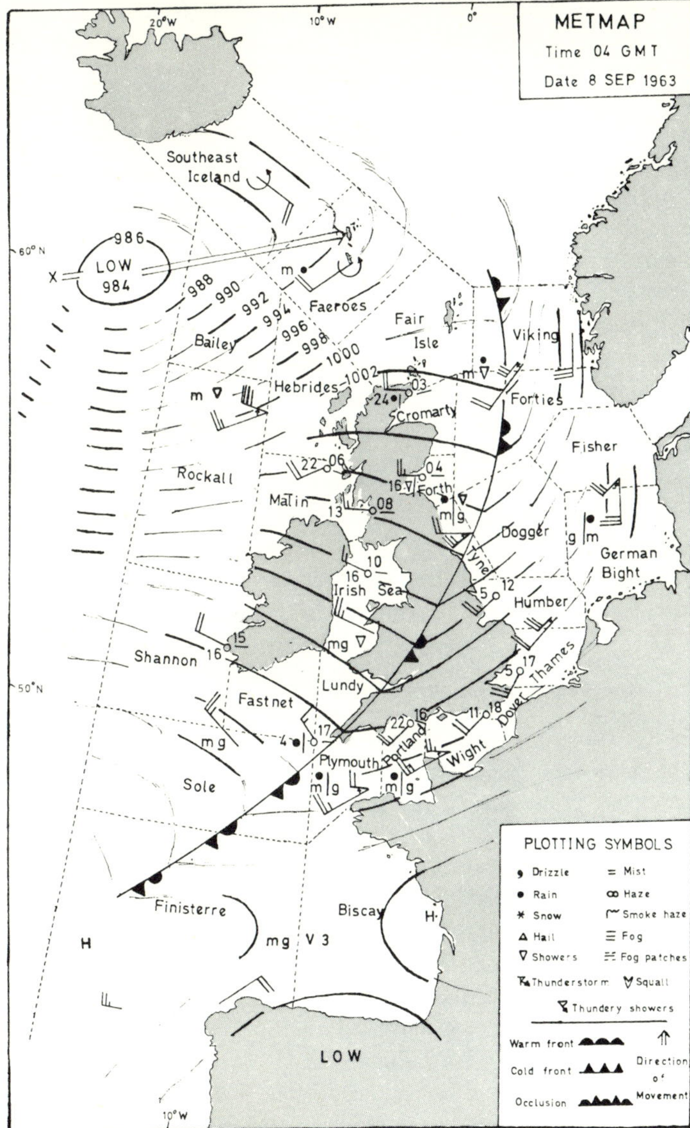

Fig. 21.8. Extending the isobars over the sea entails repeated sketching, erasing and adjusting the lines to obtain a fairly smooth and artistic pattern in which the direction of the isobars and the pressure gradients are as consistent with the present and forecast data as possible.

Now let us use the winds "later". The forecast changes in the winds east of England and over the English Channel are consistent with the eastward movement of the trough of low pressure, so these wind changes merely confirm the isobaric pattern already drawn over the British Isles. But for Bailey, Rockall, Malin, Hebrides and Minches the Bulletin stated that the wind would increase to force 7–8 and veer to W to NW, and to account for this forecast we can assume that, to the west, there is a steeper pressure gradient which will move east with the pressure pattern. Therefore, we can use the geostrophic scale to mark segments of isobars like the rungs of a ladder extending southwards from the LOW spaced at intervals corresponding to force 7–8 on the scale, and, using the forecast that the wind will veer to W–NW, we can sketch in a similarly spaced set extending from the depression towards the SSW. Figure 21.8 shows these two sets.

The "becoming West 4 or 5 in south" for the Finisterre area may appear a little odd at first sight, but this suggests that the high pressure west of Biscay is probably a very narrow ridge and that the trough of low pressure, with the westerly wind ahead, will extend towards the south during the next 24 hours.

Scales for frontal speeds

Before drawing a final version of the isobars, we should try to ensure consistency between the speed of the trough or front and the pressure gradients. In the sketches in this particular example, the trough has been marked as an occlusion. The reason for this is that a sharp trough can usually be classed as some sort of front. In this case, it is most unlikely to be a warm front, because it is difficult to visualise the air from the west or west-north-west behind the front being warmer than the SW'ly flow ahead. Furthermore, the reported visibilities of 16 to 24 miles in the W'ly airstream are much greater than those usually reported in warm sector airstreams over the British Isles. The visibilities of 11 miles at Royal Sovereign and 22 miles at Portland Bill are also higher than is likely in a really warm, moist airstream, so the front is probably not a simple cold front with warm sector air ahead of it. Therefore, we are probably justified in calling it an occlusion, or a cold occlusion—that is, an occlusion at which the cold frontal features are somewhat more evident than the warm front characteristics. The latter choice, cold occlusion, is probably correct, because, if the trough were a simple occlusion or cold front, it would probably have been described as such in the general synopsis.

The speed of an occlusion or cold front is often about the same as the "geostrophic" wind speed (at about 1,500 ft), while warm fronts tend to move at about two-thirds of the "geostrophic" wind speed. Therefore, some consistency between frontal speeds and pressure gradients can be obtained with the aid of a scale—by a similar method to that applied to the winds and pressure gradients.

The scales on the "ruler" illustrated in Figure 21.6 include scales for frontal speeds and pressure gradients. Figure 21.9 shows how to use the cold front or occlusion scale. Lay the scale along the front with the C mark on one of the isobars drawn at 2 mb intervals, and

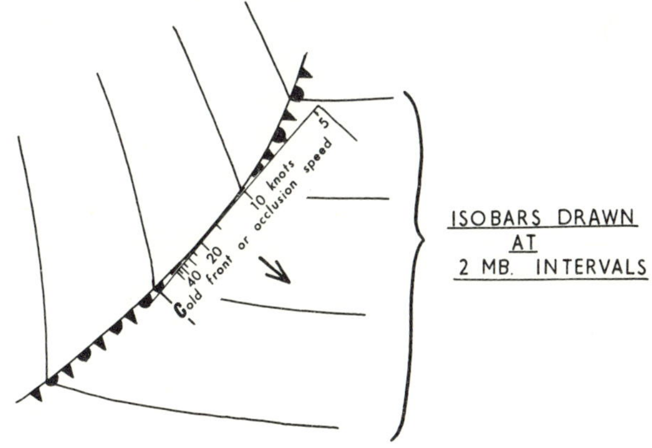

Fig. 21.9. An illustration of how to relate the speed of a cold front or occlusion to the pressure gradient. Warm frontal speeds are dealt with in a similar way with the warm front scale in Fig. 21.6.

read off the speed where the adjacent isobar crosses the scale. In the example in Figure 21.9 this is 10 knots, the probable speed of the front in the direction of the arrow.

The distances between the front's initial and predicted positions (sketched in Figure 21.5) indicate frontal speeds of between 13 and 17 knots across the North Sea, 13 knots across England and 7 knots towards the Bay of Biscay, and we should try to adjust the pressure gradients along the front to fit these speeds according to the cold front or occlusion version of the geostrophic scale. If we cannot make the pressure gradients fit these speeds then we should take another look at the initial and predicted positions first sketched to see whether they can be adjusted to yield frontal speeds consistent with the pressure gradients.

Curvature of the isobars

Experience suggests that showers are more likely in airstreams which follow a cyclonically curved track than in the flow along isobars with anticyclonic curvature, and we can use this characteristic to help shape the pressure pattern west of Ireland. In the Sea Area Forecast, showers were predicted for areas including Rockall, Malin and Hebrides, but not for Fastnet, Sole, Lundy and Shannon. Therefore, we can conclude that the isobars over Rockall, Malin and Hebrides are already or will soon become curved cyclonically around the low pressure centre, but over the Fastnet, Sole, Lundy and Shannon areas the isobars will be more consistent with the forecast if we curve them anticyclonically.

Thus, although the Shipping Bulletin information seems rather sparse at first sight, it contains a variety of clues for detecting details of the synoptic situation. Not all the clues can be fitted exactly, because the winds and weather do not conform precisely to the oversimplified guides we use. But, the more the clues that can be fitted, the more likely the map will be correct, and with this in mind we can adjust and link up the tentatively drawn segments of isobars to form the complete map as illustrated in Figure 21.10.

In this final version the occlusion has been extended from Viking to the depression centre. The reason for this is that we can easily draw a trough between the SE winds at first in SE Iceland and the SW'lies in Faeroes, and this trough appears to be a natural continuation of the trough mentioned in the forecast.

It is useful to write in the speeds of the LOW and several points of the front in little boxes with arrows, as these speeds are handy references if we wish to make a quick forecast of the positions at some specified time.

Thus it is possible to construct a fairly comprehensive and up-to-date pressure and frontal map from the Shipping Bulletins, and, with practice, an early morning map can be completed in about ten to fifteen minutes—ready for use as the key to assessing gliding prospects for the day.

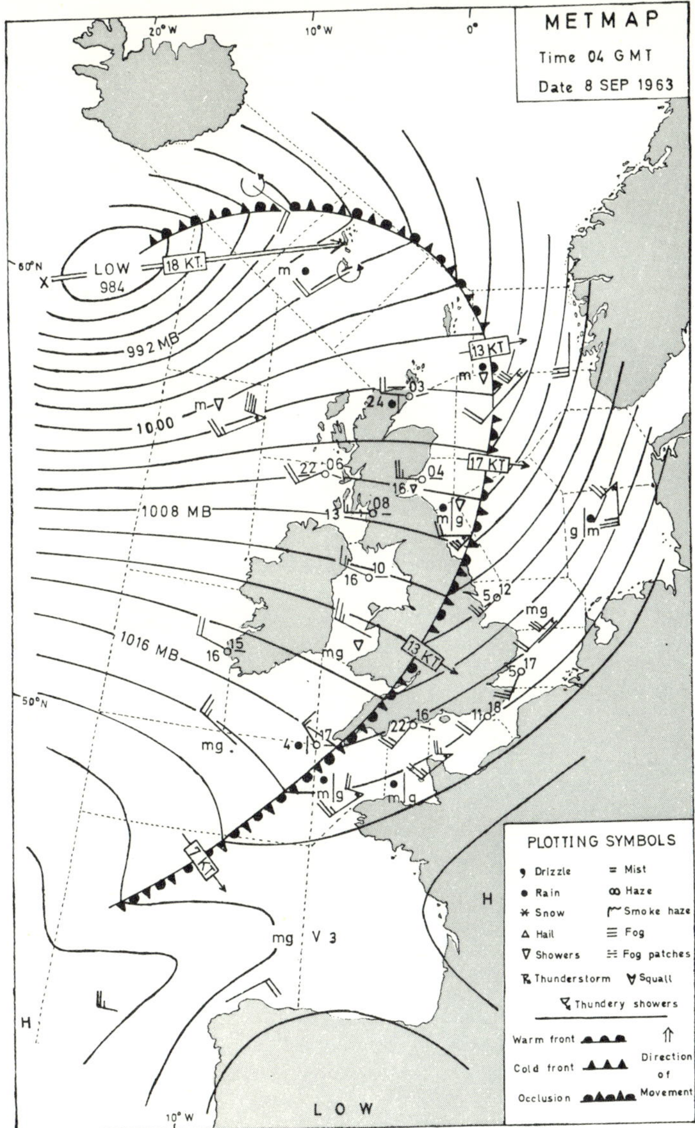

Fig. 21.10. The final pressure and frontal chart.

NOTES ON THE WEATHER SERVICE

Meanings of words used in weather forecasts for the general public

(Extracts from *Your Weather Service*, H.M.S.O.)

TERMS USED WHEN NO RAIN, DRIZZLE, HAIL, SLEET OR SNOW IS EXPECTED

FOR DAYLIGHT PERIODS

Fine	No precipitation or thick fog. Some sunshine.
Dry	No precipitation or thick fog.
Sunny	Much, or completely blue sky.
Sunny periods / *Sunny intervals*	Variable skies with considerable blue patches and corresponding sunshine.
Bright	A good deal of cloud, but considerable diffused sunlight or even occasionally some direct sunshine.
Bright periods / *Bright intervals*	Cloud rather variable in amount and thickness, but considerable diffused sunlight at times or even occasionally direct sunshine.
Cloudy	Cloud nearly or completely covering the sky and mostly thick or dense enough to reduce the daylight appreciably below that described as bright.
Dull	Cloud completely covering the sky and thick or dense enough to reduce the daylight substantially below that described as bright.

AT NIGHT

Fine / *Dry*	No precipitation or thick fog.
Clear	No fog, and little or no cloud.
Cloudy	Cloud nearly or completely covering the sky.
Variable cloudiness	Cloud varying between about one-quarter and three-quarters of sky covered.

PRECIPITATION

Drizzle	Very small generally very numerous raindrops.
Rain	Raindrops of appreciable size.

Snow Crystals of white ice apparently opaque, generally in small or large flakes of light feather structure.

Hail Pellets of ice, usually hard, partly transparent, but collectively of white appearance. There is also a form of pellet, not hard but white and opaque like snow, which is called soft hail.

Sleet Snow and rain together, or snow melting while it is actually falling.

WORDS DESCRIBING THE CHARACTER OF THE RAIN, ETC.

Shower A brief fall of rain, hail, sleet or snow, with more or less definite clearances of the sky between the falls.

Occasional (rain, etc.) Not continuous. The periods of rain, etc., are relatively short, and occupy only a small fraction of the total time. During the periods without rain the sky remains overcast or nearly so. (If clearances are expected the term "showers" is used.)

Intermittent (rain, etc.) Not continuous over a considerable period; but the rainy periods are of substantial duration, and the sky remains overcast during the intervals.

Thunderstorm Thunder and lightning with or without rain, hail, snow or sleet, which may be continuous over a considerable period and heavy at times.

Thundery rain Occasional or intermittent rain of varying intensity but heavy at times. Usually, but not necessarily, accompanied by thunder.

Thundery showers Showers of rain, hail, sleet or snow, usually heavy and generally accompanied by thunder.

TEMPERATURE

TERMS FOR DESCRIBING THE TEMPERATURE

The normal practice in forecasting the temperature is either to specify a range of a few degrees to indicate the general level of temperature likely to occur or to state a value expected to be reached. At present these temperatures are given first in degrees centigrade and then in Fahrenheit, but the degrees Fahrenheit may be omitted some time in the future.

In addition the forecasters sometimes use descriptive terms such as "warm" or "rather cool." These terms are used in accordance with the specifications set out below:

The following additional terms are employed when appropriate:

Close Temperature average or above average, for the season, with high humidity, a cloudy or overcast sky, and a calm or light wind; oppressive.

Muggy Warm damp air, but not necessarily oppressive.

Raw Cold damp air, sometimes with fog.

Temperature departure from average °C.	°F. (*approx*)	Spring (*mid-March to May*) Autumn (*mid-Sept. to mid-Nov.*)	Summer (*mid-May to mid-Sept.*)	Winter (*mid-Nov. to mid-March*)
More than 7 above average +6 to +7	More than 13 above average +11 to +13	Very warm	Very hot Hot	Exceptionally mild
+4 to +5	+7 to +10	Warm	Very warm	Very mild
+2 to +3	+3 to +6	Rather warm	Warm	Mild
−1 to +1	−2 to +2	Normal	Normal	Normal
−2 to −3	−3 to −6	Rather cold	Rather cool	Rather cold
−4 to −5	−7 to −10	Cold	Cool	Cold
More than 5° C. below average	More than 10° F. below average	Very cold	Very cool or cold	Very cold

(The Monthly Average Temperatures in the British Isles are listed on pages 289–90.]

MONTHLY AVERAGE SEA TEMPERATURES

The mean temperature of the uppermost foot of the open sea usually changes slowly (seldom more than one degree Fahrenheit in any one day). Furthermore the variations from year to year are small compared to the changes in air temperature. The average "sea surface" temperatures for any particular time of year may therefore be used as an aid to analysing the synoptic situation. For

example, when low level convection cloud is observed over the sea then some idea of the temperatures aloft in the air stream may be deduced on the assumption that the air temperature at the sea surface is approximately equal to the average sea temperature for the appropriate time. If no current sea temperature measurements are available then the average values, in °F. in Figure 20.3, may also be used in conjunction with the predicted land temperatures to assess the likelihood of sea breeze effects.

MONTHLY AVERAGE TEMPERATURES IN THE BRITISH ISLES (° F)

District	*Jan*		*Feb*		*Mar*		*Apr*		*May*		*June*		*July*		*Aug*		*Sep*		*Oct*		*Nov*		*Dec*	
	Max	*Min*	*Max*	*Min*	*Max*	*Min*	*Max*	*Min*	*Max*	*Min*	*Max*	*Min*	*Max*	*Min*	*Max*	*Min*	*Max*	*Min*	*Max*	*Min*	*Max*	*Min*	*Max*	*Min*
London area	45	35	46	35	50	36	56	39	65	45	69	50	72	54	72	54	67	50	58	44	50	38	46	36
South-east England	45	36	46	35	50	36	55	39	64	45	68	49	72	53	71	53	66	49	58	45	51	38	47	36
East Anglia	45	34	45	34	50	35	55	38	64	44	68	49	72	53	71	52	66	48	58	45	49	36	45	35
Central southern England	47	35	47	35	50	36	55	38	64	44	68	49	72	53	70	52	66	48	58	44	51	37	48	36
East Midlands	45	34	46	34	50	35	55	38	64	44	68	49	72	53	71	52	66	48	58	43	49	36	46	35
East England	44	34	45	34	49	35	54	38	61	44	66	49	70	53	69	52	64	48	57	43	48	36	45	35
West Midlands	46	35	46	34	50	36	55	38	63	44	67	48	71	52	69	52	65	48	57	43	50	37	47	36
Channel Islands	48	39	48	38	51	40	55	43	62	48	65	52	69	56	69	57	67	54	60	49	53	44	50	41
South-west England	50	35	49	35	51	36	55	39	63	45	67	49	70	53	69	53	65	49	58	44	53	38	50	36
South Wales	48	35	47	35	50	36	55	39	62	44	67	48	70	52	68	52	65	48	58	43	51	37	48	36
North Wales	47	36	46	35	49	36	55	38	61	44	66	48	70	52	68	52	64	48	57	43	50	37	47	36

North-west England	46 35	45 35	49 36	54 39	61 45	65 49	69 53	67 52	64 48	56 43	48 37	46 36
Lake District	45 34	45 34	48 35	53 38	60 42	65 46	68 51	66 51	62 47	56 42	49 37	46 35
Isle of Man	46 38	46 37	48 38	53 40	58 45	62 49	64 52	64 53	61 50	56 46	50 41	47 39
Central northern England	45 35	45 34	49 35	54 38	62 44	66 49	70 52	69 52	64 48	57 43	48 37	45 35
North-east England	44 34	44 33	48 35	57 37	60 42	65 46	68 51	66 50	63 47	56 41	48 36	45 34
South-east Scotland	44 34	44 33	47 34	52 36	59 42	65 46	67 50	66 50	61 46	55 41	47 36	45 34
East Scotland	43 33	44 33	47 34	52 36	58 42	64 46	67 50	65 50	61 46	54 41	47 35	44 33
North-east Scotland	44 33	44 33	46 34	51 37	57 42	61 46	65 50	63 50	59 46	53 41	47 36	44 33
Central Scotland	44 33	44 33	47 34	52 36	58 42	64 46	67 50	65 50	61 46	54 41	47 35	44 33
South-west Scotland	45 34	45 34	48 34	53 36	59 42	65 46	67 50	66 50	61 46	55 41	49 36	46 34
West Scotland	46 33	47 33	48 34	52 37	58 42	63 47	65 50	64 50	60 46	54 41	48 36	46 33
North-west Scotland	46 33	46 33	47 34	51 36	58 42	62 46	65 50	63 49	60 46	53 41	48 36	46 33
Orkney	44 36	44 35	45 36	48 38	52 42	56 46	59 49	59 49	56 47	52 43	47 39	44 37
Shetland	43 35	43 35	44 35	47 37	51 41	55 45	58 48	58 49	55 46	51 42	46 38	44 36
Northern Ireland	46 37	47 36	49 36	53 38	59 44	63 48	66 51	65 51	61 48	56 43	49 38	46 37

WEATHER INFORMATION BY TELEPHONE

The latest information about the synoptic situation in various parts of the British Isles and the Continent and forecasts to cover a period of up to 24 hours ahead may be obtained by telephone from the Meteorological Offices listed on the next two pages. The automatic service consists of short forecasts recorded at intervals and repeated continuously over the automatic system.

TELEPHONE WEATHER SERVICE

AUTOMATIC SYSTEM: 24 HOUR SERVICE

Centre	*Area covered by recorded forecast*	*Dial Number*
London	20 miles radius of Oxford Circus	WEA 2211
	Essex Coast	WEA 3311
	Kent Coast	WEA 4411
	Sussex Coast	WEA 5511
Manchester	S. Lancs and N. Cheshire	ASK 8091
	Lancashire Coast	ASK 8092
	N. Wales Coast	ASK 8093
Birmingham	20 miles radius	ASK 8091
Liverpool	S. Lancs and N. Cheshire	ASK 8091
	Lancashire Coast	ASK 8092
	N. Wales Coast	ASK 8093
Blackpool	Lancashire Coast	BLACKPOOL 8091
Southport	Lancashire Coast	SOUTHPORT 9541
Colchester	Essex Coast	COLCHESTER 8091
Canterbury	Kent Coast	CANTERBURY 831
Brighton	Sussex Coast	BRIGHTON 8091
Portsmouth	S. Hampshire	PORTSMOUTH 8091
Southampton	S. Hampshire	SOUTHAMPTON 8091
Plymouth	S. Devon and E. Cornwall	PLYMOUTH 8091
Bristol	Area including Weston-super-Mare	BRISTOL 8091
Cardiff	10 miles inland from Cardiff, Barry, Newport and coastal strip	CARDIFF 8091
Newcastle	Tyneside and Teeside	NEWCASTLE 8091
Glasgow	25 miles radius	ASK 8091
Edinburgh	5 miles radius	ASK 8091
Belfast	15 miles radius	BELFAST 8091

PERSONAL SERVICE: 24 HOUR SERVICE

Meteorological Office	*County*	
London (Kingsway)	London	TEMple Bar 4311
Aldergrove	Co. Antrim	Crumlin 339
Bawtry	Yorkshire	Bawtry 474
Dunfermline	Fife	Inverkeithing 266

Glasgow	Renfrewshire	City 3451
Gloucester	Gloucestershire	Gloucester 23122
Lyneham	Wiltshire	Bradenstoke 283
Manby	Lincolnshire	Louth 2145
Manchester Weather Centre	Lancashire	Deansgate 6701
Mildenhall	Suffolk	Mildenhall 2274
Nottingham	Nottinghamshire	Nottingham 55155
Plymouth	Devonshire	Plymouth 42534
Preston	Lancashire	Preston 52628/9
Southampton Weather Centre	Hampshire	Southampton 28844
Upavon	Wiltshire	Upavon 286

LIMITED SERVICE

(9 a.m. to 5 p.m. Mondays to Fridays)
(9 a.m. to 1 p.m. Saturdays)

Meteorological Office	*County*	
Aberdeen	Aberdeenshire	Dyce 331
Abingdon	Berkshire	Abingdon 1408
Acklington	Northumberland	Red Row 369
*Bassingbourn	Hertfordshire	Royston 2291
Birmingham Airport	Warwickshire	Sheldon 4747
Boscombe Down	Wiltshire	Amesbury 3331
Cardiff	Glamorganshire	Rhoose 343
Chivenor	Devonshire	Barnstaple 2241
Kinloss	Morayshire	Forres 261
Kirkwall Airport	Orkney	Kirkwall 421
Leconfield	Yorkshire	Leconfield 386
Leuchars	Fife	Leuchars 271
Liverpool Airport	Lancashire	Garston 4666
*Linton-on-Ouse	Yorkshire	Linton-on-Ouse 261
Marham	Norfolk	Narborough 398
Oakington	Cambridgeshire	Cambridge 56441
Ronaldsway	Isle of Man	Castleton 3311
St. Mawgan	Cornwall	Newquay 2224
Shawbury	Shropshire	Shawbury 335
Thorney Island	Hampshire	Emsworth 2355
Turnhouse	Midlothian	Corstorphine 2351
Valley	Anglesey	Holyhead 2288
Wittering	Northamptonshire	Stamford 2251
Wyton	Huntingdonshire	Huntingdon 251

* Office not open on Saturdays.

NOTE.—The above list is based on information available in January 1966.

CONVERSION FACTORS

TEMPERATURE

T deg. F. = $\frac{5}{9}$ (T − 32) deg. C.
T deg. C. = (32 + $\frac{9}{5}$ T) deg. F.
T deg. C. = (273 + T) deg. K. (Kelvin)

FAHRENHEIT/CELSIUS (CENTIGRADE) CONVERSION TABLE

°C	−40	−30	−20	−10	0	10	20	30	40
°F	−40	−22	−4	14	32	50	68	86	104

In English-speaking countries temperatures at ground level are usually quoted in degrees Fahrenheit while temperatures aloft are reported in degrees Celsius.

PRESSURE

Outside of national meteorological services, a number of barometers are calibrated in inches or millimetres of mercury. Such units are not precise measures of pressure; allowance must be made for variations in temperature and in the force of gravity—which increases towards the poles. The relationship between millibars and inches or millimetres of mercury (at 0°C at latitude 45°N) is

1000 mb. = 750·1 mm. = 29·531 inches

DISTANCES

1 inch = 25·4 mm.
1 mm. = 0·03937 inches
} Rainfall is usually measured in inches or millimetres.

1 ft. = 0·3048 metres
1 metre = 3·2808 ft. = 1·0936 yards
1 statute mile = 5280 ft. = 0·8684 nautical miles = 1·609 km.
1 nautical mile = 6080 ft. = 1·1515 statute miles = 1·8532 km.
1 km. = 1000 metres = 0·5396 nautical miles
= 0·6214 statute miles = 3280·8 ft.

SPEEDS

	ft./sec.	100 ft./min.	m./sec.	km./hr.	m.p.h.	knots
1 ft./sec.	1	0·6	0·3048	1·0973	0·6818	0·5921
100 ft./min.	1·667	1	0·508	1·829	1·136	0·9868
1 m./sec.	3·2808	1·968	1	3·6	2·2369	1·9424
1 km./hr.	0·9113	0·5468	0·2778	1	0·6214	0·5396
1 m.p.h.	1·4667	0·88	0·447	1·609	1	0·8684
1 knot	1·6889	1·014	0·5148	1·8532	1·1515	1

REFERENCES

Abbreviations :

G	—	*Gliding* (to Summer 1955)	Official organ of the British Gliding Association.
SG	—	*Sailplane and Gliding* (from October, 1955)	
MM	—	*The Meteorological Magazine*—Published by the British Meteorological Office.	
W	—	*Weather*—a monthly magazine	Published by the Royal Meteorological Society, London.
QJ	—	*Quarterly Journal* of the R.M.S. (An advanced level journal)	
SAR	—	*Swiss Aero Revue*—Official organ of the Swiss Aero Club containing contributions from the Organisation Scientifique et Technique Internationale du Vol à Voile (OSTIV).	

FRONTS AND DEPRESSIONS

AUTHOR	TITLE	PUBLICATION	
SANSOM, H.	*A study of cold fronts over the British Isles*	QJ	Apr. 1951, p. 96
MILES, M. K.	*A kata-front of notable structure*	MM	Oct. 1954, p. 289
POTHECARY, I. J. W.	*Recent research on fronts*	W	May 1956, p. 147
WALLINGTON, C. E.	*The problem of research into frontal rainfall*	MM	June 1958, p. 181
SAWYER, J. S.	*Temperature, humidity and cloud near fronts in the middle and upper troposphere*	QJ	Oct. 1958, p. 375

ANTICYCLONES

PETTERSSEN, S., SHEPPARD, P. A. PRIESTLY, C. H. B. and JOHANNESSEN, K. R.	*An investigation of subsidence in the free atmosphere*	QJ	Jan. 1947, p. 43
BELASCO, J. E.	*The incidence of anticyclonic days and spells over the British Isles*	W	Aug. 1948, p. 233

FOEHN EFFECTS

LOEWE, F.	*Foehn near the Balleny Islands, Antarctica*	W	Apr. 1950, p. 152
MCCAFFERY, W. D. S.	*Foehn effect over Scotland*	MM	May 1952, p. 151

SEA BREEZES

Marshall, W. A. L.	*Sea breeze across London*	MM June 1950, p. 165
Malkus, J. S.	*A formation of pileus-like veil clouds over Cape Cod, Massachusetts*	Bulletin of the American Met. Soc. Feb. 1951, p. 61
Watts, A. J.	*Sea breeze at Thorney Island*	MM Feb. 1955, p. 42
Lamb, H. H.	*Malta's sea breezes*	W Aug. 1955, p. 256
Mackenzie, J. K.	*Exploring the sea breeze front*	SG Dec. 1956, p. 294
Saunders, P. M.	*The sea breeze convergence zone*	SG Oct. 1958, p. 276

CONVECTION

Paton, J.	*Temperatures and airflow within a wheatfield*	W Jan. 1948, p. 22
	The thunderstorm	U.S. Weather Bureau, Washington D.C., 1949
Jeffersen, G. J.	*Temperature rise on clear mornings*	MM Feb. 1950, p. 33
Jeffersen, G. J.	*Method of forecasting time of clearance of radiation fog or low stratus*	MM Apr. 1950, p. 102
Broadbent, L.	*The microclimate of the potato crop*	QJ Oct. 1950, p. 439
Brewer, A. W.	*Why does it rain?*	W July 1952, p. 195
Ludlam, F. H.	*Artificial and natural shower formation*	W July 1952, p. 199
Scorer, R. S.	*Soaring in Spain 1952*	W Dec. 1952, p. 373
Scorer, R. S.	*The spreading out of down-draughts*	W July 1953, p. 198
Ludlam, F. H. and Scorer, R. S.	*Convection in the atmosphere*	QJ July 1953, p. 317
Malkus, J. S.	*Aeroplane studies of trade wind meteorology*	W Oct. 1953, p. 291
James, D. G.	*Fluctuations of temperature below cumulus clouds*	QJ Oct. 1953, p. 425
Ludlam, F. H.	*The sub-cloud layer over land*	QJ Oct. 1953, p. 430
Jones, R. F.	*Five flights through a thunder-storm belt*	QJ July 1954, p. 377
Murgatroyd, R. J.	*Investigations of cumulus cloud*	MM July 1954, p. 208
Pothecary, I. J. W.	*Short period variations in surface pressure and wind*	QJ July 1954, p. 395
Tucker, G. B.	*Mountain cumulus*	W July 1954, p. 198
Findlater, J.	*Notes on the structure of thermal bubbles*	SG Dec. 1955, p. 163
Scorer, R. S. and Ronne, C.	*Experiments with convection bubbles*	W May 1956, p. 151
Saunders, P. M.	*The formation of precipitation*	W April 1956, p. 103
Ludlam, F. H.	*The structure of rain clouds*	W June 1956, p. 187
Cunningham, R. M.	*Flight observations on the fine structure of cumulus clouds*	SAR July 1956, p. 100
Ludlam, F. H.	*Radar "angel"*	SAR Jan. 1957, p. 42
Ludlam, F. H.	*Cumulo-nimbus*	SAR April 1957, p. 213
Woodward, B.	*A theory of thermal soaring*	SAR June 1958, p. 321

HARPER, W. G. and BEIMERS, J. G. D.	*The movement of precipitation belts as observed by radar*	QJ	July 1958, p. 242
SALAMONIK, S.	*La structure des nuages cumulus et cumulonimbus à la lumière des études par radar*	SAR	Dec. 1958, p. 659
HARPER, W. G.	*An unusual indicator of convection*	Proceedings 7th Weather Radar Conference. Miami., Nov. 1958	
FINDLATER, J.	*Wind shear and dry thermals*	SG	June 1959, p. 134
KUETTNER, J.	*The band structure of the atmosphere*	"Tellus," Stockholm, Aug. 1959, p. 267	

LINE SQUALLS

LIGDA, M. G. H.	*Radar observations of pre-frontal squall lines in the Midwestern United States*	SAR	Dec. 1956, p. 557
TEPPER, M.	*Squall lines, pressure jump lines and atmospheric gravity waves*	SAR	Jan. 1958, p. 37
REITSCH, H.	*Observations during a soaring flight along a squall line*	SAR	Oct. 1958, p. 497

AIRFLOW OVER MOUNTAINS

MANLEY, G.	*The helm wind at Crossfell*	QJ	Apr. 1944, p. 197
SCORER, R. S.	*Theory of waves in lee of mountains*	QJ	Jan. 1949, p. 41
LEE, G. H. and NEUMARK, O. W.	*A standing wave at Dunstable*	MM	Oct. 1952, p. 307
LUDLAM, F. H.	*Hill-wave cirrus*	W	Oct. 1952, p. 300
ROPER, R. D.	*Evening waves*	QJ	Oct. 1952, p. 415
TURNER, H. S.	*Severe turbulence over the Inner Hebrides*	MM	Aug. 1952, p. 239
WARD, F. W.	*Helm wind effect at Ronaldsway, Isle of Man*	MM	Aug. 1953, p. 234
JONES, S.	*The April Wave*	G	Autumn, 1953, p. 130
CORBY, G. A.	*The airflow over mountains*	QJ	Oct. 1954, p. 491
SAUNDERS, P. M.	*Clutching Hands*	G	Winter 1954, p. 144
LOEWE, F. and RADOK, U.	*A wave cloud at Heard Island*	W	March 1955, p. 78
GOODHART, H. C. N.	"*. . . Gang Aft Agley*"	G	Spring 1955, p. 23
WALLINGTON, C. E.	*Lee waves ahead of a warm front*	QJ	Aug. 1955, p. 251
WILLS, P. A.	*Altitude in undress*	G	Summer 1955, p. 71
PILSBURY, P. K.	*Preliminary analysis of standing wave reports received at Northolt during the winter of 1953–54*	MM	Oct. 1955, p. 313
WILLS, P. A.	*Riding the Mistral*	SG	Oct. 1956, p. 228
CORBY, G. A. and WALLINGTON, C. E.	*Airflow over mountains: the lee wave amplitude*	QJ	Aug. 1956, p. 266

Scorer, R. S.	*Airflow over and in lee of an isolated hill*	SAR Feb. 1957, p. 83
Förchtgött, J.	*The active turbulent layer in lee of mountain ridges*	SAR June 1957, p. 324
Holmboe, J. and Klieforth, H.	*Investigations of mountain lee waves and the airflow over the Sierra Nevada*	Univ. of California Contract AF 19 (604) 1957
Berenger, M. and Gerbier, N.	*Les mouvements ondulatoire à St Auban-sur-Durance*	Monographie de la Météorologie Nationale, Paris, 1957
Corby, G. A.	*A preliminary study of atmospheric waves using radio-sonde data*	QJ Oct. 1957, p. 355
Wallington, C. E. and Portnall, J.	*A numerical study of the wavelength and amplitude of lee waves*	QJ Jan. 1958, p. 38
Kuettner, J.	*The rotor flow in lee of mountains*	SAR April 1958, p. 208
Wallington, C. E.	*An introduction to lee waves in the atmosphere*	SAR Mar. 1959, p. 187

Books used in the preparation of Meteorology for Glider Pilots

(Advanced level books toward the end of the list)

The English Climate by C. E. P. Brooks	English Universities Press
The Soaring Pilot by A. and L. Welch and F. Irving	John Murray
Cloud Study by F. H. Ludlam and R. S. Scorer	John Murray
W.M.O. International Cloud Atlas	World Meteorological Organization, Geneva
The Way of the Weather by J. S. Sawyer	A. and C. Black
Introduction to Meteorology (2nd Edition) by S. Petterssen	McGraw-Hill
Meteorology for Aviators by R. C. Sutcliffe	H.M.S.O., London
Natural Aerodynamics by R. S. Scorer	Pergamon Press
Weather Analysis and Forecasting by S. Petterssen	McGraw-Hill
Micrometeorology by O. G. Sutton	McGraw-Hill
Compendium of Meteorology	The American Meteorological Society

INDEX